fearless. free.

by Hettie Brittz

Green Hope Media
A division of Evergreen Parenting CC
Olifantsfontein, South Africa
www.evergreenparenting.co.za

fearless. free.

Published by Green Hope Media
Olifantsfontein, South Africa
greenhope@evergreenparenting.co.za

All rights reserved. Except for brief excerpts for review purposes, no part of this book may be reproduced or used in any form without written permission from the publisher.

Unless otherwise noted, all Scripture quotations are taken from THE MESSAGE. Copyright © by Eugene H. Peterson 1993, 2002. Used by permission of NavPress. All rights reserved. Represented by Tyndale House Publishers, Inc. Use of this trademark for the offering of goods or services requires the prior written consent of Tyndale House Publishers, Inc.

ISBN 978-0-620-69736-1

Translation by Willem Taute and Jodi Deetlefs
Editing by Heather Laba and Paula Senekal
Cover Design by Marguerite Gerber - Active Space Designs
Layout by Tharina du Preez - Ar-T Designs

© 2016 Hettie Brittz

Printed in South Africa

First Edition 2016

dedicated.

... to every woman who is on her way to touch the hem of Jesus' garment and to every man who believes that Jesus is on His way to stir the waters.

Even if you feel you've tried it all or have been longing for decades for deliverance from the darkness that holds your soul, please know that your time of healing will come!

"My help and glory are in God

– granite-strength and safe-harbour-God –

So trust Him absolutely, people;

lay your lives on the line for Him.

God is a safe place to be."

Psalm 62:7-8 (*The Message*)

Content

Introduction

Have you ever observed little children watching a puppet show? They sit perfectly still, staring wide-eyed at the handmade puppets. They hang on every word from the puppets' sewn-on lips, even though some of the puppets are nothing more than socks with tassels for hair and shiny buttons for eyes.

Some grown-ups are like these children. They stare at the world wide-eyed without giving much thought to who or what is behind every "puppet". Some are quietly content to seek for the meaning of life on the first level only – through the things they see, feel, smell, hear, taste and buy. They are mesmerised by puppet shows, and they identify with some of the characters in the same way we used to follow our cartoon heroes on TV. They talk and sing along with the puppets and do everything the main characters tell them to do. With full confidence, they anticipate the moment when the good puppets will catch the naughty puppets and spank them – because that's the way these stories go. If the story ends well, they clap their hands; when there is a sad ending, they cry.

For toddlers and for these adults, the front of the puppet theatre, the tangible side of life, is the only reality. But what is hidden behind the box and curtain of the puppet theatre? Can we ever fully understand the show of life without looking behind that curtain? Isn't the intangible, invisible part of life more of a reality than the décor?

As they grow in years and wisdom, the children, sitting cross-legged and looking up at the puppets, eventually see a grown-up's hairy arm peeking out from underneath the pink princess dress. They may hear someone coughing behind the theatre, or they might even hear the thump of a clumsy puppeteer accidentally bumping a knee against the wooden sides. The children soon realise there is more going on here than meets the eye, and they want to investigate. Some of the adults desperately try to stop them, but one by one the little rascals jump up and storm the theatre. They hit the bad puppets and try to rip the knight off the horse's back, but thankfully the safety pins usually hold. Others dart between an adult's legs and make it to behind the puppet theatre where they start crying with disillusionment. Some may point their tiny fingers mockingly and yell as though they've made a grand discovery:

"None of it is real!"

Grown-ups, who have for years kept an eye on the story of God and humanity, also see through the show from time to time. Appalling things happen that don't seem to fit the script any better than a hairy arm fits the princess dress. Some want to go deeper into the concert of life and investigate, but many keep guard with their backs to the reality behind the curtain. They are like the grown-ups who try to halt the children – they are either too reverent or too timid to sneak a peek behind the puppet theatre for themselves and way too impressed with the "holiness" of it all to allow others to investigate.

> *"Don't ask so many questions. Sit quietly. Cross your legs. Fold your arms. Just watch the show!"*

Seekers don't respect these types of orders. They barge through the barricades and pull aside the curtains of life. They rip the puppets off the puppeteer's hands, and tug and pull to see if the Knight of our lives is attached to reality with mere safety pins of human wishful thinking. Some see all the makeshift props and décor, burst out laughing, impressed with their own wisdom:

> *"I knew it. It's all fake!"*

The rest start crying, mourning their loss of innocence. They naively believed that the puppet princess would really marry the prince. But instead the princess is lying limp on the lawn behind the puppet theatre, her dress over her head, inside out ... The sobering reality is simply too much for them to bear.

This is more or less a picture of the mix of bewilderment, rage, sadness and self-satisfaction the readers of the headlines experienced when on Wednesday morning, the 10th of February 2010, they saw the news on the lampposts:

> *"Gospel Singer's Wife Raped."*

I concur – it's a big part of the arm showing from underneath the princess dress. It's the kind of knock against the side of the puppet theatre that makes a once unsuspecting audience fly up from their seats.

I won't expect you to sit cross-legged and look passively at me while I tell you a fairy tale. The fairy tale elements are there, because the Prince is alive, but I'm also going to invite you to walk around the puppet theatre as often as you like and to tug and pull to your heart's content, because the story I'm going to tell will make the flimsy puppet theatres topple anyway. You will see puppets turned inside out and you will hear disturbing noises from behind the curtains, because these sights and sounds are part of real life. I'm going to try and gently force the respectfully religious amongst us, who try to conceal the back of the theatre, to look where we were taught never to look. I do this not in an effort to shock people for effect. Rather, it's my hope that those who are compelled to gaze into the hidden places will find the answers, the peace and the comfort they've been looking for all along.

I will allow you to ask the forbidden questions. In fact, I will even ask them on your behalf. Surely you must realise that I, too, lost some of my innocence that night. I thought I was somewhat like the princess, only to be turned inside out and left on the floor. I asked questions – tough ones, unspoken ones that you only dare whisper. I also asked difficult questions with dangerous answers that hold the power to topple the puppet theatres many of us naively hold dear.

Since that fateful night, I've been spending more time behind the theatre box than I have in front of it. I've been peeking over the Puppet Master's shoulder, trying to make sense of the script He's been writing. Since we started telling our story, many men and women have joined us behind the curtains. We have found so much life and liberty here!

Although I may clumsily trip over words and could never express all that's in my heart – with an understanding that is far from complete – I will try to share the affirming joy, deep healing and fearless freedom that we have discovered behind the theatre box.

Hettie Brittz
Pretoria, South Africa

1 *Across dark waters*

My husband is standing at the foot of our bed with his hands tied behind his back, surrounded and held back by three dark figures. Robbers. A fourth is standing to my left with a revolver to my head. I'm on my back in bed, still coming out of that in-between place – half alert, half asleep. Fully frightened. A voice commands me to roll over onto my stomach. They tie my hands behind my back. It feels like shoe laces.

In the story that ends here, I was a precious princess who lived happily in a safe, gated community east of Pretoria, South Africa. In my mind, the bad guys never came close; they were only in newspaper stories, not in my story. In Pierre van Ryneveld, a suburb where we once lived, they ran through our yard a few times. I remember one specific night when my husband, Louis, was out of town. Just after midnight the back door's alarm started wailing. Quick footsteps decrescendoed past the kitchen windows, the bathroom, then past our bedroom's sliding door and on past the swimming pool, into the shrubs in the corner of our yard. Thankfully, the armed response was quick to arrive. Like bloodhounds, the security guards followed the trail in the same sequence. On both sides of the garden wall they discovered bricks that had been stacked like stairs to create an escape route. It reminded me of those plastic stepping stools toddlers stand on so they can reach the sink to brush their own teeth. It said, "Look, we have made it easy!" The barbed wire on top of the garden wall had been cut and folded back in advance. From the house the whole project was invisible – completely disguised by the trees and shrubs in the corner of the yard. From the street the criminal construction had the inviting look of a welcome sign. The arrogance astounded me. Then it reminded me of the sneaky shortcut we had mapped out through our neighbour's yard to the candy store when we were kids, with only one big difference – we streaked through the yard with things we had *paid* for.

In this unfenced neighbourhood we even heard shots fired on our street from time to time, which is precisely why we moved. Because that's what reasonable people do, isn't it? We move from one story to the next if we find our forest to be frequented by too many wolves. If our houses prove to be made of straw, we move to brick ones.

So that is how we ended up in a brick house in a wolf-less forest. The estate agent and previous owners promised, with faces so innocent they could make Goldilocks look sly by comparison:

"We haven't seen a single wolf in this neck of the woods in seven years."

Behind the scenes of our new story, beyond the fence we trusted, waters were rising – literally. Two months' worth of incessant summer rains had steadily seeped into Six Mile Creek, and — on this very night — the creek burst its banks and swept away the fence between our sleepy hollow and the neighbouring fenced community.

Just a few hours ago, at eleven o' clock, the night guards completed their first fence patrol of the shift, and they didn't notice anything suspicious. Our lights were still on, but they know our lights seldom go off before one in the morning, with a few of them remaining lit through the night. They had no cause for alarm.

The clock passes 2 a.m. and Louis is still in his home-recording studio editing the music CD for the Turn2God Movement. He has every intention to work through the night, as he needs to hand in the master copy for duplication before flying out on a three-week tour to Dubai, Australia and New Zealand. He has nine hours left before the morning flight and a lot more to get done. His bags are already packed and on the floor next to our bed.

A gang of four armed robbers, who had been evading the police while causing havoc in the neighbouring community, unexpectedly run into exceptionally good luck: a house with no wall. How convenient. They cross the river and two neighbouring properties before cutting our chain link fence with wire clippers and crawl through an open window into our house. They go to where they hear the music. They catch Louis off guard, order him to the ground with the gun to his head, and tie his hands behind his back with shoe laces.

At 4 a.m. the security guards complete their second round. A guard notices the broken fence on the edge of the complex and immediately reports it. Everyone is informed via text messages, but by now the burglars have been in our house for almost two hours. Our cell phones can't beep anymore, and we don't dare make a peep either. Nobody around us suspects anything. The front of the theatre box seems intact.

Louis tries not to look at their faces and promises to cooperate. He senses the Lord giving him step by step instructions on what to do and not to do. He prays out loud – non-stop. Pleading prayers for God to spare us. Rebuking prayers directed at the demons he imagines must be in these men.

The men threaten to kill him. As if in response, God preaches Louis's own sermon back to him, the one he has preached to thousands of people across our country, quoting Charles Spurgeon:

> *"Stop fearing for your life! You are immortal until your work on earth is done."*

With the gun held to his head, he hears God's voice reassuring him:

> *"They hold the gun, but I hold the keys."*

Louis is not sure whether or not he will survive this night, but at the end of all of this he will know for certain whether there is still work and a calling for him on this earth. If not, this is the perfect opportunity for the end. In the midst of the fear that shakes his body, he is certain of one thing: These men cannot give or take away life at will. They cannot administer death. God will have the final word.

> **"Don't fear: I am First, I am Last, I'm Alive. I died, but I came to life, and my life is now forever. See these keys in my hand? They open and lock Death's doors, they open and lock Hell's gates"**
>
> (Revelation 1:17, *The Message*).
>
> *"Where are your guns? How many people are in the house? Where are they? Are they asleep? Take us to your wife. Wake her up and make sure she doesn't scream."*

Scream? Why do people always assume that women will scream? I despise those shrill high-pitched yells girls sometimes utter: 'Eeeeeeeee!' My three brothers tried in vain to elicit such shrieks from my mom and me, using the usual toy spiders, slimy frogs and huge fluttering moths. We are not screamers. We make a unique sound. Something between a goat's bleat and a lion's roar. And we add flailing arms for effect.

This exact sound escapes my throat as they finally bring me completely out of my daze. But the sound lasts just for a second or so, because then I hear Louis's calm voice filtering through:

> *"Honey, these men are here to take our stuff, and we will give them everything they want. But in the Name of Jesus they will not harm us. Don't look at their faces."*

I squeeze my eyes shut, but somehow the puppet theatre's curtains refuse to shut along with my eyelids. I want to bring the story to a stand-still, but everything keeps on moving. The puppets from other people's stories, puppets that use scary words and deadly guns have come alive and are standing in my room tonight. It's not a dream. It's not a nightmare. It's worse. My whole body is shaking, and in my mind's eye I see fire-breathing dragons like the ones in fairy tales. Horrifying newspaper headlines and the gruesome details of every kind of inhuman crime run through my mind like a colony of stinging fire ants.

In this moment, Louis's words become the antidote. I'm so glad they were in the script. His words start sinking in as I lie gasping face-down on my pillow. The ants stop biting. His words call out all the characters in my story to line up in front of the curtain, like actors taking the final bow. It's not only Louis and me, and our three vulnerable children and four dangerous men in this story. Jesus is here, too. As a Good Shepherd, He is always in my story.

In fact, Jesus has been playing the lead role in my life for quite some time. With hundreds of story episodes behind me over the past twenty years, I already know that we may encounter dragons in this life. Sometimes they arrive when I make big mistakes. Sometimes I run into them in dark corners where I'm not supposed to be. Sometimes they simply arrive uninvited. Regardless of the reason for their appearance, Jesus always chases them away. Still, I regularly forget that the story always ends in victory, so I keep getting scared, like I am again tonight. I should know by now that this fear is unfounded, because among the things I have learned so far are a number of unshakeable truths that will remain forever, even if my whole theatre box gets turned upside down tonight.

I grew up in a safe, carefree and loving home, with a dad who led me to the face of Jesus, and a mom who faithfully provided everything my three brothers and I needed – whether it was resources for a school project on the solar system, a basket of goodies for a picnic on the beach, or a Station Wagon load of necessities for a camping excursion in the mountains. She always had the details under control. Even now that we are grown and have kids of our own, her help is still a phone call away. This is how I got to know what love is – by looking into a gentle, caring face, and being cared for by an ever-present helping hand.

Love, I learned from experience, sometimes entails a shake of the head, a serious look, or even a frown. The same caring hands sometimes had to discipline me or remove me from the swing I didn't want to get down from. They had to pry sweets from my sticky fingers before dinner and, later, close the wallet so I could learn to stand on my own two feet. These things never made me doubt their love. They simply taught me that love had many faces, and love may include painful actions – not just bed time stories or a hot flask of tea with cookies on a cold winter's morning.

The same hands that rubbed my feet on cold winter evenings also plunged me into cold baths to break a tonsillitis fever. They even dabbed acid onto my skin when I was seven years old; the doctor said it was the only thing that would kill the uncommon type of wart I had on the soles of my feet. The hands had to apply the acid one drop at a time, using the back of a match. Then they scraped off the dead skin with a pocket knife until it started to hurt, repeating every twelve hours until one day they could scrape out the core from the bleeding crater which the treatment made in my foot. I cried every time. It was for my own good, though, and I knew it. Everything healed perfectly, and there were no recurring warts. The pain was necessary.

Love, I learned, is sometimes painful, bloody and even grisly. Love is not erased by pain. In fact, the two are often closely interwoven. In the birth of a baby we hear two screams – one of agony followed by one of life. On the cross of Jesus we see extreme pain and indescribable love rolled into one.

A very important truth, one I would need to lean on now, was already written on my heart: children will never ask their parents for pain – not even for necessary, healing pain. Good fathers and mothers must look past the temporary pain for the sake of their children's future. Fathers do not give snakes when children ask for bread, but sometimes inexperienced children are given bread that in their eyes seems like a snake. Fortunately, fathers know best. Good fathers give what *is* good, not what *feels* good.

I got to know fatherly hands as saving hands. I was a very scared girl as a child. When I needed to go to the bathroom at night, my heart was in my throat. Our hallway seemed like a deep, dark river which I could not cross alone for fear something would leap at me in the dark.

"Daddy, Daddy!"

I regularly cried in desperation. He would get up every time to help me across the dangerous river without complaint and without resentment. Afterwards he always tucked the blankets in tightly around me. The room didn't even seem dark anymore, simply because I felt assured he was always just one call away.

To me it was a logical conclusion: my heavenly Dad would be the same – close by when I called. The certainty of my daddy's love for me and my mom's care spilled over easily into an assurance that God the Father loved me in the same way. I did not doubt it. I just knew. I remained sure He was at the very least as merciful as my own dad. He would always provide everything I needed, even better than my mom could. During any dark night He would hear my half-bleat, half-roar distress call. He proved it countless times. He was not deaf. He was there whenever I needed to cross dangerous rivers.

He provided faithfully, even when my earthly parent wasn't present, like the time when my children and I ran into trouble in a foreign land. It happened in 2004, at the end of a four month concert tour through the USA and Britain. We were almost out of money. We ended the tour with a 36 hour non-stop trip, which entailed driving a minivan from Iowa to Chicago and then a flight from Chicago to New York.

A trip is only romantic if you don't have an almost two year old stepping on your lap as if it were a pile of dirty laundry. What makes it even less romantic is being eight weeks pregnant!

We tried to find the cheapest possible accommodation. As we opened the door of our hotel room at the YMCA in Manhattan, my five year old daughter complained about the foul smell. I picked up the smell, too. It smelled of late night parties, an old smell that seemed to have permeated the bedspreads, the rug, even the paint on the walls. It told of the after effects of binge drinking. The next moment she vomited right there in the doorway. Then as if on cue, our two year old son started screaming for food – suddenly too hungry to wait another minute.

The air-conditioning didn't work, the windows wouldn't open, and the floor space allowed for only one bag to be opened at a time. We had to alternate between digging for pyjamas and digging for clean diapers. You might wonder why we didn't just put some bags on the beds. Only Tarzan could have picked up those heavy bags high enough to swing them onto the bunk beds! When you travel with a band, the CDs, guitar pedals, drum sticks, cymbals, cables and reverb units are dished out equally among the travellers to ensure that everyone runs an equal risk of breaking their backs. To make matters worse, I could not find my son's baby bottle. Then and there I stopped fighting the urge to help and proved to all of them that I could whine and wail the loudest.

Escaping with a few dollars, Louis almost looked relieved to be the one chosen to go hunting for an affordable dinner for four. He spent the dollars very carefully, so after a whole hour he returned with one foot-long sub of wholegrain bread with ham and cheese. I tried to look impressed. In the meantime I had found the baby bottle and prepared green Cool Aid for me and the kids. We took turns sipping it from the only available container – the baby bottle. It was long after dinner when everybody finally stopped crying.

The next morning Louis had to leave us to fly back to Nashville, and we stayed behind with a whopping $5. It was an error in translation that got us into this financial trouble. When we booked the tickets we heard that we would land in New York and depart from what sounded like "New Ark." Ah, their strange American accent makes it seem like two separate places, but why would it be? Upon arrival at the airport, we discovered it was not the American accent but our own that let us down. We were at the wrong "New." Newark did exist after all and due to the fact that we were eight people with sixteen Tarzan bags and a truck load of sound equipment, the taxi ride we booked to get us to Newark two days later set us back a scandalous $800! Add to that figure the $400 we had set aside for Louis's roundtrip flight to Nashville and subtracted from what we had left, you end up with the measly $5 I found remaining in my pocket.

When Louis's taxi left, we looked brave and walked to the breakfast corner only to make a horrible discovery:

YMCA = BED – BREAKFAST!

Someone leaving the dining area noticed my son's longing stare and gave him the remainder of his oily doughnut from his typical American breakfast. Of course I wouldn't normally allow my children to take food from strangers, but at this point beggar me was not about to be a chooser.

With my son tucked into the carry bag on my back and my daughter's hand clutched tightly in mine, we tackled the streets of Manhattan. With our mighty $5 we headed out to find lunch, dinner and tomorrow morning's breakfast, keeping in mind that we should probably save a little to survive at the airport until our flight's departure the following evening at seven.

On the first corner, the Burger King beckoned us to *have it our way*. Determined, I walked in and ordered the smallest burger. At least it came with fries and a soda to share; it added up to $1.50. I ate the tomato slice and lettuce, dividing the rest of the burger between my children.

The waiter held herself back for a whole five minutes. She couldn't stand it any longer. I suppose such pathetic sharing goes against the American dream. She promptly served up two more burgers, fries and sodas, and when we had finished that, each of us got a piece of their famous cheesecake – all for free. God bless America!

With a skip in my step and $3.50 still in my pocket, we moved on to the next part of our mission – diapers. I was going to need at least four to get us to England, provided my little boy's stomach stayed stable. At the Dollar Store it was the first thing I noticed – a packet of half a dozen diapers for a dollar. We also noticed little children's books for just 25 cents each. My son dearly wanted the one about the magic snowman. We were broke anyway; a quarter wouldn't make a difference, so we added the snowman to our party.

I made my calculation. I had peanut butter in my suitcase (which I never leave home without), but I still needed to find something for us to eat that night and the next morning.

Around the first corner we discovered a deli. I asked if they sold "half loaves". Everyone in South Africa does. The man frowned. I could not afford a whole loaf of bread, so I tried saying with my fake American accent:

"Do you sell any 'hahf' loaves, sir?"

But still the same frown. It must be the idea of half a loaf of bread that troubled him, not the pronunciation, I thought to myself. I explained to him all I needed was a few slices of bread, a bit of butter and maybe something meaty. My pitiful request broke another American heart, and I walked out of the store with a loaf of bread, some butter, a few slices of deli meat, four bananas, and the same $2.25 in my pocket.

That night I managed to pry the hotel window open. Natural Manhattan air-conditioning. With my husband's luggage now out of the room I was even able to open two bags at the same time. Just like the comedian, Mr Bean, I used my worthless South African bank card to butter our slices of free bread. It was all the card was good for, because it had a five digit pin code instead of the four digit one required in foreign countries. I could stare at my bank balance on a screen while all I owned remained locked behind virtual bars.

That evening the three of us sat on the top bunk bed and read *The Magic Snowman* together. Nobody cried.

The next morning we ate the rest of our bread with peanut butter for breakfast, and the taxi we booked fortunately came as promised. After a few hours at the airport, I started rolling the last money around in my pocket. The children began to beg for bites and sips from the other band members, but I was too proud to allow that to continue. I had to go and buy something.

Everyone knows airports do not make their money by selling flight tickets; they make it by selling food at the price of gold. I searched for a packet of popcorn to divide between the three of us and found I had just enough money left for it. I observed the man standing in front of me at the cash register. With a fancy sandwich and a cappuccino in his hand, he suavely handed over an exclusive credit card to pay for his meal. He had clearly never stayed at the YMCA. Curtly the woman behind the counter motioned at a notice on the wall:

A minimum charge of $10 when paying by credit card.

Without making eye contact he turned to me and asked:

"What are you having?"

In that moment I understood what the twelve disciples must have felt when Jesus told them:

"Whatever you ask in My name, I will give to you."

I grabbed three energy bars, a coffee, two sodas and blurted out an overly dramatic,

"Thank you so much."

A few moments later I was sitting on an airport bench with all this food and $2.25 still in my pocket. It finally dawned on me that I had experienced the multiplication of our five dollars. I had been buying almost everything we needed over the course of two days with a heavenly credit card with no limit.

This is why I knew I am never abandoned. This is why I believe Louis's words as he says:

> *"These men are here to take our stuff. But in the Name of Jesus they will not harm us."*

Acid may drip on the soles of our feet, knives may scrape off dead skin, we may bleed profusely, we may walk the streets with a heavy load, but my Dad is always here to make sure everything heals. My Dad is always awake and hears me crying when I need to cross a deep river. In the centre of our being, in our spirit — where we already have eternal life — we carry a treasure that no one can take. They are welcome to take the rest. Just as my mother provided for my needs, the Spirit of the Living God will not forget to provide in the tiniest detail. If I search in the right places, I will surely find I already have everything I need for this unexpected situation.

In the days when I was seven years old with the painful feet, my dad's choir sang a hymn based on Psalm 121. Now I hear it replaying in my head:

> *"Indeed, He who watches over Israel will neither slumber nor sleep."*

Our three children are watching a puppet show in dream land.

The rest of us are awake: God, the burglars, Louis, and I. The theatre box is rocking precariously. A dark side of life behind the curtain is coming into view.

In at least five different homes, friends of ours are rolling around in their beds – unable to sleep. Some wake up to pray. One is only twelve years old and writes down a Bible verse for Louis. One feels he needs to pray for us, even though he hasn't seen us in almost a decade. He is unsure of what to pray for but believes God tells him to drive to a gas station to buy a newspaper. He obeys. It's full of crime stories. He prays that we will be protected from violent crime and goes back to sleep. Two women believe they hear the Spirit of God saying my name and blindly pray for all the usual things like our family's safety, our marriage, and that our hearts will be near to God. The next day one of them posts Psalm 23 on my Facebook page ...

In East-London, an artist who does not even know me also can't sleep. She gets up, creates a necklace rich in symbolism and calls it 'Mary'. She returns to bed.

2 Not forsaken

I still have my face buried in my pillow. I expect the worst as I hear one of the robbers bending over my back. I feel his breath on my arms. He lifts up my hand and pulls my wedding ring off my finger with his teeth. Vivid images crowd my mind again like those teeming fire ants of a minute ago. They threaten to overwhelm me – images of women with cut-off fingers and chopped-off hands in black trash bags ... I suddenly regret having seen so many episodes of CSI. As he struggles to bite off the other ring, I propose to take it off for him. I intend to give them everything they want. All I want is for them to leave my husband and children alone. I don't care what happens to our belongings, as long as we can all manage to survive this; most people in our country don't survive this type of robbery. Survival is as much as we should hope for.

If they give me a choice, I would rather choose to be shot in the head than to be stabbed to death. And if that happens, then may it be my husband first. No husband should have to powerlessly watch his wife die. If I survive, I will continue with my life for the sake of my children, but if they die I would also rather go with them. If Louis and I both get shot, then I still want my children to live. I just hope they won't have to go through life with bloody images imprinted on their childhood memories.

I wonder what my children's reactions will be to all of this, especially if Louis and I are murdered tonight. I pray they won't hate God. I pray the stories of God's bigger picture, the transience of life, and the immortality of love that I've read to them during our home schooling days have cut a deep enough track of truth in their hearts. Our youngest is only three. In time she will forget about us and will simply have to trust that the people in the photos, the ones everybody cries nostalgically about, were her people.

The various possible scenarios and final wishes keep churning in my thoughts. The seconds feel like hours.

With my eyes shut, I lie face down and hear the bedside drawers on my left and right opening and closing. They find our cell phones but are still looking for guns and more jewellery. I explain to them that everything I own is on the dressing table, and the only other jewellery worth anything is my grandmother's diamond ring in the drawer. They don't fully comprehend what I'm saying, so they pull me to my feet and insist we take them through the house to find everything they want to take.

For more than an hour we move up and down the stairs with them, back and forth between the bedroom and the study looking for firearms, jewellery, and computers. My dad's gun safe in the dressing room is empty since we handed the guns in at the police station. There are two lone rounds left inside, in the place of the .22 rifle that would have been there. I hope they don't see the rounds because it could rouse their suspicion.

If I remember the newspaper stories correctly, people are often beaten to a pulp until they hand over their weapons and money. How will we explain an empty gun safe with bullets still inside?

> *"We don't own a gun."*

They believe us and nobody gets hurt.

The robbers and I simultaneously think of the cash in the house.

> *"We know you white people have safes. And you women spend the money. Where is it?"*

I explain to them where to find it, but they want us to show them. Once again we are lifted to our feet. I refuse to look at them. One of them tries to lift up my head with his hand under my chin, but he wants me to look where I'm going so I won't fall down the stairs. I insist that I don't want to be able to identify them. He grips me firmly by the shoulders and takes me down the stairs.

When we bought this house, the safe had already been installed but was in bad condition. It's still in the same condition, coming out of the wall – bolts and all – essentially useless. It would serve better as carry-on luggage! A few weeks ago, when Louis applied for his Australian visa, we tried in vain to open the safe, thinking that his misplaced passport might be in there. The previous year we occasionally kept petty cash for our home office in there along with our passports. After seven months of not using it, however, nobody in the house or the office could remember what the combination was. Luckily the passport appeared elsewhere.

Now I find myself on my knees in front of the safe with a revolver against my head.

> *"You have one chance to open it. If there is no money in it, I will blow your head off."*

Another truth comes into focus. I realise that this part of the script is not an *ad lib* movie moment. This is not *Whose Line is it Anyway*? Someone wrote this story and is making sure every actor is playing his part correctly. This is the moment when I'm convinced Jesus is not just another puppet in my story, but Someone behind the puppet theatre – Someone bigger than us all and in control. Not only is He here with me right now—He has already been here.

Just ten days ago, I suddenly decided that friends who owed me money should be reminded of their debt. I wanted to have curtains made for the bedrooms and living room. It was a year since we moved into the house, and the rooms' windows were still bare. I felt guilty asking for money because I still had a few thousand South African Rand in my account, and by April I would receive royalties for a parenting book. It was strange for me to act this way, knowing my friends weren't in the same position. I asked Louis why I had suddenly become such a terrible person who wanted to shake down people in need – and for a few pieces of cloth in front of a window! The debt was already a few months overdue, however, and so he felt it was probably my right to ask for it ... even though I could see a question mark on his face. This behaviour was out of character for me.

I phoned my friend and asked for the money. Her husband arrived a few days later with R10 000 in cash. I didn't want to sound ungrateful, but, goodness me, did he expect me to pay the banking fee for the cash deposit as well? I complained. Why did he not simply transfer it electronically into my bank account?

"Don't you have a safe?"

I glanced at the useless metal box which used to be a safe before it came out of the wall bolts and all.

"I suppose I could keep it there. But it is so easily carried off as hand luggage. It's like a lucky packet for whoever finds it, Besides, I don't know the combination.

I consoled myself that nobody would find it. It was safe behind the bookshelf in my study. After all, our side of the forest doesn't have wolves, does it?

My friend left and I simply had to make a plan. I went through a great deal of trouble to find the previous office assistant who sometimes used the safe so I could finally figure out the combination and put the money in the not-so-safe safe. My new assistant made me memorise the code. She knew I forgot numbers all the time. Thankfully I had to recall it again the following week in order to give one of our employees a few hundred Rand advance on her salary.

Here I am on my knees in front of the safe. Louis is praying aloud in the background.

"Jesus, please!"

With the alien looking hand-made revolver angled above my left eye, I ready myself to punch in the code on the little keypad. They untie the shoe laces so I can use my hands. I know the code! There are thousands of Rands in cash in here. They are going to be very happy. This is very good. I punch the four keys in the correct order. The safe door swings open willingly.

They tie me up again and command us to lie down on the carpet while they distribute the cash among themselves as if they were dealing a deck of playing cards. I can smell the dirt trapped in the rug in my study and curse our miniature Dachshund who leaves his mark everywhere. I think of everything else that is dirty and untidy in the house. I can't die tonight. My mom would hate to clean up my messes. At least she will be able to inherit my scrapbooking materials. It dawns on me that my thoughts are awfully trivial. Shame on me for thinking about such things at a time like this. I should rather be praying non-stop like Louis.

They seem to be very happy with the cash. They call me 'Ma'am.' Then, once again, they drag us upstairs. I peek through squinted eyes; I can see only my bare feet and their threadbare trousers and shoes. They push Louis and me down onto the floor next to the bed in our bedroom.

"Sleep! Sleep!"

Louis's feet are pointing eastward and mine westward, our heads together.

"Honey if this is the end, I'll see you on the other side."

Louis is the realist. He reads the daily newspaper and knows the probability of this night going awry. We pray together out loud in an unsynchronised fashion like a poor speech-choir. They have had enough and silence us. I pray in tongues in my head because I don't know what to ask any more.

Once again they start searching through everything. One of them asks me why we don't have an alarm system.

"We didn't think we needed one. We thought we were safe."

He sarcastically spews the words back in my ear:

"You thought you were safe!"

His taunting triggers verses that I memorised from Psalm 18. I memorised them, because as I read the Psalm on New Year's Day I believed it to be my key scripture for the year. I repeat it to myself:

"I love you God. You make me strong. My God is bedrock under my feet, the castle in which I live, my rescuing Knight. My God – the high crag where I run for dear life, hiding behind the boulders, safe in the granite hideout. I sing to God, the Praise-Lofty, and find myself safe and saved."

I lie there thinking, 'God is my castle. No burglar bars, alarm, electric fencing or weapons can protect me anyway.' It's also not Louis's responsibility. He already moved our family to a safer area, and he pays a levy for the extra security patrols. He is the knight in my puppet show, but when this puppet theatre crashes in, as is happening now, he needs Jesus just as much as I do. I'm going to run into the granite hide-out tonight. I'm going to wait for my Knight to come and rescue me.

I recall the rest of the memorised verses from Psalm 18:

"The hangman's noose was tight at my throat; devil waters rushed over me. Hell's ropes cinched me tight; death traps barred every exit. A hostile world! I call to GOD, I cry to God to help me. From is palace He hears my call; my cry brings me right into his presence – a private audience!"

Now I know why I felt prompted to memorise this Psalm! It was the first time in more than a year I had memorised scripture. I wondered then what "hell's ropes" could refer to, and I couldn't imagine I would ever find myself in a place where it would feel like death lies in waiting for me at every exit. But here I am in exactly such a situation. I can choose to focus on hell's ropes and the robber's fire arm or on the One whose complete attention I have. I can cry out to Him.

If the first part of the Psalm is true — and if we as God's people can end up in death traps with devil waters rushing over us and death traps barring the exits — then the rest must be true for us as well. When we call out in this hostile world, then even a soundless scream on the inside, like mine right now, will be heard! I can make my bleat-roar sound or cry "Daddy," as I did as a child, or I can jabber in incomprehensible tongues ... either way I have my God's attention.

Many people assume difficult times and God's attentive presence don't go hand in hand. According to them, a watchful God should do one of two things: get rid of all difficulty and hurt, or prevent all difficulty and hurt from coming near us in the first place. I'm glad the Psalmist David refers to both extremes in the same breath and drags us in behind the puppet theatre where the truth is clear: devil waters *and* an attentive God in the same picture. If He does not prevent the devil waters from rushing in, as He did not prevent the rain water from flooding the river banks and washing away our perimeter fence, many people reach a damaging and erroneous conclusion: He looked the other way. They believe something or someone more important than them must have diverted His attention. If He had seen it, if He had been there, if He knew, He would have stopped it, wouldn't He? Or is He not really God? Perhaps He couldn't look our way because something in our lives put Him off ...

I've seen this pain before. In victims of hurt and abuse it's a pain that continually screams:

> *"You weren't valuable enough for Him to pay close attention to what was happening in your life!"*

It's an unbearable insult piled on top of the present injury. Not only did they get hurt, they also have to face the possibility God doesn't really care.

This type of intense pain throbs with disillusionment, rejection, and powerlessness. This is just the smoke, though. If we follow the smoke trail it takes us to the fire which is fuelled with lies from the pit of hell. There is no pain as excruciating as the pain caused by the lies we believe. The lies we choose to believe are like swords we voluntarily and even intentionally fall into like Saul. It takes us to the same dark place where we, like Eve in the Garden of Eden, continually doubt God's intentions. We wonder if He truly has our best interest at heart. We wonder whether He really sees us. As a result we make choices that lead to death.

These are a few lethal lies which most victims of trauma believe. It's not God's fault we get confused about God's stance on pain. The Bible never sugar coats trauma. The Old and New Testaments both plainly exhibit the truth about this; so if we read, believe and apply these truths we can dispel the lies we believe. We can find the antidote to our heartache. Yet many Bible readers never listen to the truth with the ears of their hearts, and this deafness for truth is even more pronounced in those who don't read their Bibles at all.

Paul writes to the Corinthians that he and his fellow Christians are hard-pressed on every side, yet not crushed; struck down, but not destroyed. He defends a fundamental truth: this temporary life's toughest blows can never crush the Eternal Life inside of us.

Sometimes life leaves us feeling crushed and in tatters. It might be because we don't believe, or that we've forgotten the truth exhibited in the same verse – a truth of such cardinal importance that we won't be able to stay spiritually or emotionally intact unless we believe it. *We are persecuted, but not abandoned.* Once again: God's presence and our pain in the same picture; persecution with God right next to us.

It's a lie that God wasn't there when we got hurt. The power of this lie is that it not only leaves us with the pain of loneliness, but also with the fear that we will be betrayed again in future crises. We erroneously think, "If God abandoned me once, then what will prevent Him from doing it again?" If that were true, then we should rightly shake with fear every day wondering what awaits us around the next bend.

But the actual truth is: *God did not forsake us.*

It's physically impossible for God to forsake His own. How could an omnipotent God withdraw His presence in our darkest moments? It's also not spiritually possible because Jesus bought us something very special: *God the Father's face.* On the cross He paid for abandonment when the Father turned His face away from His son. Only Jesus could truly cry out:

> *"My God, my God, why did You forsake me?"*

Because Jesus paid the price so dearly to be sure it will never happen again, we will never have cause to repeat that cry. Instead we can stand tall and cry out in victory and hope: Never again will anyone who believes in Jesus be forsaken by God.

Many Christians entertain the lie of abandonment even though they merrily sing along with worship songs in church:

> **I'm forgiven, because You were forsaken**
> **I'm accepted; You were condemned**
> **I'm alive and well, Your Spirit lives within me**
> **Because You died and rose again!**
>
> [Billy James Foote, *Amazing Love*]

Obviously these words sung dutifully on a Sunday morning do not automatically trump the lie, but they should, because it is the healing truth. There is a firm anchor for the soul and an indestructible steadfastness of spirit in every Christian that knows: I have God's full attention – always.

Instead of crying tears of abandonment as the devil waters wash over us, let us rather call out:

> *"God show me where You are! Open my eyes so I can see You in every storm of life."*

Let me ask one of the forbidden questions: Why our house? Couldn't God have prevented these men from coming into our home? Many people believe this: *God can't prevent what bad people decide to do. People have free will against which God cannot act.* It's a lie, too – a lie that leaves us with the most terrifying fear of all: that we're either left in the hands of evil people without an effective Helper, or we have a powerless puppet god who is not who he claims to be. People who spread this lie imply that we have a God who continually invites us to build on Him as our Rock, to keep our eyes on Him, to trust Him with everything, to unswervingly believe in Him and His good plans for us, but who should probably have pointed out the fine print disclaimer that He would unfortunately not be able to help us when evil people have evil plans for us.

This couldn't be further from the truth.

In his book *Growing with Christ*, J.I. Packer explains that when God introduced Himself to Moses as YAHWEH, which means "I am," He was telling Moses something much more profound than a simple mysterious name. God revealed something of His being.

> *"I am the One whose being cannot be manipulated by anyone. I will be who I will be and no one can thwart or distort it."*

His being would never be controlled, restricted, predicted or contained by people. Moses would soon see a practical demonstration of the "I am" playing out in front of him: A strong arm twisting Pharaoh's will to become stubborn and yielding and stubborn again many times over according to God's own plan. The mightiest ruler of the time had to play along like a puppet in God's show. He would feel his lips move with words he hadn't thought of himself. Exasperated, he would see a nation, which he didn't want to let go, walk away laden with the riches from his own kingdom. God would have His way and people – believers and doubters alike – would have to look on.

How then could we believe today that the malevolence in mortal men is what determines when and how God can be God to you and me?

If it's not true that God looks the other way, and if it's also not true that He is at the mercy of evil people, then it leaves us with some very uncomfortable conclusions: God is always present. He sees and hears, and yet He doesn't always stop these things even though He easily could. Many stop right here, grab their precious theatre box, plug their ears and storm off swearing that all the lies they believe are more bearable than this! They feel it would be better for them to fall forward onto the swords of their own lies. They'd rather believe God did nothing because He couldn't.

This is actually just half of the story. There is a truth we often forget which makes a tremendous difference. For those who only acknowledge it theologically, it will not relieve any pain or fear. But for those who grasp it in their deepest being – in their spirit – it is the truth that changes everything.

This truth is: *Jesus in us*.

Those of us who have built our lives unconditionally on the completed work of Jesus Christ have an indestructible spirit – unbreakable by the events of this life. God made us this strong by His Spirit. God made us supernaturally sturdy. He gave us so much inner strength that when we are pressed hard enough, what flows out will be the rich deposit of God's Spirit in our lives ... not our own weakness but the power that raised Christ from the dead (Ephesians 1:19-20).

The truth is: God could have stopped our four robbers in their tracks. If their actions would in any way have limited God from being God in our lives, He certainly would have kept them at bay by ordering an angel to stretch out just one arm. It would have been enough. Easy. If they had the ability to steal Jesus away from us or to destroy everything He is to us, then God would have tossed them out by their collars. The fact that He didn't tells me God saw them for who they were – troublesome, dangerous, full of evil – not unlike Pharaoh of old – but nevertheless unable to thwart His good plans. They were weaklings swinging their fists at the Creator, which is laughable from God's perspective. God saw them as they were. They were not and still are not able to enslave those who are in Christ or able to take away the Promised Land of milk and honey that awaits us.

Glimpses like these behind the puppet theatre shake our theology, don't they? Especially if our theology doesn't embrace what David embraced in Psalm 18 – suffering and a loving God right next to each other in the same photo frame. If our theology doesn't give us this hope then it really needs to be shaken. If our theology cannot free us from the lies that bring so much pain, all of us need to plead for a shake-down that would rid us of every sham. If our theology presents us with a God whose hands can be tied behind His back by mere men, we need to light the match beneath it ourselves and let it burn.

Why is the above-mentioned theology so attractive? Because it gives us a handle to hold on to and a theatre box small enough to carry around. We enjoy holding on to theology that allows us to fathom our unfathomable God. We love explanations that rest on the elementary logic of cause and effect. According to such a theology, there must be a reason why our house was chosen for this criminal act. Louis or I or both of us must have done or owned something unholy.

There must have been a reason why God's arm was too short to help, a reason for His apparent absence. Maybe some secret sin drove Him away, maybe some African *sangoma* buried *muti* in the garden, or perhaps the objectionable object that kept God out was a souvenir we brought home from a trip to Egypt. What if He couldn't come in our hour of need because our forefathers had committed an evil deed or left idolatrous artefacts in the attic? Perhaps everything could have been prevented if only Louis and I had remembered to put on the armour of God and to plead the blood of Jesus over the house. Or maybe we should have anointed the windows also and not just the doors on the day when we moved in. Maybe that would have convinced God that we qualified for special help. In our human fickleness we desperately want to hold on to a conveniently pre-packaged theology such as this one.

If our God was this small and subject to His own creation and creatures, we had better march around the Jericho walls of our religion until the earth quakes and everything implodes. Such theology waters down the perfect and complete work of Jesus on the cross to a mere brave attempt. The cross of Christ was not a good try — it was a resounding success!

These ideas reek of Old Testament sin-offering theology which doesn't take into account that Jesus became a curse for us. During Old Testament times, God explicitly asked His people whether or not they realised that it was their sins that had become a wall between Him and them. The sin caused them to feel His ears were deaf and His arms too short to help, but the wall came down when the veil was torn in two. Now, because of what Christ has done, we who have cast in our lot with Him, stand in a place where our sin no longer determines our fate. We stand in righteousness before God, covered in the blood of Jesus whether or not we plead or profess it daily.

God's name is 'I will be who I will be.' His name is not 'I will be whatever you need Me to be.' Nor is it 'I will be who people allow Me to be.'

A theology that can withstand the trauma and violence of life in South Africa needs to contain this one truth at the very least: *Immanuel. God with us*. Even though we are sinful, even though there is nothing more we can do to be more acceptable ... *Immanuel*. That is the difference between a people plodding along heads down with their peace offerings sent ahead in the hopes of finding a morsel of favour ... and us. We are in Christ. Jesus is in us. Nothing can separate us from His love.

I cannot resist paraphrasing into my own words the promises of Romans 8:31-39, which were already beautifully penned by Eugene Peterson in *The Message*:

> **You have to state where you stand on this so let me help you get your thoughts straight: Is there ever really the danger of defeat with God on our team? If God, ticking every box of what it cost to save us, broke through every barrier, scaled every wall and plodded through the stinking swamp that kept us stranded in our sorry state, is there anything He would regard as too much trouble? Will He hold anything back until we can afford it or qualify for it? Would anyone even dare to orphan us if God proved us adopted like this? Could anybody make our shame stick to us? Our Sacrifice, the Risen One, the Victor over death, is ready before the throne, convincingly stating our case and defending our favourable standing before God. Is there anyone who could counter such a defence by making God suspicious of us or making God suspicious in our eyes? Impossible! Trouble can come, we can have a rocky road beneath our feet, be hated by all, emaciated by hunger, deceived by homelessness into forgetting that we have our home in the King's palace, taunted by terrorist threats, hung out to dry by so-called friends, surrounded by enemies who move in when we are at our weakest because by hurting us they hope to bring God agony. When all of this has been hurled at our faith, what will the damage be? There will be none! Our faith is in this: Jesus loves us! We will bet our life on it that no stinking grave, nothing that walks on the earth, nothing with angel wings or demon fangs, nothing from the old days or the New Age, nothing hidden deep or flying high, nothing understandable or incomprehensible – I mean nothing – can sever the bond of love between us and God. And there is only one reason for this: the way in which Jesus has always loved us and always will love us: unconditionally.**

While looking away from the robbers and revolver that taunt and lie to me by saying my God is not present, I can see Him. It's a good thing to close our eyes from the immediate reality in order to stare into the one that lies just beyond it. I see my God's fingerprints everywhere – in the provision of cash in the safe, in the invisible barriers that keep the burglars out of my children's rooms hour after hour and in the fact that all of the scurrying about has not awakened them. I experience Him in the inexplicable hope in my heart, because I know that Louis's whispered words are the truth – if this is the end, we still have the other side. We're already living in eternity. The truth liberates me even though I am tied up – they can take everything from us except the indestructible treasure of Jesus' love for us.

> *"In the Name of Jesus they will not harm us."*

The Name of the Lord is a strong tower

The righteous run into it and they are saved!

(Proverbs 18:10, *New International Version*)

3 *Hidden*

I hear one of them come up the stairs. At first my heartbeat follows the rhythm of his footsteps, then it accelerates. His footsteps taunt me: *Trouble is on its way!* He says he hears a beeping noise in the studio, and Louis must come along to switch it off. After taking the computers earlier, they unplugged the lightning protectors. These were now emitting a low battery signal that sounded to them like a panic alarm of some sort.

Three of the robbers go with Louis and one stays with me in the bedroom. He sits on the bed. I hear zippers whizzing as he repacks Louis's luggage that was set out for the trip. I imagine him separating it into the bag he would take and the bag he would leave behind. I wiggle myself forward until I am halfway under the bed in order to look as harmless as possible. I stare at the grooves of the laminate flooring. He needs to know that I am not memorising his features or doing anything else of the sort. And I pray. I'm very relieved that the robber is ignoring me and seems to be much more interested in the luggage than in my exposed legs – which must be visible from where he is sitting.

Usually it makes you feel good when someone is attracted to you or interested in you. It's flattering. It's affirming. But lying here now I'm incredibly thankful to be, for the moment, unobtrusive. Invisible. I have no desire to catch the eye tonight.

During spring break of the previous year the Lord had urged me to come and sit at His feet. I knew how to fight for something, and I knew how to work hard, but I didn't really know how to sit still. It was an incredibly daunting command when God instructed me to clear my schedule for one full year. No public speaking. No training. No doing what I had been doing for years. A clean break from the very things that had become my identity.

That was the whole problem. While reading the book *Shame Off You* by Alan D. Wright, I become aware of the pathology of my subconscious motto – busier, better, bigger! These were the symptoms of an orphan mentality. It characterises somebody who needs to create rain for himself by dancing before his idol of choice. In my case I thought that the harder I worked, the more my ambition idol would provide me with approval and fulfilment — only to realise later that I could only dance so fast and my idol could never make quite enough rain. The result was experiencing even more of the shame I thought I could get rid of in the first place. I felt especially ashamed the day I got a rear view perspective on the silly rain dance that had become my life. Instead of dispensing a sense of worth, my work only mocked me by screaming a silent *Never good enough!*

God wanted to release me from the need to perform and my need to earn recognition for it. This was my idol. The applause from people, the number of books I sold, the number of people attending my talks – these were all things by which I measured whether or not I still made it. I had been like this since school days, and God knew. It was time to stop the rain dance.

At first I tried really hard to negotiate with God while driving down to a small town where I was due to present a parenting course followed by a sermon on the Sunday morning:

> *"Lord, I know I do things for recognition and it has become an idol. Since I've repented and acknowledged this, I feel I can keep on speaking and training. Now that I know what to watch out for, I'm OK. Surely now that I understand this, You don't still intend to take me off the stage for a whole year, do You?"*

God has a way of speaking once and demonstrating after that in case we are hard of hearing. I was given a little demonstration. I arrived at the little town only to be sent to an old couple's house around the corner since the pastor's wife reportedly did not feel up to the task of receiving me in their home. Upon entering their house, I heard the disconcerting sound of the old gentleman throwing up in the bathroom. Politely, they offered me tea. Graciously, I asked for coffee – my drug of choice. They had no coffee in the house. I instantly knew it would be a very long headache of a weekend. Pun intended. After an exhausting evening session, I lay sleeplessly shivering in my icy room listening as the dear old man vomited intermittently throughout the night. I wondered when the incubation period of this old man's tummy virus would catch up with me: Would it be on Sunday morning behind the pulpit? Or maybe on Sunday afternoon on my drive back to Pretoria?

Saturday morning began with an intense withdrawal headache. To add insult to headache, the audience seemed decidedly bored. Nobody asked questions. There was no participation whatsoever. Everybody just wanted to make sure I finished on time so they wouldn't miss the kick-off of that afternoon's rugby match. My books and CD's, which usually sell very well, lay gathering farm dust on the table. Before storming off to the TV screen, the minister offhandedly reminded me that he would not allow the house of God to be turned into a den of thieves — I, therefore, shouldn't bring my products with me to church the next morning when I come to deliver the sermon.

Upon my arrival on Sunday morning the other minister closed the vestry door in my face. I was harmless enough to preach to his congregation, but joining a church council meeting was one step too far ... I belonged outside those holy walls. While they prayed for the morning service I stood behind the pulpit in a small passage waiting for my cue to preach. I tried to suppress the unease rising up inside me. I hadn't had any coffee and my head was pounding, but the intense agony in my heart was due to a withdrawal of another kind. My other addiction hadn't been fed – I hadn't received any appreciation.

I preached my heart out. Yet all I saw were puzzled faces. I had barely stepped down from the pulpit when the minister helped me pack up my laptop and walked me to the car. There was no 'thank you', no 'we learned so much from you!' Only this:

> *"Don't take the road through Parys. It's in bad condition."*

Even if there had been potholes I wouldn't have seen them through the tears of self-pity that flowed freely. It hurt so much. I blurted out at the top of my lungs:

> *"OK, God. I get the message. I'm addicted to approval! I enjoy being treated well and being appreciated. So, it's fine. Put me on a one-year detox. Clearly I have a big problem. I'm not going to negotiate any more. I'll clear my schedule for 2010. I'll go off my drug – cold turkey!"*

While driving and wondering how on earth I would survive it all, I heard a question inside of me:

> *"Hettie, why did I create all this?"*

I looked at the bushes and hills along the road and gave the Sunday school answer:

> *"You made creation to declare Your glory."*

> *"No. I made it because that's just who I am."*

That's true, I thought. My God is so full of beauty that He can't keep it in. Creation and beauty burst out of his being.

The revelation and jolting realization tumbled over me like buckets of cold ice: I've always done things because it helped people, because it was interesting, because market research showed the need, because my publisher insisted on it, or maybe even because it glorified *me*. Had I ever done anything because I couldn't stop myself, because it was busting out of who I was in the Lord and who He had become in me? I found myself afraid to answer and cried unashamedly.

A gas station appeared on the horizon just as my fuel light turned red. My nose was the same colour red from all the crying and my eyes were puffy. I was very relieved when I seemed to be the only client at the little station. 'If anybody sees me like this...!' I thought. I handed the attendant R200 for the fuel. 'If I had sold something during the weekend then I would have at least been able to fill up the tank with fuel', I thought bitterly. I rushed into the shop for coffee. At least this was one comfort I could have. The attendant called me back before I reached the shop.

> *"Are you from church, Ma'am?"*

Irritated with the man who was keeping me from my coffee I turned around to face him.

> *"Yes, I've just preached at a church, but I don't understand your question."*

He stood leaning with one hand on my dilapidated Toyota's roof and the other on the fuel nozzle.

> *"I feel like I'm serving an angel. I have never seen such love and power."*

There I was, looking like a mourner with a migraine and feeling sorry for myself. But finally I was small enough that somebody could see right through me and past me, straight into the face of the Puppet Master himself. I used to be the wannabe star, in my own eyes, anyway. Now I saw the truth – I was more of an eclipse, really. If I could move aside, God could shine His glory past me. I heard the Lord whispering: 'This is where We are going with you – to a place where you don't have to teach people to get their children to sleep through the night or get their toddlers to stop biting the other kids at the nursery. You won't have to go on selling parenting books so that people can see you. It's only the show. It's not real life. If you would just get out of the way, you'll have the joy of people seeing Me through you. It's so much better.'

I was stunned. After a brief discussion with the attendant about Jesus, which was probably not that necessary, I got coffee and returned to my car. I understood now. I would have to give up my artificial rainmaking for a heavenly torrent which I wouldn't have to dance for. What I had thought was God wanting to spitefully hold me back from ministry was in fact a very gracious offer.

In the week that followed, God kept on confirming He wanted me at His feet. I would have to exchange my Martha coat for a Mary one. I was convinced it would not fit. Mary coats usually didn't come in my style, cut, colour or size, and they were allegedly not made for speed ... I liked speed.

During a weekend retreat with five other women, one lady read something from her journal that the Lord had supposedly told her to tell me: 'You've been playing Martha-Martha for a long time. You have to be Mary for a year.' She didn't even know who I was or what I did for a living. Immediately another woman added: 'I saw you at the feet of Jesus and your wrists were handcuffed to His feet.' I hear the unsaid warning: 'You have to come willingly so He won't have to use circumstances to tie you down.' I was still staggering from the initial warning when a third lady shared a vision she had of me. In the vision I sat for a little while, stood up, walked away, burned my hand on a hot stove and then returned to sit again. The message was obvious to me: 'If you stand up, you will get hurt.' It was all too clear to doubt any longer. I cleared my diary for 2010 and gave my assistant the instruction to say: "Hettie is taking a sabbatical for the entire 2010. Please apply again later for talks in 2011."

In December 2009 I decided to start practising my sitting skills. I probably wouldn't magically transform into a Mary on the 1st of January, would I? I had been so proud and independent for so long that my knees wouldn't even bend. I was used to a McDonald's style spiritually – grabbing a Bible verse on the run like grabbing a burger at the drive-thru. How would I ever learn to kneel and digest slowly? I bought myself a journal, convinced I would write for a week and then shove it into a cupboard in between half-read diet books, half-done sewing projects and unfinished scrapbooks. But I was going to give it a shot, anyway.

I decided to start writing down whatever I thought I heard, or at least what I knew I read. Since I hadn't attended a journaling workshop, I wasn't exactly sure where to start.

Within days something happened to me that eventually shackled me as if I were indeed handcuffed. I thought my marriage to Louis was the one area in life where I was covered in plates of double thick armour. Over almost eighteen years our relationship had become watertight, I believed. But one fair evening a man I didn't even know well gave me a compliment coupled with a cry for help ... and with that he stormed through my feeble defences as if with a battering ram through a paper wall. With every secretive message we exchanged in the days thereafter, I felt my head and heart shifting. For the first time in my life I held on to Jesus daily as if my very life depended on it.

I thought I would have a choice whether I came willingly or in chains, but I soon realised that I, just like Paul, needed a firm hand and a good shake-down from the Lord in order to hear which way to go. I discovered things within me I didn't like at all. My holiness and pride lay like shattered glass around my feet, because I had never thought I would be involved in anything sneaky like this. The fact that the content of the messages were innocent enough and mostly aimed at helping him through a crisis did not dissipate the underlying emotions of guilt. If it was all innocent, why was I hiding it? It was the frequency of the messages and my emotional dependence on them that soon set off the alarm.

For the first time in my journey with the Lord, I would sometimes lie face down on that same dirty carpet in our study that smelled of Dachshund and cry:

> *"If You don't keep me, Jesus, I'm lost!"*

I felt like a fluttering flag clinging to a pole, soon to be ripped apart by the howling wind. I enjoyed the intellectual challenge of the riddles and arguments this man and I exchanged in between our formal discussions. It simultaneously felt as if I was taking part in a treasure hunt and I, myself, was a treasure being hunted. I rationalised that I was just helping this man, but my heart belied it.

I looked for anchors in the Word and in my daily Charles Spurgeon devotional. I read strange messages, which I dutifully wrote down in hopes they would protect me from being completely swept away.

In retrospect, I can see two puppet show stories intertwined over a period of months. I was learning about the mysteries of temptation and tests. I was learning what a temptation and attack from hell looked and felt like, but also how it looked and felt when the Silversmith stokes the fire more and more to burn away all the impurities until He can see a semblance of His own face in the reflection.

I jotted down what I was learning.

December 11

> **All who are in union with the Lamb are safe; all the righteous will hold on their way, and those who have committed their souls to the keeping of Christ will find Him a faithful and immutable Preserver. May He assure you that your name is engraved on His hand and whisper in your ear the promise, 'Fear not; for I am with thee'.**
>
> (Spurgeon)

This probably means that Jesus will not allow me to slip through His fingers in this test. I can trust Him. But one only preserves that which can rot; therefore I really need His preservation, because as a person I'm unfortunately perishable. I can't stay unsullied on my own. Even though I can trust Him I should not trust myself. It's the bitter truth, and for the sake of survival I need to swallow it. I have to see the connection between my proud, independent self and my inborn tendency to rot.

December 12

> **You have dealt treacherously with Jesus, your First Love, but He stands even now with your name engraved on His breastplate, interceding for you in the throne room.**
>
> (Spurgeon)

If I don't protect my heart carefully, the danger of unfaithfulness towards my husband is not nearly as great as the danger of betraying Jesus. I call myself a Christian ...

While I thought about this I heard Jesus:

> *"Hettie, I'm praying for you."*

Of course it's an undisputed Biblical truth and is written everywhere in Hebrews, but my honest, instinctive reaction was: 'Oh my goodness! If even Jesus is praying for me then I'm in serious trouble!' Yet the words also brought me tremendous comfort. Surely Jesus would pray effectively. He would certainly ensure that I remained standing.

December 13

> **Some things in the economy of grace are measured; for instance our vinegar and gall are given to us with such exactness that we never have a single drop too much, but of the salt of grace no restriction is made ... You need much. Seek much, and you will have much.**
>
> (Spurgeon)

Here once again is the guarantee that temptations and pain will never be too unbearable. While writing down this truth I wondered exactly how much gall I would have to drink and how much vinegar my sponge would contain. Maybe it depended on me. Maybe the proudly self-sufficient ones among us receive more of it because we can handle more, or maybe we get more because it's difficult to break us into submission and humility.

December 15

> **The kiss of outward profession [of faithfulness] is very cheap and easy, but the practical cleaving to the Lord, which must show itself in holy decision for truth and holiness, is not so small a matter. How does the case stand with us? Are our hearts fixed on Jesus? Is the sacrifice bound with cords to the horns of the altar?**
>
> (Spurgeon)

One would probably never know how strongly someone is clinging to Jesus by just listening to the words from her mouth. One probably has to tug here and pull there to find out. If her grip loosens easily, she probably needs to be tied down more tightly ...

December 16

> **You will be panting for nearer and closer communion with Him ... Your response to Him will be, 'Come, and occupy alone the throne of my heart. Reign there without a rival, and consecrate me entirely to Your service.'**
>
> (Spurgeon)

Kingship without competition? The picture of my heart is probably: the King sits on the throne but is barely visible through the sheer wealth of ideas, desires, plans and loves trying to dethrone him by force. In the deafening noise, the King's voice is lost. I wondered what it would take to convince someone who is flattered by the contest for her heart, to call out: 'Only you, Jesus!'

December 18

> **Heartrending is powerfully humiliating and completely sin-purging; but then, it is sweetly preparative for those gracious consolations that proud spirits are unable to receive.**
>
> (Spurgeon)

If my spirit is too proud to receive these graceful words of consolation, it would actually be grace if a test crosses my path that is so challenging that I voluntarily tear my own heart in two, ripping out the love that does not belong there. I desire a heart that is gentle enough to be consoled.

December 19

> **My soul, rest happy in thy low estate,**
> **Nor hope nor wish to be esteemed or great;**
> **To take the impress of the Will Divine,**
> **Be that thy glory, and those riches thine.**
>
> (Spurgeon)

January 4

> **Grow likewise in humility. Seek to lie very low, and know more of your nothingness.**
>
> (Spurgeon)

By this time I'm completely aware of my nothingness. I realise that every temptation and battle we fight results in precious humility. It's the same powerlessness Paul had experienced with his thorn in the flesh, and Moses with his poor speech, and it will help me to stay weak and small.

However painful it may be, lying under this bed with shoe laces for cuffs takes me to a place where who I am, what I know, and what I've achieved in the past is burned away. Bound up I become smaller and smaller. Hopefully I become as concealed as I was when the fuel attendant didn't see me but looked right through me. Hopefully I'm invisible to this man sitting above me on the bed. In fact, to be invisible to all men, except my own husband, becomes my deepest desire in this moment.

4 Father, forgive them!

But it seems the young man does see me after all. The bags' zippers go quiet. He's thinking, or looking, or something. This silence does not bode well.

I hear the voice of Jesus I came to know it in those weeks at His feet:

> *"Hettie, remember you're My bride."*

For a few moments I am with Him behind the puppet theatre and am reminded of how we human puppets are knit together – spirit, soul and body. I remember my immortal spirit is engaged to be married to Him. The wealth of revelations which I had gathered in December and January like sheaves of wheat, were unknowingly tied together for this moment under the bed. They were all read and copied into my journal. Written into my spirit.

December 20

> **R. Erskine declares: "He does not think it enough behind her back to tell it, but in her very presence, He says, "thou art all fair, my love" (Song of Solomon 4:7). It's true that this is not His ordinary method ... but there are times when He will make no secret of it – times when He will put it beyond all dispute into the souls of His people."**

Lying here I realise that if there was ever a time I needed to be reminded of His love – that time is now. It's a strange collision of images. She – a bride in white satin; I – a scared hostage dressed in humble pyjamas. She – a bride honoured and admired on her special day; I – a body that's being looked at inappropriately, as if I were a cut of meat. She – a bride dancing on the dance floor; I – tied up, lying still on a cold floor.

Towards the end of December I continually stumbled upon many similar contrasting images in the Bible. On New Year's Eve I penned some of them down even though I didn't understand them; they captivated and repulsed me at the same time. I did not know what to make of them. I felt compelled to study them.

"I'm not doing this for you, Israel, I'm doing it for me, to save my character, my holy name, which you have blackened in every country where you went ... Then the nations will realise who I really am, when I show my holiness through you so that they can see it with their own eyes. For this is what I am going to do ... take you out ... bring you back. I'll pour pure water over you and scrub you clean. I'll give you a new heart, put a new spirit in you. I'll remove the stone heart from your body and replace it with a heart that is God-willed, not self-willed. I'll put my Spirit in you, and make it possible for you to do what I tell you and for you to live by my commandments. You'll once again live in the land that I gave your ancestors. You'll be my people. I'll be your God ... I'm not doing it for you. Get this through your thick heads!"

(Ezekiel 36:22-38, extracts from *The Message*)

God's Church – His bride – truly blackens His name in every country where we live. It's not an unfair accusation. Our silver is faded; our reflection of the Silversmith distorted like a Picasso. We are self-willed, not God-willed, and we really think it's all about us.

On the same day that I read this passage, a friend sent me a text message saying I should also read Ezekiel 16:6-14. My goodness, did that make my stomach turn! A passage of Scripture like that makes you wonder what you did wrong, or are going to do wrong, if you read it the way I read it. I thought it pertained to the emotional bond to the man I was involved with. I would later see in it the most accurate description of how God would reach out His hand to me on this night.

Part of the passage read:

And then I came by. I saw you all miserable and bloody. 'Yes,' I said to you, lying there helpless and filthy, 'Live! Grow up like a plant in the field.' And you did. You grew up ... But you were naked and vulnerable, fragile and exposed. I came by again and saw you were ready for love and a lover. I took care of you, dressed you and protected you. I promised you my love and entered the covenant of marriage with you. I, God the Master, gave you my word. You became mine. I gave you a good bath ...

(*The Message*)

I realise that I, an individual who is part of the bride of Jesus, am not really the main character in this puppet show. The story I'm a part of is as old as time itself. It's the love story of Jesus and His bride. Through the ages His bride has been filthy and tied up, not white as snow and dancing exuberantly as she is supposed to be. Still He remains at work in her every day. He scrubs her clean and brings her back. Just as Ezekiel 16 explains – her light fades and her heart hardens. But what is the Bridegroom's reaction? He washes her clean with pure water and removes her heart of stone. He melts her hardened heart by showering her with love.

December 30

> **The rough-looking diamond is put on the wheel ... It loses much – much that seemed costly to itself. The King is crowned; the diadem is put on the monarch's head ... a glittering ray beams from that very diamond that was recently so sorely vexed by the lapidary. You may venture to compare yourself with such a diamond, for you are one of God's people; this is the time of the cutting process. Let faith and patience have their perfect work, for in the day when the crown will be set on the head of the 'King, eternal, immortal, invisible,' one ray of glory will stream from you.**
>
> (Spurgeon)

While God reminds me that I am His bride, the truths come together like the stems of a flower bouquet. I realise this sort of thing is part of why the church throughout the ages could not escape the dirty fingers of the world. What is going to happen to me next might not be a direct result of the fact that I'm part of His bride, but it's still going to happen - *in spite of it*. Like all others before me I may also be cut like a diamond. What a privilege if the Lord could use this night as a polishing process, and what a joy if I could, in some way, shine brighter for Him after this.

All of these thoughts about what it means to be His bride take only about a minute to settle in my mind. Why these words? Why now? Could it be because I will need to put on this truth like a piece of armour? Everything that a bride can be is shattered and challenged by rape. A bride is white and pure and loved. She has her bridegroom near. It is her big day. Her new life starts now. Rape screams: 'You are devastated and destroyed, dirty, despised. You are not loved. Your bridegroom is nowhere. Life as you know it ends here.'

Suddenly I know. It is going to happen. After almost three hours in our house and ample opportunity, this is now the moment I dreaded. My youngest daughter's room is so close I can usually see her feet when I'm on my bed and she's on hers. Her room does not have a door. It used to be a study nook. If I were to fight back now, she'd surely wake up. What she would see would stick in her three-year-old mind for who knows how many years. And down the hall are my eleven-year-old daughter and eight-year-old son. Do I really want to wake them? If I were to scream, Louis would probably come running. What would they do to him if he tried to help me? Would they take it out on him or on me? I know the answers. I make my decision.

As the robber walks around to my side of the bed, I hear God's promise:

> *"I hold your spirit and your soul safely in My hand. All the enemy can ever touch is your body."*

I remember how Jesus prayed for His disciples, a verse I had written in my journal on the 2nd of January: 'Father, I want those You gave Me to be with Me, right where I am, so that they can see My glory, the splendour You gave Me, having loved Me.' Jesus can be with us in soul and spirit, even when our physical bodies are caught up in the evil of this world. We can look into His glorious face while the puppet theatre crumbles all around us. Our life is hidden in Christ, as I had written in my journal on the 1st of January: 'Your old life is dead. Your new life, which is your real life – even though invisible to spectators – is with Christ in God. He is your life. When Christ (your real life, remember) shows up again on this earth, you will show up too – the real you, the glorious you. Meanwhile, be content with obscurity, like Christ' (Colossians 3:3-4, *The Message*).

The true you and me are hidden in God. We're out of reach of the one who hates Jesus, and therefore hates our souls. The true you and me are hidden within a piece of flesh – whether chubby or skinny, attractive or plain, with cellulite and varicose veins or without. The true you and I are not clearly visible on the surface, and we're not that easy to take hold of. The attacker may hurt my body – but that is all he can hurt. What my body may suffer as a result I will have to overcome by what Jesus has put in my filled spirit and my saved soul.

The man kneels next to me, rolls me over onto my back and puts his hand on my body.

> *"I want."*

I pretend that I don't understand. He just repeats the same two words patting me impatiently on the part of my body he is now interested in.

> *"I want!"*

I reply, quite sure that his English is too poor to really understand what I'm saying:

> *"I understand. You won't hurt me and I won't make any trouble for you."*

My head and chest are still under the bed. I can't and don't want to see if he is armed. He is in a hurry. He hastily tears my underwear on both hips. He pushes his head in under the bed, but my eyes are still closed and I don't see his face. He kisses me on the mouth a few times. He smells like beer and sweat. He is still nothing less than a rapist, but I'm thankful at this moment that my worst nightmare of being violently stabbed with a knife is not materialising. He seems full of lust, but not full of hate. He doesn't have any respect, but he also has no rage.

I turn my head to one side and purposely choose to look into the face of Jesus. Jesus is looking at both of us, seeing.

Suddenly I see what He sees. This rapist's words are actually quite true: 'I want.' It may well be the motto of his life. A very succinct summary of his soul. I saw it six months ago when I worked in a prison. Young men just like him: rapists, robbers, hijackers. Some as young as fourteen. They stood up one by one to state their dreams. One said: "When I get out of prison I want to become a social worker. I want to make sure every boy grows up with at least one parent." It doesn't take a three figure IQ to read between those lines ... Those men wanted. They wanted everything. They took everything they could find to fill a void left by absent fathers.

The summary of my soul is quite the opposite. I can sing my motto. It sounds like this: 'The Lord is my Shepherd. *I shall not want.*'

This man will take from me what he wants, and when it is all over I will still have all that matters. I will still be me. I will still have everything that makes life worth living. He can

take nothing eternal from me. He, on the other hand, will have even less of himself after doing this to me – hollowed out by sin and lovelessness.

I manage to remain calm. I become aware of God's love. It is overwhelming and almost tangible in my room. I'm not only aware of His love for me, but also caught completely by surprise by the certainty of His love for this rapist, who is living with so much evil, so much fear and emptiness. I know God hates the actions of this man, and yet somehow God loves him.

However disturbing it may be, this is where we need to walk around to the back of the theatre box to remind ourselves of how unprejudiced the story of God and humanity really is – how colour blind, how overflowing with undeserved grace for every person from murderer to thief. In the words and actions of Jesus we see proof that God's love is not held back from anyone except hypocrites. The only people ever to encounter the sharp edge of Jesus' tongue were those who dared to pray for grace for themselves while dishing out judgement upon others. Forgiving love is available to all except those who don't think they need it. The gentle words of Jesus are for those who realise their own need for grace. Such people know better than to point an accusing finger at a fellow sinner ...

I look at us on this floor. 'You sinner, me sinner. Do we ever need a Saviour!'

I wonder how this man grew up, and I don't even want to imagine the childhood that led to such desperate choices and foolish living. A thought crosses my mind, and I wish I could speak his language properly, or he mine, so that I can look him in the eye and tell him:

> *"I wish you knew the Love that I know. If you did, you never would have done this."*

He knows so little of love that he needs to break into my house, tie me up, and strip me naked in his search for an unfulfilling counterfeit. I know parental love, the love of a child, the love of a husband, a friend's love, and most of all Jesus' love. These loves are my preservatives. They are the reasons why I am not the wanting one.

Ironically Rob Bell's book, *SexGod*, is right above us on my bedside table. It's no coincidence that I read it in January. I never read for relaxation, but during the holidays Louis reads considerably, so I thought if I also had a book to read I could 'keep him company' during those lazy evenings. I figured a title like that by a writer like Bell would probably be worth it, too. It was. Bell claimed in the book that '*this* is really about *that*' when it comes to sex. He said every dysfunctional expression of our sexuality, every uncontrollable sexual desire, every sexual aversion, and — I suppose by implication every abuse of sex, such as this rape – reveals a person's separation from God. *This thing* is actually about *that thing*. What we do to our own and other people's bodies echoes with heart-wrenching notes what has already happened to our spirit. The good news is that our spirit will harmoniously echo outwardly when we intimately meet with God. This will permeate even our hormonal glands that would otherwise have propelled us from urge to urge like animals.

January 22

> **Great believer, you would have been a great sinner if God had not transformed you ... Therefore, be not proud, though you have a large estate, that is, a wide domain of grace. Once, you did not have a single thing to call your own except your sin and misery. Oh, strange infatuation, that you, who have borrowed everything, would think of exalting yourself!**
>
> (Spurgeon)

I've never before looked at a criminal this way. I usually look with a judgemental eye. It's very natural. Therefore I truly believe that in these early morning hours God is lending me His eyes for a few moments. If I don't see what He sees, I will not be able to forgive. Then I will fear this young man as the one who can destroy me, instead of pitying him as the one already destroyed. I cannot afford to see two bodies under this bed. To become one like this is scandalous, unlawful, but that is not the important thing to notice here. "*This* is really about *that*." What would be unlawful is if my spirit and his spirit became one. Our spirits clash more than language, culture or bodies ever could. My spirit is alive; his dead. Mine is safely locked up in Jesus; his is in danger.

When Jesus hung on the cross, He looked at the Roman soldiers and the people who had requested His death and Barabbas' release and cried out: 'Father forgive them, they know not what they are doing.' What do you think He saw in them? Do you think He feared them? I'm willing to bet He knew that they could not swing the whip even once without the Father's consent. Why would He fear them?

What do you think He sees in you and me while He defends us before the Father? Do you think He is put off by our uncleanness? I believe He sees us free from the destruction and the pits inside us which we refuse to let Him fill. He sees beyond people's grossly misplaced hatred of Him – misplaced because they're hating the One who loves them more than His own life. He sees how deceived we really are. I'm sorry if it offends you, but isn't this the truth? Aren't we, like the people in the crowd on Golgotha, mostly ignorant of what we are doing? I am convinced that the same prayer still rings out daily in the courts of heaven.

> *Father forgive them.*

Forgiveness can only come if we look in the right direction and listen to the right Voice. When our eyes are on the weapons, we react with fear. When our eyes are on the faces of our enemies, we hate. When our ears are listening to their threats, our hearts shudder. But, when our ears are against the mouth of God we can, even in these horrendous moments, experience His love. If our eyes can see the brokenness of our attackers, we can even forgive them, with God's help. We need to see them as humans, though. We cannot forgive monsters, only fellow human being. I am grateful for the little time I spent working in that prison. I am grateful that I saw rapists without their gangster friends, their knives, their arrogance and their anger. I saw them fearful and lonely, heading off to the courtroom where their fate would be decided by a judge whose language they don't speak after testimonies they would not fully understand. I saw them carrying their food for the day in one hand, hungry eyes darting wildly and alertly ahead, vigilant against those who would love to snatch a slice of bread from them.

Ten years ago I learned not to trust my own eyes when it came people. In 1998 God led us to start a community project in Pretoria West. Despite our disgruntled family and friends, we moved to live amongst people who were some of the poorest we had ever known.

I grew up privileged in the East of Pretoria. I never had any reason to venture west of Church Square. I think our only daring excursions in those days had been to *Kaap Krimp* – a wonderful dress fabric shop between Laudium and Proclamation Hill. As privileged kids we always stared wide-eyed at the poor people in those decrepit little houses. We thought who we were seeing were dirty people, bad people, dangerous people and 'stay-far-away-from-them' people.

A few years later we were living just blocks away from *Kaap Krimp*, in 1 Manganese Street, West Park. Our house used to belong to the Iron and Steel Industrial Corporation. It had the industrial look as opposed to the inviting look – inside and out. It was fitted with Novilon vinyl tiles and from the floor skirting to the roof it was painted with a yellowish cream gloss enamel. Throughout the two years we lived in that house, the smells of urine, cigarette smoke and another strange smell I could never quite put a name to fought for dominance of the indoor air space, especially when we dared to keep the windows shut for a day or two.

But I was thankful for this house, because the only other available option triggered every snobbish cell in my Lynnwood Manor body: 8 Coke Street, Danville. That's where I had to draw the line: 'Lord, I will live amongst the poor. I will serve the community in any way you command me to – free of charge. You can even show me the most humble home that is out there and we'll take it, but at my school reunion one day I'm not going to tell my swanky Menlo Park High School friends that I live in Danville. It's too much to ask. We joked about Danville people. I can't become one!'

I was eight months pregnant with our first daughter when we moved in. Everything made my skin crawl. I was scared of the neighbours. Some ladies had more hair on their chins than Louis had on his head. Some men wore the same pair of sweatpants every day as they stood in the same place at the grocery store buying the same marked-down junk food. I was too ashamed to live there, because I was looking at my surroundings with my own eyes – deceived, prideful, prejudiced eyes.

One afternoon I was driving around in my Volkswagen Jetta with its leather seats (I have to add in my defence that the car had been a gift) and wondered if I would ever be able to help someone here. I prayed that the Lord would help me to see people as He saw them, because I knew that as long as I judged them I would never be able to help them. The very next moment I noticed an old lady shuffling alongside the road with bulging shopping bags on each arm. I realised she had already walked about ten street blocks from the grocery store, up and down a few hills. I could see the heavy plastic bags cutting into her flesh.

Then, one by one, I noticed more people walking. It was as if all the invisibles, people who for years I had successfully filtered out, suddenly emerged as one from the shadows into the foreground. I started feeling compassion for them. I realised that nobody had vehicles, and that everyone seemed to live way too far from the shops, homes and schools they were walking to. Without a public transport system and without cars or bicycles their lives were so small and getting around was so incredibly hard. The very basic things were almost impossible.

I cried for two days. Suddenly, all I was able to see were rusted prams, threadbare school uniforms, which seemed to have been passed down not by siblings but by previous generations, children with bare feet walking on hot tarred roads to help along their parents' begging efforts, and mothers trying to appease their crying kids by buying them a packet of Romany Cream cookies that had been marked down after falling off a truck. Along with the stream of tears, a stream of love for these people started flowing inside of me.

Every kind of sorrow and brokenness imaginable was present in our community. Good people around us were suffering horrendous hardship. Late at night moms came knocking on our door, begging to heat up baby bottles in our microwave oven, embarrassed that their power had been cut off again. I stood with them in line at the pay phone a few times, as we took turns to report that the whole street's telephone lines had been cut, all because one person hadn't paid his bill.

But inside these unsightly, foul smelling homes with their permanent head lice infestation, I found friends who were spiritual giants. Amid their worn-out furniture and mountains of hand-washed laundry, these woman rejoiced in the Lord's goodness and love. They were women who clearly understood that you do not use circumstances to measure the Lord's goodness. They were women I had previously looked down upon because their hair had been dirty and their dresses old-fashioned. I didn't realise some people could only afford to wash their hair with body soap. I didn't known that some people used newspaper instead of toilet paper. I didn't know a lot of things. I had a lot of opinions about people, though.

After a while in this community I reached a point where I was no longer ashamed to live amongst them. Instead, I was thankful – thankful I had been able to see a side of God that had been obscured by the easy life and affluence of the eastern suburbs of Pretoria.

Another side of God I got to know in Danville was His concern for the little things. My afterschool care centre was barely surviving on donations, and my salary of R1 500 was paid by a good friend of ours. There was never much money but ever so much generosity! One winter's morning I went looking for a particular kind of hair curler, of all things. I remember hearing that the R5 shop on Mitchell Street had some in stock. They sold lots of other thingamabobs, but not what I was looking for. Heading out of the shop I noticed a pharmacy across the street. I thought I could go and ask for advice since the children here seemed to get terribly sick every winter. The combination of no electricity, no nutritious food, the bitter cold weather, and insufficient clothes and blankets made the winters deadly. I thought the pharmacist could perhaps recommend a cheap supplement to strengthen their immune systems. He jumped as I walked in.

> *"I know you! I want to visit your afterschool centre to find out more about what you are doing. I've been working here for thirty years. I actually live in Waterkloof Ridge and don't make any profit here. This pharmacy is my ministry. The people here are incredibly needy."*

The pharmacist went on to explain that he had seen a short TV-broadcast the previous day in which I was talking with Sunday school teachers and briefly mentioned that I worked in Proclamation Hill. He had been thinking of this broadcast and wondered if I shared his heart for these needy people. Imagine his amazement as I walked into his store. All of this due to a failed attempt at finding hair curlers!

I shared my need with him, and he promised to let me know what he might be able to do for the children. A few days later, the school phoned to ask me to kindly remove my boxes from their reception area. I didn't know of any boxes and explained that it must have been a misunderstanding. They insisted that the boxes had my name on them and were in their way. When I opened the first box, I saw the heart of Jesus. Inside the box was proof of His love for the poor: several two litre bottles of vitamin syrup, thousands of vitamin C tablets, bottles of cough syrup, and lastly – my favourite – bottles and bottles of lice shampoo!

Does He care for children who cough so much during the night they can't study the next day? Yes. Does He care for teenage girls who are too embarrassed to go to school because their black hair is covered in unsightly nits? Yes. He cares for people who are making an effort with the little they have and still don't get anywhere.

There were, however, also some children and parents doing unthinkably desperate things. One boy discovered that his neighbour's eighteen year old disabled daughter would do almost anything for a cigarette and absolutely anything for a pack of them. He fixed the price per visit on a pack of smokes plus R50 (his commission) and started a thriving brothel on the roof of their apartment block.

A mother of five, a prostitute, asked me one day which one of her children I would advise her to send away to the orphanage. She couldn't care for all of them anymore. She had been considering giving away the youngest, because she reasoned that the older ones would soon be able to stand on the street corners with her and earn their own living. This mother was white and spoke Afrikaans. I had a friend by the same name. She could have been me. I could have been her.

Both the boy who ran the brothel and the mother who put her own daughters on the street were damaged, not evil. With them, and so many others in similar circumstances, I saw how much harm this suffering, hunger and fear can cause a person. It broke down their self-worth until they could no longer recognise themselves as people created in the image of God. It also broke down the image of God in other people, up to the point where they could ignore everyone else's worth and human rights. This is what made them act like animals and treat others like animals. Where their conscience was supposed to cry out "no!" there was only an empty cavity, hollowed out by suffering. A love gap created by completely loveless living. And don't think for one moment that a white skin is a tougher barrier against this dehumanising process than any other skin.

During the time we lived in Danville and managed the after-school centre, the Lord impressed on our hearts this very important warning:

> *"You who know comfort and love can never judge someone's deeds who lives without love every day. Leave that to Me. Only I can read hearts and know those hidden things."*

If we claim to be Christ-followers, we are not allowed to look at people with condemnation or hatred. 2 Peter 1:7 clearly commands us to add to our faith love for one another – for *all* people. In verse 9 we read that if someone does not have love for all people, such a person is blind and forgetful. Such a person has completely lost sight of the fact that his own sins have been wiped away.

Still feeling this man's weight on me, I'm praying that Louis is unaware of what is happening. Not resisting is such an unnatural response. Knowing that resistance could trigger in this man a wave of rancorous violence helps me to stick to my decision. Who knows what he may be armed with?

Sometimes when swimming in the ocean, you see an approaching wave so high and powerful that you dare not take it on. Jumping up against such a wave throws one into a dangerous churning that can slam you into the sandbanks or rocks. When such a wave approaches, the wisest thing to do is to plug your nose and drop down low into the still depths until the violence has passed overhead ...

> *"... devil waters rush over me." (Psalm 18:5)*

Naturally my thoughts are not all spiritual as this is happening. I am intensely aware of the implications of this vicious reality. I realise that I have just become a South African rape statistic. Unlike some women who have experienced themselves standing outside their bodies like spectators, everything happening to me is very real and close: body temperature, texture, everything registers as though my body feels a need to memorise it all. Because I'm not fighting, he is not holding me down or using any force. I'm thankful it's happening calmly and slowly so that I can keep my head together. My natural response when I'm threatened is to react with aggression – exactly what I should not be doing right now. I fight the flood of adrenalin. No fight. No flight. I worry about sexually transmitted diseases and possible tearing. I position my body in such a way as to minimise physical damage.

He is done with me.

In the dimly lit room I can only see his shoes and his pants from the knees down. In the way he gets up, shuffles around and makes hasty, fidgeting movements I can see the shame that he has just heaped on himself. The shame is his. Not mine. He hides as much of the proof as he can. He rolls me back onto my stomach, shoves me neatly back in my familiar place under the bed and pulls down my nightdress as far as it will go. He leaves me quickly to join the others downstairs.

A short while later two of the gang members rush into the room. One lifts up my nightdress, notices my underwear is gone and starts feeling me up to establish whether I had been raped. He probably suspects that the young man was left alone with me for a little too long ... The gang leader sounds angry.

"What happened here?"

"He raped me."

"Are you okay, Ma'am?"

"He didn't hurt me."

I stick to my strategy to remain as calm and non-threatening as possible. It's better to fight in court than in my bedroom, I think to myself. I don't want to come across as a raging, vindictive woman. He may have realised that the rape and the rude probing by the other gang member, which also amounts to rape according to our sexual assault laws, could lead to a charge of gang rape or accessory to rape against any one of them if they were ever caught. He also straightens my clothing. The two of them leave as hurriedly as they had entered, probably to keep an eye on Louis.

I just wish they would all finish what they came for and take everything they want so I can get up and go to hospital ...

A few minutes later one of them returns to get me. He is clearly agitated, judging by the force with which he yanks me out from under the bed, helps me to my feet and thrusts me out the bedroom door and onto the landing next to the children's school room where the rest of the gang is still disconnecting computers to add to their plunder. The next moment an argument ensues of which I can't make head or tail. After a short but hefty exchange I hear the following welcome words in English:

"No, we are not doing that. Put her on the floor; make her sleep."

The man grips my shoulders a little tighter than is necessary and shoves me back into the bedroom. I kneel down next to the bed and bend my head towards the floor. I'm tired of lying on my face on the cold floor. I want to just sit in a little bundle. He grabs my feet and pulls my legs from under me. I can't help but think he might take his turn with me. Instead he shoves me back under the bed wheelbarrow-style. He spits out the word as though he wants me to know he doesn't agree with the decision:

"Sleep!"

The gang leader returns a while later and asks again:

"Are you OK, Ma'am?"

I take care to use a calm voice.

"He didn't hurt me and I will not cause any trouble."

"And your husband?"

Unsure of exactly what he is asking, and with the intention of making my husband seem just as harmless, I answer:

"He doesn't know, so he won't cause any trouble."

They leave, scurry down the stairs and their footsteps and voices fade away within minutes. I have no idea what is going on or what will happen next. Then I hear a car starting up and driving over gravel. Whose car is it? It can be our relatively new Renault, as I don't know its distinctive hum, yet. Or it could just be a neighbour leaving early for work. The day will break soon. Will I surprise one of them and get shot if I get up in order to see if the children are OK? Perhaps they are all still downstairs with Louis. Or did they abduct him? They may have taken Louis and the car to go and withdraw cash at a nearby ATM. Would they then bring Louis back? They can't drive through the security boom without him and his security tag, so he must be with them.

Everything is so quiet. I feel alone and unsure. I talk to Jesus:

"Please let me know when it's safe to get up from under this bed."

While I wait, in my mind's eye I suddenly see the word 'fear' to the front and left of me and other words – 'power, love and a sound mind' — to the right. They look like those neon lights that usually mark a motel. They seem like two options. I have to choose one or the other. I'm *allowed* to choose. I can leave my fear beneath this bed if I want to. I don't have to walk with it for the rest of my life. In its place I can choose power, love and a sound mind, which literally means consistent, clear thinking. The well-known verse comes to mind:

God hasn't given us a spirit of fear, but of power, love and a sound mind.
(2 Timothy 1:7)

"Lord, I choose love."

I knew those words meant I choose to make fear the enemy; not people. It meant I would choose to love my rapist; not hate him. This would only be possible, I knew, by the kind of spirit God can give – the kind that deposits in our hearts a godly love for the unlovable and supernatural power, along with the ability to keep our wits about us, when the natural response would be to lose our mind ...

I am reminded of some verses in Psalm 18, the psalm I had memorised:

But me He caught, reached all the way from sky to sea; He pulled me out of that enemy chaos, the ocean of hate, the void in which I was drowning. He stood me up on a wide-open field; I stood there saved – surprised to be loved.

It's quite unexpected indeed to experience the most overwhelming awareness of God's love during a burglary and rape. Is it possible? I feel it. I can truly echo the Psalm: *Surprised to be loved.* I thought a rape would make me feel hated and would make me doubt God's love for me, but I am surer of His love now than ever before — not because of the rape, but because of how Jesus was with me through it.

The bride of Jesus, His Church, will also be yanked out of the sea of hate and enemy chaos one day, like someone saved from drowning. She will then stand astounded in the wide open field of grace, surprised by the reality of Jesus' love for her. The world hates Jesus' bride, sees her as worthless, persecutes her, destroys her, and yes, even rapes her. Yet no destruction can separate us from the love of Christ. Here I lie like a puppet behind the puppet theatre, tossed out, yet in this unlikely place I experience the Lord's tremendous love for me.

Knowing that love does not need to prove itself by giving me my every wish, I am suddenly uncertain whether God would love me tonight in the way I am hoping for. I want to believe that my husband and children are unharmed and that soon we will all be safely together. I want to know how it will play out in the hours ahead. I am putting off my tears of mourning or joy to that moment when the curtain will come down to announce *"The End"*, be it a good one or a tragic one. I cannot exhale yet.

5 *Fingerprints*

It feels safe to crawl out from under the bed now. The shoe laces are fairly easy to wiggle out of. Before I leave the room I collect as much DNA on my pyjamas as possible, but I don't change because I vaguely remember from CSI forensics that one shouldn't. I only put on clean underwear in hopes that it will help keep the rest of the DNA evidence intact and because I'm acutely aware of how short my nightdress is ... Oddly I feel as if I need to be dressed appropriately for the moment of truth, like people wearing hats to a funeral. I should at least wear underwear. It seems improper to be half naked on your way to face a possible discovery of a loved one's corpse.

My first stop is the children's rooms. My youngest is sleeping on her side, as always, with the corner of her knitted baby blanket caressed between the usual two fingers. The opening to her room is double door-width and faces towards the scene of this night's crime. Only the Lord knows how she remained sound asleep despite the repeated trips past her doorway as all six of us went to and fro, up and down the stairs. I remember now how a robber had stepped into her room with one foot, turned to me and whispered: 'Shhhhhh!' With that, he echoed my wish and perhaps the command of all the unseen angels, too.

I cross the landing where they held me a while ago, fighting over what to do with me and all the evidence in and on my body. It dawns on me that it could have been so much worse. They could have decided to complicate the DNA evidence ... or to kill the witness. My son's door is shut. I open it quietly. The covers are pulled over his head, and I can only guess which way his feet are pointing. He loves sleeping in this cosy bundle. It served him well as a sound barrier tonight.

A faint sound becomes audible as I slowly open my eleven year old daughter's bedroom door. Worship music comes softly from the CD player. She must have fallen asleep with it still playing. The fan is blowing cool air over her sweet face. I swallow at the lump in my throat as I realise the worst was spared us. The children are unharmed. Thank you, Jesus! I realise the Script Writer left them out of this episode of the story on purpose. I am so thankful for this mercy.

I hurry downstairs, now fully convinced the robbers had left. I half-heartedly call out,

"Honey, are you here?"

I'm not surprised that only silence replies. I run out the front door and once around the house with my bare feet. I do what I saw the investigators do in *CSI* – I look in the bushes and the little store room near the back door. People can be shot silently through a pillow or something and dumped outside. No-one dead or alive. I notice my car is still there, but the Renault is gone. So they did drive off with Louis, which means he's kidnapped, but I'm unsure whether or not that also means he is dead. I don't know what I should expect – should I fear or hope? I want to believe the grace we have received up to this point has not run out.

The doors to the production company's office are still open. All the computers and sound equipment are gone. It's not the way it goes in Hollywood movies, where the thugs cut the telephone and power lines first. They left the whole switchboard untouched and all the lights on. This is South Africa. It is no use calling 911 in South Africa, so I dial 10111 and wait. It rings eight or nine times before a bored voice answers. I state very clinically what had happened and don't give our home address at first; instead, I give the address to the nearest ATM, in hopes that this is the only reason they took my husband. Maybe they just want to empty his bank accounts. The police promise to drive past the ATM on their way to our house.

I ask for the number of the ER24 paramedic service. A friendly nurse gives me the name of the best and nearest trauma centre with a specialised rape unit. I am not to comb my hair, brush my teeth, change, take a bath or shower or wash my hands. I should try not to even go to the toilet. She has clearly memorised the list. I wonder how often she has to recite it. Too many times, for sure. Still, she manages a little concern.

"Are you sure you have been raped?"

Well, I don't think this is something most women would just suspect. Then again, I am unusually calm, I realise that. Is this what a supernaturally sound mind feels like or am I just in coping mode? I assure her that I am not making it up.

All the important numbers are saved on my stolen cell phone instead of filed in my memory. I now realise how foolish this is. I can only remember my mother's mobile number. I pick up the phone and try to formulate what to tell her and what not to. She's never been called at such an hour – not even about a broken arm or a flat tyre. I simply can't figure out how to string together soothing sentences to explain the shocking truth, so I hang up halfway in the first ring. It would just be too cruel, I decide. Perhaps I'll never have to tell her. The neighbours could help instead. If my dear neighbour could be with my children when they wake up, I could drive to the hospital on my own. I start thinking what I should advise her to tell the children until we all know if their dad is coming back or not. Parenting advice is second nature to me, but nobody ever taught me how to tell children that their mom was raped and their dad kidnapped.

All the house keys as well as the gate's remote control are still in the usual place. Dawn is breaking, and the air is crisp. I'm not wearing enough, but it has become irrelevant. I think of the women in reality shows on TV who run screaming from burning buildings in only their underwear. I always thought: 'Nope, not me! I'm the kind of woman who will get scorched or swallowed up in toxic smoke while combing her hair so she looks decent when the firemen arrive.' But today I'm one of those less respectable women, and I really don't care. But I have enough vanity left to hope that my friend answers the door and not her husband.

As our gate rolls open I hear another sound to my right. I look and there in the dim light I see the shape of my husband. Louis is running home! In an instant the dragon is slain, and the nightmarish ending that I came to expect as the inevitable and most likely outcome, is averted. I feel ashamed of my earlier thoughts. Practical, clinical thoughts about insurance policies that were thankfully in place and wills and testaments that were basically in order. A most unlikely happy ending plays itself out on the theatre stage. The curtain comes down – finally! Now I can cry. All I can get past my lips are the same words over and over:

> *"You're alive! It's all I asked for. You're alive!"*

My legs give way, and I drop to my knees in the driveway. I just want to cry because the relief is almost unbearable.

The automatic gate closes behind Louis, and for a few moments I ponder whether I shouldn't just bar him from discovering the princess puppet's misfortune behind the theatre box. I should be like those forbidding ladies now. I should shield the truth, because not all truth is helpful, is it? Everything is over. I'm alive, he's alive, and our children are alive. Louis has picked me up from the paving. I am in his arms. The rest is irrelevant, isn't it? If we start talking about this, more dragons may come out and plant themselves between us ...

The lie that puts a sock in our mouth is an evil whisper from the deadliest snake in the garden. But it feels so right. It feels wise. It even feels selfless. I want to agree with the lie and keep silent – it's surely better if no one ever knows.

Louis informs me that the police will arrive within five minutes. When he ran back through the security gate he told the guards to sound the alarm. The guards didn't suspect foul play when he drove out earlier, because Louis had a revolver in his ribs and was forced to nod, wave and swipe his security chip. The kidnappers threatened to kill him or the guards if he aroused suspicion.

Louis promises to tell me the rest of the story later.

> *"Let's go inside and have a cup of tea just to settle down before the police get here."*

Louis notices my slight hesitation and gives me an inquisitive look. It's 4.45 in the morning, and I don't want to stay here for hours and give statements while a virus may be crawling around in my body. I want to get to the hospital. If I had a stab wound or gunshot wound I could use it as an excuse. But I don't even have a scratch on me. How do I explain that I need to go to the emergency room? There is no other option but to tell him. I couldn't really look into those darkest brown eyes of his and lie – not even for a day. How could I possibly hide this from him for years to come?

The words come out in clumsy spurts like school kids filing out of a bus:

> *"You can wait here for the police. I have to go to the hospital. The guy that they left me with in the room raped me. He didn't hurt me. I'm OK. God really spoke to me and helped me. Please don't be mad."*

Calmly he replies:

> *"I may feel differently later, but now I'm going to stay calm so that we can do the right thing."*

I thank the Lord for a husband with self-control. He is not the Rambo type and he's not a racist, and I realise this very well may have saved all of our lives tonight. Now, it may save our marriage as well. The way Louis looks at me as he tries to determine whether I am really unharmed is not the way one looks at damaged goods or at someone with a contagious disease. He looks at me just the way he always does, only with a bit of added concern.

Louis has been colour blind for a long time and helped the rest of our family to follow suit. In the early nineties, before Nelson Mandela's release from prison, he was already quite comfortable with black musicians in his band. As African Americans in basketball circles jokingly say that 'white men can't jump,' we in the South African music industry willingly admit that 'white men can't groove.' Louis simply picked the best young musicians, irrespective of their skin colour. Over the years it caused a few interesting incidents at hotels and guesthouses in small towns where apartheid sentiments still ruled. Louis was always able to diffuse these with grace and humour.

When we lived in Proclamation Hill, a very conservative white community, a black musician lived in our living room for a few months, as he was temporarily homeless. When our neighbour saw the young man out in the yard, sipping on a cup of coffee, she leaned over the fence and asked if he worked for us, assuming that he was our gardener. He answered affirmatively, meaning that he played in Louis's band. She proceeded to ask if he would mow their lawn as soon as he was done in our yard. He answered with a gobsmacked, 'Hell, no, Ma'am!' He was used to entertaining the rich and famous on luxury liners around the world, not mowing people's lawns! We had the privilege of having these stereotypes purged out of us before racial integration became a policy. Since those early days, we had the privilege of sharing life with friends, colleagues and fellow church members of every race. I am so glad that racism, which could have twisted this rape into something it need not be, had been dealt with in time ...

Less than a month before the robbery, one of our staff members at the production company died of AIDS. People asked whether she was black or white. We saw then that too many people still make a distinction between white suffering and black suffering, white sin and black sin. What did it matter? A young woman in the prime of her life died of a sickness that her knife-wielding, blackmailing, promiscuous boyfriend had given her along with a few punches. It was a tragedy without colour. And the truth is it happens in every community. Some are just more sophisticated at covering it up ...

We go back into the house and kneel on the carpet where the cash was distributed just two hours ago. Louis wants to pray. It is the first time we have knelt together to pray since our wedding almost 18 years ago. We do pray together, but we don't kneel.

"Lord, thank you for saving our lives and the lives of our children! We pray that your Name will somehow be glorified through all of this. We cannot see how, but we know You promise in your Word that all things work together for good for us who love You and who have been called according to Your purpose. And we forgive these men in the Name of Jesus. Amen."

Someone is at the gate. The blue police car lights are flashing through the study window. We get up to let them in. As the policemen get out of the patrol and Flying Squad cars I notice a distinct expression on their faces. The mark of numerous trauma scenes is clearly etched on their faces, and they look at us with sincere concern, scanning us for signs of violence. They are clearly relieved that there is no blood or hysteria. Tonight's crime scene is nothing compared to what they've experienced before.

I explain to the inspector that Louis will give the statements but I need to go to the hospital. One of the officers is trained in forensics and offers to immediately seal my nightdress as evidence so I can change into clean clothes before going to the hospital. An ex-member of the Flying Squad (a special crime unit) who lives close by, arrives and offers to send his wife with me to the hospital. I explain that I would rather my neighbour's wife, who has become a good friend, go with me. I go upstairs to change, while Louis crosses the road to wake up our neighbours.

Our neighbour lets out a scream. It's not rage. It's the realisation that it could have been his wife.

I'm wearing a long skirt, the only skirt in my cupboard, and a button-up top, thinking it would probably make things easier at the clinic. I probably need money or a credit card, my medical insurance card and such. I have the lazy habit of leaving my purse in the car, so I go to the garage to find it. They found it first. The entire contents of the bag are strewn out on my Toyota's hood. The cash is missing. My gym bag is still in the boot with everything I took to the gym the previous morning. I'm planning on swimming the Midmar Mile in five days, and I have been following a tough exercise routine. I can survive with the contents of the bag, so I take that as my hospital kit bag and just add my lipstick. I then remember I'm probably not allowed to put anything on my lips. Searching, I can't find my bank cards, but my medical insurance card luckily shows up. I don't know if treatment for rape is free or if I will have to pay for it, seeing that our hospital plan already has so many exclusions. I won't need to be admitted, so the medical insurance probably won't cover anything. I find the bank cards under the car. I look for my cell phone, then smile at myself for having forgotten they took that first. All set.

My dear neighbour is crying as she walks across the road to come with me. Despite the tears, she is still as radiant as always. That's why I picked her. She is what Charles Bunyan calls a 'shining one.' We hold each other for a few moments; I know what the unspoken words would be if she or I could utter them. The former policeman and one inspector offer to drive behind us to the hospital. They still need to take my statement and will complete it there. I like both of them immediately. I get the impression they are the type of policemen who can help to change our country.

I suddenly remember our domestic helper, Letta. She has her own little apartment separate from the house. She slept through the whole thing. She is snoring so loudly that I almost have to break down the door to wake her up. Like an archetypal African mama, she immediately starts wailing with both arms flung over her head like limp palm tree branches. She cries her African funeral cry. Her knees wobbling, she asks:

"And the children?"

I see a near heart attack avoided as I reassure her that they are still sleeping soundly. I feel closer to her than ever before, knowing rape is also part of her frame of reference and now one of the few things we have in common. I realise that to her, and all her 'sisters', news like this is almost old news. It's familiar news, regular news, news usually followed by a resigned phrase:

"Sorry my sister. At least you're alive."

Before leaving for the hospital, I make it extremely clear to everyone what the children are and are not allowed to hear. This is the preferred story: Criminals stole mom and dad's computers, money, cell phones, and daddy's car. Mommy is talking to the police at the hospital because she had quite a fright.

The first time I can convey to someone how real the Lord has been to me tonight is on the way to the hospital. I tell my neighbour about the encouragement from Psalm 18 and the love I felt. She is the first to hear. I didn't even have time to tell Louis. Then I start crying because Letta's motherly reaction made me think of my parents. I cry for my father and mother who could be in for the worst news of their lives. I decide I should ask the trauma counsellor at the hospital whether or not it's truly necessary to tell them. Do I really have to knock over two other people's puppet theatre boxes along with my own? Can't I just let them sit cross-legged and enjoy a beautiful story? I am their only daughter.

In my absence the house is processed for evidence. Louis points out that the men wore latex gloves and would therefore not have left any fingerprints. Louis, being less emotional and more practical than me, does the inevitable. He phones my parents, wakes them up, gives them the highlights of the story and asks them to take our three children away to the Bushveld where they live so they won't have to experience the turmoil that was sure to ensue at our home once the media and our friends become aware of what has happened. He made the right decision.

The emergency room isn't very busy, and everybody can see that I'm not bleeding and don't have any obvious injuries or symptoms that would justify a visit at this hour. Maybe my dishevelled hair betrays the rest of the story, because I receive several sympathetic glances. The doctors and nurses probably know the signs. Imagine if I had arrived in my nightdress ... I'm led to a little room that I would get to know all too well in the months to come.

To my amazement, the little room is lovingly dedicated to the late husband of a good friend of mine. He was a well-loved and brilliant emergency room doctor. I never met him, but his wife was a member of our small group at church until she got remarried and emigrated to Canada. She is a brave woman. The Lord carried her through the death of a child and soon thereafter the death of her husband. She is one of the most joyous people I have ever known. Seeing his picture on the plaque and her face in my mind's eye, I feel like I'm in good company. It also puts matters into perspective. In that moment I am certain that our family will be made whole as theirs was made whole, after the much harder road they had to travel on. What Jesus did for their family, He would do for us – He would restore our joy.

I get onto the crisp white hospital bed and wonder how many women have sat on this spot. I wonder what they looked like and how they felt. They were probably much bloodier than I am. I wonder how the doctors must feel. I suspect most of them may have lost their taste for puppet theatre a long time ago. Perhaps they've had to pick up far too many torn puppets behind the theatre box.

Everyone comes in and out of the room in mechanical fashion. Papers. Folders. Clipboards. Tablets. They speak in robotic tones. Safe, clinical questions. It's probably the only way they can survive the rape clinic's assaults on their own hearts. Then nothing happens for several minutes. I ask my neighbour to inquire what happens next. Apparently no one is allowed to continue until I've seen the trauma counsellor, and he is a 45 minute drive away from the hospital. The only thing they are allowed to do until he arrives is take my pulse and blood pressure. Pulse: 65; Blood pressure: 113 over 85. The nurse double checks. These aren't normal measurements for someone in shock. I tell her about how the Lord had been with me in my room, and I can see she pities me. I realise she probably hears lots of wild things and undoubtedly sees every sort of delusion and denial. She's not going to believe me.

I wish someone else could have heard what I heard. I wish I could retell it exactly as it happened. Spirit things are beyond words, I realise. The harder we try, the emptier the words sound. I think these dear people would stop fighting back the tears and giving cheap words of comfort if they could only see that my Father has always come for me.

You came

When I was just a baby Your angels cradled me
Already precious in Your sight, already Yours to be
On little legs I waddled, my footing faltering
You came to lead me by the hand
You came to dance with me

And no-one saw, not even me, Your hands around my heart
No-one heard the words You spoke: "We'll never be apart."
You called me Yours
You sang my name
You planted hope within my heart
Just because You came

As I grew up You found me and taught me to believe
Patiently transforming me by all that I received
I often needed guidance, my footing faltering

You came to teach me where to walk
You came to stand by me

And no-one knew, not even I, the dreams You had in mind
No-one heard the words of love, the promise – true and kind
You called me Yours
You sang my name
You planted joy within my heart
Just because You came

Then one night danger found me – defenceless, overpowered
I called The Name I knew so well, and hoped You'd pull me out
Instead, You came to be with me, to bear the fear and shame
I love You for the words You said
I love You, 'cause You came

And no-one saw, not even me, Your arms around me then
No-one but I heard the words You whispered once again
You called me Yours
You sang my name
You planted peace within my heart
Just because You came

(Hettie Brittz, August 2010)

Dejected, I realise that the only proof I could offer that He was really there is my pulse rate and blood pressure measurements. It may not be enough proof, but to me it is all the proof I need.

I borrow someone's phone to call our cell group from church to tell them what had happened and to ask for prayer. One of our neighbours already contacted the head of an international prayer network, so we are already being prayed for all over the world. Maybe that is why I experience such peace in this little room. My neighbour and two policemen are still waiting outside the room like my three personal bodyguards – guardian angels, even.

Finally the counsellor arrives. I first have to agree to speak to him. They could not find a female counsellor. I imagine us having to wait another 45 minutes for a female counsellor if I dare object even nonverbally ... so I take care to smile convincingly:

> *"It is quite all right with me, thank you. I am comfortable speaking to a male counsellor."*

I couldn't care if he were a cross-eyed, drooling taxidermist with garlic breath. I just want to get this over with so that they can start my treatment. It seems crazy that they have not done a single medical intervention yet.

I'm asked to tell what I can remember of the morning's activities. I think to myself, *could I actually forget any of those details within two short hours?* I tell the story, as he keeps a straight face and makes his notes. He tries to explain to me that the peace and calm I'm experiencing, the forgiveness, and the idea that God had talked to me are all indicators of how deeply I am in denial. I explain that I am familiar with the classical stages of trauma and passed Psychology 3 as part of my studies. I know this knowledge does not make me exempt from the process, but I also know that I am not in denial. Once again I notice the unmistakeable look of pity. More secret scribbling on his notepad.

He cautions me that the next stage of trauma will be hyper-vigilance, which means I will be extremely on-edge and tense like someone facing imminent death around every corner. He explains that certain smells, sudden movements, people stepping into my personal space without warning or similar stimuli could elicit a sudden anxiety attack and fight or flight response. I mustn't be worried, since it's normal, but I should phone him if I struggle to control my anxiety. I try to think what might trigger me. Nobody grabbed me suddenly. The rapist didn't really smell that bad. I'll be OK.

When I start experiencing rage, he cautions, I must not feel that as a Christian I'm not allowed to become angry. I can see he is very concerned that I might sweep everything under my religious rug. Clearly he has never seen me drive. There is no rug big enough for how angry I can get while driving.

When we still lived in Pierre van Ryneveld, to the bafflement of my less bloodthirsty passengers, I always drove past our driveway to see whether or not someone was hiding behind the bushes, ready to hijack me as I came home. This is a safety tip the police gave the South African public. In some ways I was almost disappointed when the headlights shone smoothly over the bushes revealing nothing sinister. After doing a U-turn, I always pressed the remote for the automatic gate to slide open and waited in the street, not in the driveway – just as the police had taught us – so that I couldn't get locked in between the gate and an unfriendly vehicle that could come from behind. Waiting for the gate to open, I always prepared myself to fearlessly knock over anybody who would dare try anything. I visualised how I would select with lightning fast reactions either R or D on my automatic gearshift. I was ready for an attack from any direction.

And I believed I had it in me to drive over someone or even pull a trigger if I had to. I have hunted before and was really OK to see an antelope bleed. If an antelope could threaten me in any way, I would have been more than OK to put him down with a head shot right between the eyes. It's probably much harder to kill a human being, but whenever I heard strange noises in our house I always armed myself with the sharpest available weapon. Then I visualised how I would rip open the enemy's skin all the way from their belly button to their chin in one Samurai-like sword motion. Are you convinced yet? There is no rug big enough for the rage I used to feel at the mere thought of someone harming me or mine in my car or in my home. Even thoughts of revenge wouldn't have surprised me.

That is, until today...

Everything changed today. Today I love with a love that is not mine. Today's peace is also not mine. The absence of rage, even though much of our earthly possessions were stolen, is also beyond me.

It comes as a surprise to me that aggression, something in myself which I have had to fight on a regular basis, is not present at all now. It's equally unbelievable that I'm sitting on this bed, knowing deep in my heart that during the whole night's events — the white hot rage I always experienced before putting my hand on the gearshift or kitchen knife — does not well up in me now. It's difficult to imagine that I would ever experience that calibre of rage again.

Maybe it has something to do with the fact that if your Knight carries the swiftest, sharpest sword in the entire Kingdom, you, the princess, might as well leave your dagger at home ...

The counsellor advises that it's important for me to continue with life as usual as soon as possible so I don't experience an unnecessary sense of a loss of control over my life. I explain that I'm planning on doing exactly this by swimming the Midmar Mile in Natal in five days. He thinks it's a brilliant idea, and tells me he is busy with his Master's degree in the therapeutic value of diving and water. It's the end of his efforts to counsel me. Now we're talking about *his* passion, his interests and calling.

In all the friendly banter he completely forgets the part of the counselling I actually needed to hear – the details about the treatment and blood testing process for HIV, and the nature and duration of the forensic examination I'm about to endure. We're probably equally relieved when he eventually leaves and sends in the doctors because, despite both of our best intentions, neither of us have any idea of how to handle the other.

The examination begins. A surgical pack is wheeled in on a trolley. The doctor unfolds the green sheet under the supervision of a police officer. I realise that we're dealing with a criminal and legal process, not just a medical process. Inside the sheet is a sterilised metal bowl which they proceed to fill with sterilised water. A second pack contains gynaecological instruments. Next in line is the most important thing – the forensic pack. It's sealed. I have a first-world-feeling about this whole procedure and realise grimly that Africa is probably the best place to develop such a protocol. Ironically our rape statistics put us at the forefront of such an intervention.

I ask how long everything is going to take. *'Usually about two to three hours,'* is the reply. In the meantime I wonder what is happening inside my body. Can't they immediately administer some sort of neutraliser or sperm killer? Or would it destroy the evidence?

First, they draw blood, as my baseline test for HIV will show whether I was HIV positive before the rape or not. The result of this test is probably the only thing I don't have to stress about. But needles and I are not friends. The nurse suddenly notices that I'm shaking and babbling faster and faster. Even now in adulthood I sometimes still get a fight-or-flight reaction when I see needles. They're my biggest fear. There must be more f-reactions than just fight or flight to choose from, such as freaking out or fainting. I mumble unrepeatables under my breath ...

> *"Nurse, if you put the rapist next to the needle and force me to choose, you may be surprised ..."*

She looks pale at the very thought that someone could utter such crazy nonsense. 'She should ask my dentist,' I think to myself. 'He will confirm it.'

They start at the crown of my head. I can quickly see that if they are going to work this thoroughly, they will be lucky to make their way from my head to my toe in three hours. A thin tuft of hair is plucked out apologetically and folded into a small paper sleeve as a control sample for my own DNA. Then another paper sleeve is held below my hair while they comb it out carefully with a fine-toothed comb. Every one of us is hoping for a strange hair or other trace element. I don't see much falling onto that paper. Maybe some dandruff, dust particles, and more of my own hair. It's gently folded up and sealed, as if it were gold dust. Everything is still happening in the presence of the witness' watchful eye.

Now they examine my face and take swabs of my mouth – at the back of my throat, on my tongue, inside my cheeks, on and around my lips. It doesn't predict comfortable things for the rest of this process. Every swab goes back into its own marked wrapper and then back into the evidence box. They don't see any bruises or scratches on my face, and I explain that he hadn't hurt me. Once again the looks of pity. I understand. They've seen too many black and blue women to believe that rapists sometimes don't use the kind of violence that leaves visible traces.

Next are my neck, my shoulders, my chest and my back. They discover bruises on my shoulders that are difficult for me to explain. Like peas lined up in a little row, the rest of these bruises would become visible only later, as if my body wanted to help me remember. Four front fingers left the marks when they held my shoulders and guided me up and down the stairs.

The doctor now scrapes under my fingernails and folds the little fragments away carefully as well. She takes samples between all my fingers and in the palms of my hands. Next are my dirty feet that still have red dirt on them from my lap around the house. My legs are not properly shaven, but right now that's the least of my worries.

I notice the metal speculum for the vaginal examination and quickly decide I won't be able to bear it. It looks sharp and big and simply dangerous. This could be the counsellor's prediction of hyper-vigilance kicking in. All I know is this is not going to happen. I demand they get a smaller one and preferably a plastic one with rounded edges, because my logic tells me if that thing breaks my skin, I will possibly have a more dangerous and direct exposure to the virus than during the rape itself. The virus could enter my bloodstream directly.

Now the sympathetic glances turn into glances of annoyance. At last the slightly deranged patient's blood pressure and pulse are climbing! They don't have anything smaller or less threatening, and they're not in the mood to go and look for something else. I don't budge. I want my gynaecologist's opinion about the risk before we proceed. Apparently it's my right, as they explained to me at the beginning. I could stop at any time if I didn't wish to continue – which I don't.

They call a gynaecologist from the hospital. She enters in a business-like, doctoral fashion and explains that she will handle the speculum very carefully, as she has done many times before. I'm unnecessarily worried. She acknowledges that if the skin should break, however, it would not be good. But she doesn't think that will happen. I'm not satisfied with that answer and insist my own gynaecologist be contacted. Someone leaves to phone him.

Unfortunately, he is in surgery but agrees about the risk. Finally the gynaecologist goes to the consulting room and comes back with the teenage version of the dreaded instrument. I wonder to myself what other women in my position do when they are totally in shock and can't speak for themselves. Do they just submit to whatever the doctors see fit? I decide there and then to do something about this someday.

They're first going to examine my legs, she explains. She switches off the light. The assistant shines an ultraviolet light over my legs and purple smudges become visible on the insides of my legs. They carefully take photos of each bit of evidence. With clinical precision she works through the series of samples. Each time she boldly announces the source location of the sample, while handing it to the assistant with an outstretched arm, who places it back in the box in its assigned place: 'Left upper thigh ... right inside leg ... left buttocks ...' I'd rather not mention the names of the other samples.

She looks up for the first time, as if she suddenly remembers I'm a human being, and holds up the last swab in front of my face.

> *"Where does this blood come from?"*

I explain that I'm at the end of my menstrual cycle. Her jaw line and expression change.

> *"That's a pity. The cervix is slightly open and raw for a few days, and on this day especially the risk of infection is much higher than on any other day."*

She's right – it is a pity.

While we're talking away the horrors of the morning hours, she suddenly turns on her heel and goes out into the hallway. I assume she went to fetch more forms. She comes back with a new face – flushed, damp, and softened. She recognised me from the picture on the back of my parenting book which she is now reading. We start talking about children. She adds her faith to mine that it will go well with me. She hands me her business card along with the invitation to phone her anytime – day or night. She stays with me for the rest of the process and hands me two handfuls of capsules and tablets to swallow. She tells of her own accidental needle prick with an HIV infected syringe and then recounts the tales of her reaction to the drugs. She lists their common side-effects: nausea, disturbed balance, weight gain, hair loss, mood swings. This is not going to be fun.

Now I'm protected as thoroughly as possible against most sexually transmittable diseases; I'm slightly nauseous from the sheer volume of pills, yet craving coffee. I'm very, very tired. The doctors start cleaning up the medical waste from my forensic exam. It forms a small mountain in the corner of the room and completely fills up a large trash can. This must be expensive.

> *"How much is it going to cost?"*
>
> *"The government pays for it. It's free."*

The gynaecologist refers me for a series of Human Papilloma Virus (HPV) vaccine shots that will cost an arm and a leg. It's the most common cause of cervical cancer and can be transmitted sexually. The government doesn't pay for immunization against that.

She explains that I need to come back the following day to collect more medication and to find out the results of my baseline HIV test. They don't give medicine in advance and don't give test results of this nature over the phone. I think they want to constantly monitor you to see if you are still acting sane. I'll receive enough medicine for three days, then enough for ten days, and then enough medicine for the rest of the month. Another blood test after six weeks will determine if I need to continue with the medication. And after that there will be re-tests for HIV after three months, six months and a year.

For at least the first six months Louis and I will have to manage our intimate life as if I were HIV positive.

My mother cannot bear the idea of leaving for their home two hours away without seeing me, so she's waiting outside the emergency room. I tidy up a bit and go out to greet her. She is brave but pale. This time around she wasn't able to pack me what I needed, or bring anything along that could help. The pain of this powerlessness is clearly visible on her face. She gives me a hug and asks the burning question that has been gnawing at her all morning:

> *"How many of them?"*

My neighbour's wife already confirmed it to her, but she wants to hear it from me. Years ago a friend of hers answered 'four', so she knows how grateful I am to be answering,

> *"Just one, Mom, and I am not in any pain."*

She will take the news to my dad. He is having a milkshake with the children in a nearby restaurant, waiting for my mom, the scout, to report on how I am doing.

I'm back in the exam room. The doctors go out, the police come in. My whole statement is taken from the top. Everything is noted in the dossier, and in between my answers I hear of the inspector's own trauma. Our story is a fairy tale compared to the nightmares he experiences regularly. I see a knight rising up in him. I realise this man would slaughter seven dragons if need be. He promises to do his best police work for our case, and I know he means it.

Now I can finally go home. The doctor asks me if I want to shower first. I do have my whole gym bag with me, so I go into the adjacent bathroom and look at myself in the mirror. Not too bad, but I need to wash my hair. My dad has now also come and brought the kids just to reassure them I was OK. They will say goodbye to mommy and then go to the Bushveld with Grandpa and Grandma. I step into the shower and start washing my hair. Hair? Is my grubby hair really what's bothering me? Shouldn't I feel like I want to scrub the very skin off my body?

> **I took care of you, dressed you and protected you. I promised you my love and entered the covenant of marriage with you. I, GOD, the Master, gave my word. You became mine. I gave you a good bath, washing off all that old blood, and anointed you with aromatic oils. I dressed you in a colourful gown and put leather sandals on your feet.**
>
> (Ezekiel 16:9-11, *The Message*).

That's why I don't feel dirty, I realise. So this must be what God's fingerprints look like. They don't leave any bruises on my shoulders. Instead a peace and lightness not of this world invade my soul. It clothes me. The same fingers tapped me on the shoulder the morning before the burglary and urged me to review my entire journal instead of reading my daily devotion as usual. I read through two months' entries, rereading the words I had transcribed from the Bible, from my devotional and from my heart. Everything I needed for this frightful night – words of love, hope, freedom and truth – were virtually bundled together and packed into a backpack with the same meticulousness as my mother's picnic basket for a road trip. That is why I felt prepared. In this way the Lord also dressed me in a garment – even an armour – of words that kept me from ever really being naked.

In my journal the last morning before my rape, I responded to all I reviewed by penning down this prayer:

> *What is love, Lord? Where are its limits, Lord? How many people can one truly love before one's capacity is exhausted? Jesus, take my heart today and make it primarily yours. May I know no other, bigger, sweeter love. Help me to focus on You, Jesus!*

I can hear the doctors talking. With the towel wrapped around me I slide open the bathroom door and join their conversation. Suddenly I realise it's not entirely appropriate and close the door again. That's strange. I'm usually very private and discreet. Someone barged through my boundaries this morning and left me with my fences and defences down. The examination subjected me to many more hours of the same invasion of privacy. My spirit is snugly tucked away, but the effect of the violation shows up clearly in the extent to which my boundary lines have shifted.

I get dressed, comb my hair and even put on a bit of make-up. My neighbour waits for me and tells me my dad is eager to see me.

He only manages a courageous smile and "Poppie", his nickname for me, before we hold each other for a few seconds and put on our brave faces for the sake of the children. The sight of his pain rips my heart out. He wasn't there to carry his little girl over the dark river.

He explains that everything is under control at home. Louis is already managing a steady stream of visitors – special detectives, members of our cell group from church who came to lend their support, and neighbours who had heard the news.

Louis's band would depart for Dubai, but Louis was considering cancelling the rest of the three week tour. I don't want him to. I am eager to get home to try and convince him to take the soonest flight out. If he ever had a message to take to former South Africans, many of whom had fled the country for fear of exactly a night like ours, it was now. We finally have the authority to say that the God who is in us truly is greater than he who is in the world. I want Louis to do this.

My children are chirpy. My oldest is always chirpy after a milkshake. The youngest tells me how the police had stolen all our stuff. Her brother corrects her and chatters on about the police cars that were in the driveway when he woke up. He is going to set traps in the yard in case the thieves ever come back, but first he and his grandpa are going to shoot baboons with slingshots in the Bushveld because Grandpa says they have been pulling the grass out of his lapa's thatched roof.

No fingerprint bruises on my children. Thank you, Jesus.

As my family walks out, our cell group leaders and other cell group members walk in. One of them asks my dad,

"Are you OK, Sir?"

My dad hesitates for one moment before he responds with the deep faith of which I am an heir:

"We will be."

One of my cell group friends hands me a cell phone just like the one that was stolen, along with a charger and ample airtime already preloaded. They are like family, and I realise how privileged we really are. I know that with my parents and my cell group drawn around our family like a laager, everything will be easier. They will pray with me in a few moments, and where they can't reach, God will – to heal and to help.

What have I to dread, what have I to fear,
Leaning on the everlasting arms;
I have blessed peace with my Lord so near,
Leaning on the everlasting arms.

(Anthony Showalter and Elisha Hoffman, 1887)

6 *Wedding flowers*

I arrive back home by lunch. The travel agent in our cell group is already here to help cancel or adapt Louis's travel plans. I try to convince him to go for the entire three weeks. He knows me so well. I have brown eyes with green specks. The darker my eyes, the darker my soul. Louis loves it when the brown lightens to an ochre tone. He says it gives away my secrets. Ochre lioness eyes mean I am mellow and unarmed. He looks me in the eye; he will go. We decide to arrange it so I can join him in Australia halfway through the tour. But just when we're done re-arranging everything, we remember that I have to report at the hospital for my follow-up medication right around that time. I'll have to stay.

Someone brings lunch. My personal assistant and one of my colleagues are also here. Louis's production company's staff are all still in shock. This morning they walked into an empty shell of an office and recording studio. I have to tell them where I just came from and why. Louis wasn't sure what and who to tell. Everyone in the room starts crying. The accountant turns pale. She tells us how her daughter could not sleep, woke her up and showed her a Bible verse that she believed was meant for Louis. The verse promises the priest and worship leader, Aaron, a new anointing on his ministry.

The signs of shock and sympathy are evident in the mounting number of flower bouquets accumulating on our dining room table and in the constant ringing of our two landline phones.

My assistant wants to know what she can confirm and how much she can tell the e-mailers and callers. Some things just don't come across well, no matter how you formulate them. It's like certain parcels. Even though you may try and wrap them beautifully, they still look untidy, awkward, and you can guess what's in them from a mile away. The standard email reply I give her to send seems like that type of parcel – gawkily wrapped in inadequate words with the ugly truth hanging out.

I decide to phone my big brother. He should be told personally. It's a very difficult call to make, but I can't risk him hearing via someone else, or worse, through the media. He answers in his usual cheerful voice. I dump the parcel in his lap.

"Hettie, no!"

He loudly bursts into tears. I hear him sob, and I cry for his pain. It's unfair that I'm causing others more pain than what I'm experiencing myself. It feels like I'm pulling them all into a hurricane, only to assure them that it's just a light breeze blowing. I try on alternati phrases like 'sexual assault', 'molestation' and 'violation'. It makes no difference. Th hear 'rape'. I might as well say it.

I desperately want to have a few moments alone with Louis. Having been separated for most of the night, we have some stories to share ... scars to compare. It seems impossible to get two words in. Someone wants to start installing an alarm system right away and would prefer we stayed elsewhere. Arrangements have already been made for us to stay in a guesthouse for the next two nights until Louis can get a flight out to Dubai. There are many gracious offers for the children and me to stay elsewhere during Louis's tour, but I'm unbending: This is my home; it's our safe haven. I'm not going to let it go. I want to return as soon as possible. What if after three weeks I didn't want to come back like someone falling off a horse and not getting back on quickly enough? I clearly recall those moments under the bed when I made my choice between fear on the one side, and power, love and a sound mind on the other. I'm not living elsewhere – not temporarily, not permanently.

It's getting dark. Everyone who should know have been handed their awful parcels, and at long last we have some privacy. We never ate lunch, so we take a few bites from the containers full of food which have arrived. This proof of so much love moves me.

Louis hasn't even had a chance to shower after his long run home. He wants to soak his sore and stiff muscles in a hot bath. I don't want to give in to the assumption that to be naked or close to him would be uncomfortable for me, so I join him in the bath even though I have had my shower for the day. Finally, we can tell each other what took place during those hours when we were apart.

Louis tells me how the robbers forced him to help them load the computers and sound equipment into his car. Initially they wanted to drive the car out of the complex themselves, but they couldn't figure out the Renault's key card. Louis tried to explain it, but their English comprehension was inadequate. God alone knows how they completely overlooked our minivan, which would have been a much more ideal get-away car! They would have been able to lug off so much more and probably would have known how to drive it. Our best guess is that being dark blue, the van was hidden by the dawn's blue shadows. They decided that Louis would have to drive the car through the security gate himself in order to rouse as little suspicion as possible.

A new guard was on duty and did not know what normal behaviour was and what it was not. The lights at the exit revealed only the outlines of five passengers – not enough to suspect anything was out of the ordinary. Feeling the revolver in his ribs, Louis went through the required motions. They were out the gate and down the road, headed for a stretch of unlit road towards the informal settlement on the outskirts of Tembisa. Oddly enough, Tembisa is derived from the Zulu word *thembisa* which means 'there is hope.'

Louis studied law and had enough time last night to determine quite rationally on a scale of probabilities, that the reasonable robber would have to shoot him. He didn't really see their faces, but how could they be certain he would be unable to identify them? They were in our home with us for more than three hours. They wore gloves, but their faces were uncovered; some lights in the house were turned on and the sun was now rising, making them more and more visible. Recognizable. The stretch of road between us and Tembisa was as abandoned as always. There are fields on both sides, a factory and what looks like a quarry. For Louis there was also the reminder of a businessman who had been shot there recently, after pulling over with a tyre that was blown out by an unexpected pothole. Louis knew it was a case of motive, means and perfect opportunity.

He talked to the men, to the demons within them, to God and about God. He prayed for grace for us to have the privilege to see our children grow up. He thanked the Lord for the exciting adventure of his life of more than forty years. He confessed that he believed if his work on earth was done and he was at the end of his numbered days, God would come for Him. He prayed for us — that God would take care of us if this was indeed the end for him.

One of the robbers, the one with the best English, suddenly said:

> *"We know you are Christian. Stop the car and get out."*

They took his shoes and ordered him to face away from the car. He expected an execution style shot in the back of his head. There were a few moments of silence, and then he heard the wheels spinning on the gravel as they sped away. He started running home.

Louis sits in the bath tub wincing as he rubs his sore calves. It is my cue. It's difficult to read his face. It's normally difficult to read his expressions, and after being married to him for eighteen years, I've learned not to fill in the silent spaces, since my conclusions are often wrong. After relaying the rape and forensic process, I explain to him that the medical visits and blood tests will continue for a year, and that we will have to be cautious for a long time in order to make sure he is protected in case I'm infected with HIV.

Both of us are too tired and too thankful that we're alive and the children unharmed to get upset about little things like compulsory condom use. We finish our bath, pack two overnight bags, and go to dinner with two couples at our cell leaders' home. We talk about the greatness of God, because we all realise something extraordinary has happened. Our joy comes from a heavenly place. We celebrate our being alive, having a second chance, and the reality of the Christian life. Slightly sacrilegiously, we even toast the celebration with champagne – not recommended as a condiment to anti-retroviral medicine, so I pass on the bubbly and drink juice instead. One of my friends jokingly offers me her excellent veins when I reveal my biggest fear is the repeated blood tests I will need to go for, as my veins always disappear, collapse or blow up like little water balloons whenever a needle comes near them. I'm humbled by the love shown by these friends who would gladly bleed for me. No-one could deserve such generosity. Church is such a God idea! Being part of a body never felt more real.

We depart for the lovely guesthouse where we have just enough energy left to brush our teeth before flopping into bed. Louis lets slip a flattering comment about a new pink item of underwear I'm wearing, and it doesn't make me uncomfortable in the least. No signs of serious trouble yet, I think to myself. I lie snugly in my husband's arms and fall asleep feeling safe. I sleep right through the dreamless night.

It is early morning. Every now and then, in between half-lucid moments, I hear my new cell phone beeping. Only a handful of people have this new number – close friends, family and the police. It's probably important. Maybe the police have tracked down the robbers? Louis is still sleeping soundly. The cell phone starts ringing again, so I grab it and run into the bathroom to keep from waking him. It's just past seven. Who would be calling at this early hour? I don't recognise the number. I wonder if people realise how exhausted we still are.

Reluctantly, I answer. It's a magazine editor. She heard something terrible in the news and would like to know if it is true. Are we 'the Gospel singer and his wife' that this horrible thing happened to? I confirm it bluntly, wondering what lies she must have told to get a hold of this number. She thinks it would be very therapeutic for me to give their publisher the exclusive rights to a book about my experience. Seeing as I have published through them in the past, she feels strongly their company almost has the right to my story, based on what she calls "the relationship". I don't think so. I am not interested. I end the conversation quivering with disbelief.

The first vulture has landed.

I crawl back in bed, all innocence and belief in my fellow man's goodwill gone for the moment. The cell phone beeps again. It's a warning text message from a friend:

Your story is on the lampposts.

It can't be true. No newspaper has spoken to us. Half our friends don't even know yet. My parents informed my other brothers before I could, but they wouldn't have contacted the newspapers. Louis is still sleeping. I don't want to wake him, but I'm hungry. I decide to go to the guesthouse's breakfast nook to eat something and to look for a newspaper. Many women are raped in our country every day. One woman every 17 seconds, not counting children. Usually the story barely reaches page five. I'm sure our case couldn't be front page news. We came off lightly. No shots were even fired. No-one shed a drop of blood. It is non-news.

I enjoy a wonderful breakfast, then finally see someone walking in with a newspaper.

"What's in the news?"

"A Gospel singer's wife was raped."

She tells me this with shock evident on her face. I frown and shake my head appropriately. This sweet lady is not getting slapped with a wrapped hurricane from me today. My cell phone rings again. A friend gives the report: our story was broadcast on the radio. I have to know what was said, so I borrow the woman's newspaper. There are extracts from my statement, but they have twisted some of my words and the details are inaccurate – sensationalised, of course. Louis was supposedly tied up helplessly downstairs while I was being raped violently upstairs. Even though the article was published without our names, there are many details such as where we live and how many children we have. Hundreds of people must have pieced together the rest by now. I have no idea who leaked this information to the press. Thanks to Christian radio stations nationwide and the normal grapevine, everybody seems to know. I can't get through to my parents to warn them. Their phone is ringing off the hook already.

Back in the room I inform Louis that our initial plan to keep everything private is not an option anymore – it's already public. But the undertones and the spirit of what was written and reported is taunting. The report seems to say: 'If even Gospel singers' wives get raped, what type of a God are they singing their songs to? If *they* don't enjoy His protection, then who is safe?' The article is sowing fear and blasphemy. This is going to shake people's faith. The Puppet Master is accused of sloppy work. We pray about it in the guestroom and decide we should respond in some way.

We decide to give our statement to Neels Jackson. We came to know him as an excellent journalist who has been reporting Christian news with objectivity, open-mindedness and accuracy for years. He agrees to meet us in a coffee shop so he and Louis can have breakfast, too.

We talk with Neels for a long time. We explain our experience and our convictions. We don't believe the Author of our lives has had His pen snatched from His hand; we believe this episode fits neatly into the story. Louis is deeply involved in the Turn2God movement, aimed at getting South Africans to acknowledge and submit to Jesus as the ultimate authority over our nation. A day and a half before the burglary, Louis called a prayer meeting in our house to pray for breakthroughs in our country and for the success of the Turn2God event to be held at the Union Buildings – the seat of parliament – in less than a month. The organisers gave us a worrying report. While preparations for the event were underway, *sangomas* started visiting the site, making proclamations, pronouncing curses and planting their *muti* on the perimeter of the grounds against any other rule but the rule of the ancestral spirits. The resistance on a government level and from traditional leaders was very strong, too. We prayed prayers of spiritual warfare that night. Elza Meyer, the founder of the movement, reminded us that one always pays a price for breakthroughs in a country. There often is bloodshed before there is breakthrough. She urged us to be courageous. We tell Neels that we see a link between these events and the attack on us.

I explain what I experienced throughout the night, and Neels takes notes, even of the scripture passages I quote. He is willing to write down the strange-sounding statements: the Lord warned and prepared and comforted me by calling me His bride and promising to hold my spirit and soul safely in His hands.

I don't expect anyone to consider our statements strange theology. For years, Louis and I have regarded believers as the bride of Christ. We believe every Christian can claim that precious title, because Jesus gave His life to make it possible.

I explain to Neels that I believe there is a battle raging between light and darkness, but even though we get scarred in the process, the war has already been won. Louis and I don't have delusions of grandeur when we claim to be fighting this war. Ephesians 6 is not written for a selected few super-Christians. It gives no believer the option to stand outside this war. There are no selectively chosen fighters with exclusive credentials. It says everyone in Jesus' camp is part of the fight, and we won't be able to stand without our spiritual armour strapped on tightly.

Neels promises to report everything the way we explained it, but he warns it's not up to him whether the story gets published in full, partially, or not at all. He says he will write three short articles instead of one long report in the hopes that perhaps one will make it into the newspaper. We understand. In fact, tomorrow is the commemoration of Nelson Mandela's release from prison – a much more newsworthy event. The grim truth is, however, the rape statistics have skyrocketed since that day and, by tomorrow, other women's rape reports might be more newsworthy, too. Each day brings enough horrible front page news that even sensational news like ours has a very short shelf life. The secular press is not in the business of accurately representing God's image. My guess is they don't have to print corrections or retractions simply because we feel God's name was dragged through the mud in the first report of our story.

Neels phones a newspaper photographer, and we take a few photos at the nearby creek in Waterkloof Ridge just in case they do decide to publish the article. I hate photo shoots. I've had to do a few over the years, and after every one I felt nauseous. Even here in the soothing surroundings I hate it. I pray they use a tiny, passport sized photo, if any at all. We look at the photos on the camera screen. My T-shirt seems a little tight and Louis asks if they would crop the photo. You never know. It could elicit that hackneyed reaction:

Well, dressed like that – it's no wonder ...!

In truth, I could have never imagined how much antagonism this impromptu little photo of Louis and me would evoke. The simple fact that I was smiling in one photo and contentedly looking into Louis's face in the other caused unmasked fury. One reader decided I was an exhibitionist, smugly displaying my 'battle scars' and preying on the publicity by having my picture printed 'large and prominent'. As if I had any control over that. Another reader said my smile was proof of my insanity, while yet another commented our smiles were the idiotic ones of 'typically stupid Gospel people'.

It turns out to be another day full of very emotional people and crisis management. Louis urgently needs a new cell phone, laptop, and worship software, otherwise his performances overseas are going to be virtually impossible. Several volunteers scurry about to make it happen.

I have to go back to the hospital for the next few days' medication. They congratulate me on my negative HIV test results. It's somewhat of an insult that they are so happy, since this result only implies I didn't sleep around before the incident and, therefore, hadn't accidentally become infected somehow. Louis was the first and only man I'd ever had intercourse with, so I would not have expected any other outcome. I guess at such a clinic you celebrate every bit of *negative* news anyway! Some people are infected without being promiscuous, of course.

I have my old mobile phone number back so many more calls are coming through. From time to time someone phones who hasn't heard the news and merrily starts talking about everyday things, asking me favours, or complaining about their work load. These are welcome islands of normality, and I jump at the opportunity to chat about trivial matters. I do realise they will soon discover they were unknowingly very insensitive, but I can't bring myself to be the one to tell them and spoil their day. I'm even relieved when someone phones to ask why I haven't replied to her email about changes to one of my parenting books.

'I've had a busy day but will do it immediately,'

I reply. I use the only computer that wasn't stolen, read through the changes and proposals, and email answers to her questions. I reply to a few other emails – mostly parenting questions. Other messages cautiously probe whether we know anything about the Gospel singer and his wife. After all, we are in the same circles and are the logical sources ... They will know soon enough, and I don't feel like answering now.

There are several text messages on my cell phone, too. One friend's message catches my eye.

> *Dear Hettie, no words can express my sorrow for the ordeal you have been through. I am ashamed to be a black man right now, to say the least. I know that in your heart you have forgiven them, though the trauma lingers. I once more apologise on behalf of all black men. Thank you for your forgiveness. I am sure that from this trauma the Lord Jesus will use you mightily to help thousands upon thousands through your writing and counselling. You will never let the enemy triumph.*

I ask myself how we managed to make rape into an issue of race. How did we manage to load the guilt of Apartheid, an invention of a few white men, onto the shoulders of generations of white descendants? And why does this black man willingly assume the shame of my rapist? Is it because he is already carrying the shame of merely being black along with forty million other South Africans? It's bitterly unjust and unnecessary that our entire rainbow nation is bent down by burdens of blame.

We spend a second night in the guesthouse, grateful to come to the end of day two *post facto*. Another sound night.

Not again! It would be lovely to be awakened by bird song or anything but the phone. I read the text messages streaming in:

> *'Jesus' is on the lamp posts.*
>
> *Today's headline is: Jesus talks before rape.*
>
> *We read your testimony. Praise the Lord for He is good!*

It's front page news, but our goal was never publicity. We wanted to bring glory to God, to tell what He did for us, and to help people understand that fear is from the enemy who wants desperately to be feared. It seems God is always openly ridiculed. It should also be the case that for once someone openly declares He is not ridiculous. While we are happy the news made the front page, we also immediately think of how this will affect our children, but then we realise the first article and radio bulletin took away our anonymity in any case. Louis is understandably angry at the reporter who wrote the first article. We still don't know who it was. It was mean. This gross misuse of writer's liberty was the real rape. It forced us to go even more public.

We sit on the guest room bed, a little shell shocked as the implications start to sink in. For the rest of their lives our children will also have to endure the knowing looks of pity ... I read out loud for both of our comfort today's extract from my Charles Spurgeon daily devotional:

> **A Christian should model Christ's boldness. Never blush to own your faith. Your profession [of faith in Christ] will never disgrace you; take care that you never disgrace it. Be like Jesus, very valiant for your God ... Best of all, as the highest portraiture of Jesus, try to forgive your enemies, as He did; let those sublime words of your Master, 'Father forgive them; for they know not what they do' (Luke 12:24), always ring in your ears. Forgive, as you hope to be forgiven.**

We pray together. We have forgiven the robbers but not the informant and the first journalist. They forgot that the puppets whose story they plastered on the front page can actually get hurt. We agree that they did not know what they were doing and choose to forgive them together.

Printed just below our story in the newspaper is the story of our former president, Nelson Mandela. I suddenly realise both are stories about cross-racial forgiveness, and both are vivid examples of the disgrace of extreme injustice we as South Africans are trying to crawl out from under, as we try to build a hopeful future together. On the second page is our report about the spiritual war we believe Christians are fighting in South Africa. The third report, the one about the support our church members gave us, is also published. Every word Neels wrote down made it onto page one and two.

Naively, Louis and I believe this brings an end to the newspaper saga. We have no idea of the war of words about to erupt. Our comments send shock waves through the bastions of racism, prosperity teaching, demonology, psychology, nationalism and theology. Everyone feels they have a right to react, and so they do.

The article is translated from the original Afrikaans into English for the syndicated newspapers. A word in the initial report describing me as surprisingly upbeat is translated as *beaten-up*, because I surely couldn't have been upbeat. This leads to a rumour that I was badly injured and admitted to hospital. The conflicting messages become laughable: I was beaten to a pulp but insisted my attacker wasn't violent and I was in no pain ... all thanks to Jesus. No wonder people thought I had lost my marbles!

A committee of vultures descend upon us in a flurry.

> *"Will you do an exclusive radio interview?"*
>
> *"Will you sell the story to Huisgenoot magazine for a check with many zeros?"*
>
> *"Won't you reconsider the idea of an exclusive book?"*
>
> *"Don't you think the exclusive podcast on our magazine's website is appropriate on the grounds of our past collaborations?"*

We give the same responses many times over:

"No, we don't think so."

"No thanks."

"Not right now."

"Not ever in exchange for any amount of money. "

We rush back home to try and put out all the flames. On the way we warn our parents about the front page photos, which we don't believe our children should see yet. Dr Marietjie Yssel, a specialist in the field of child trauma, has already agreed to be at our home tomorrow when the children return. Our children are eleven, eight and three. We think professional help is needed to communicate everything clearly on each one's level of understanding. She is the expert. She helped me long ago with trauma debriefing when children from my afterschool centre in Proclamation Hill witnessed a motorcycle crushing their friend's tiny body after the drunk driver attempted a stunt called a 'doughnut.' I remember the children's' horrifying questions: *'Teacher, why were his eyes still open even though his chest was so flat?'* I'm anticipating such questions from my eleven-year-old. I don't have all the answers, so Marietjie will have to help.

More people await us at the house.

"What colour would you prefer for the burglar proofing – black or brown? Is it a good time to demonstrate your new alarm system? It has a complicated zone design ... No, you don't need to pay for anything.'

Fort Knox turns out to be a free gift by a group of sincerely concerned friends and neighbours from around the globe. I'm sad when I think of how families who aren't in the public eye must go through similar crises all alone, with very little chance that people will help them in practical ways. It's unfair. I feel ashamed because of the help we're receiving, but then I remember that the Lord has different ways of showing grace. He will surely show grace to others in different ways.

The telephone rings, and Radio Pulpit would like to know if I will share my testimony with their listeners who have been earnestly praying for us since yesterday. I agree to do it because I know Radio Pulpit isn't sensation-driven, and I want people to be encouraged by our testimony. They do the interview with me, and then allow Louis to pray for the country while on the air. His prayer is short and passionate. After the interview is over, Louis quickly continues to run his errands, as it is now only hours before he flies out to Dubai. He is still waiting for his new laptop to be delivered. We hug each other in passing every hour or so while running around in a mild frenzy.

A friend arrives to take me for my first HPV vaccination. Apparently it was set up by a friend-of-a-friend who is a doctor, and all I need to do is hop in the car and go along. I'm glad someone is taking me, because I refuse to head in the direction of needles voluntarily.

My friend is the most jovial person I know, and so we sit laughing in the waiting room while they open a file in my name. The nurse assigned to give me the immunisation tells how her son-in-law was shot and killed in their driveway. Once again I realise how much grace we were given. I'm so thankful my husband is alive! I'm told to take a seat again because something needs to be signed off before I can leave.

My friend cracks a joke, and we both let out real belly laughs. The next instant a doctor with a concerned face appears next to me; I get that familiar pitiful look. Goodness me, do they teach this *'poor-thing-is-on-the-verge-of-a-nervous-breakdown'* look in medical school?

"You must see the doctor first before you can leave. That's our policy."

I realised quickly that we had laughed too loudly. We should have sat and cried — then maybe the policy would not have included a compulsory visit to the doctor. I object, because I want to greet Louis before he departs for Dubai. I know if I have to wait for a consultation, then I will probably miss him. The more I protest, the more pitiful the looks. They insist I should calm down. My husband is not leaving for Dubai. He would not do that. Everything is going to be OK as soon as I see the doctor. I need to be thoroughly probed probably because they think they see hysterical cracks, and they want to prevent me from falling apart completely.

So, I walk into the doctor's consulting room. I see Bible verses and Christian artwork on the walls. This doctor is clearly not just a doctor. The first questions probe in a very therapeutic manner. I suddenly realise this is not about me anymore. It is about her, and so I accept the fact I will not be able to see Louis off. I share the whole story. Her eyes well up with tears. She tells me that she does a lot of trauma counselling – in fact, she sees all of the rape cases in this area. My story is not what she usually hears.

"I can see you are calm and rational. I can see you are in touch with reality. This is the sort of healing I know that the Lord can do and that I have often prayed for on behalf of my patients, but it's the first time I see it so clearly in front of me."

As I leave her office, I pray that she will never again quit on a broken woman until she sees the sort of healing that I have received, even if it takes a long time.

My friend drives me home. Apparently *Huisgenoot* is not impressed with the refusal of their offer to buy our story. Instead of staying home where they were sure to pitch up, I decide to go to a tea garden for lunch. At the security gate one of the guards walks towards my car. He kneels on the ground with his chest pressed against the car door and his hands on the half open window. His face is so close I can see the tears on his cheeks.

"Ma'am, I'm so sorry I couldn't protect you. Please don't be angry."

I'm good friends with this guard. When I shot a blesbok a while back, I frequently gave him some of the biltong, and in turn he kindly opened the gate for me on the many days when I accidently left my security disk at home. During some chilly winter nights he came to our driveway gate to beg for tea bags and sugar so he could make tea for himself and the other guards. I can see the trauma on his face now. It is the same as on my white friends' faces. I get out of the car and put my arms around him. He starts shaking. He had a tough day. He was the victim of a few angry white people who decided to make him the scapegoat of their anger even though he wasn't even on duty the night of the robbery. His skin colour and security uniform justified it. In their view he was just the same as all the thieves and rapists who shared his skin colour. They thought nothing of this humiliation and kept him accountable along with the other guards. What infuriated me almost more than their actions is the fact that he carries this false guilt willingly. I want to scream, it makes me so mad. I try to comfort him:

> *"It's not your job to protect me. God protected me. I really am okay now. The rapist is not your brother any more than he is mine. How can I be angry with you?"*

He loosens his shoulders from my grip and replies with the identical words the fuel station attendant used that day on the road between Klerksdorp and Pretoria:

> *"I have never seen such love and power."*

'So, this is the second way in which God can shine through us,' I think to myself. 'The first being when we see ourselves small enough, and the second when we allow Him to give love through us to people who expect retaliation.'

I enjoy my lunch at a tea garden and keep ignoring *Kwêla's* office that is now phoning me for the third time about a TV interview. Louis and I decided we would only talk to the media again when he was back home from the tour ... and then very cautiously and selectively. A friend phones me to say a radio presenter would like to interview me on how a woman should protect herself physically during a rape. It's for a secular radio station; it's not to exploit us or even to tell our story. It seems safe and would probably help other women, so I agree to meet her and immediately drive to the appointed place.

A beautiful woman with long black hair, a big old-fashioned voice recorder and a microphone walks towards me. I feel a warning crawling up my spine. We sit at a little table in the courtyard of the open air shopping mall. I ask her not to switch on the recorder until she has explained her true agenda. She practically spits the words back at me.

> *"My agenda?! I want to know what your agenda is! You owe the listeners an explanation. After I did everything possible to protect your identities, you go and splash it across the front page with photos and everything! What do you want to sell?"*

The lights in my head all go on at once. I'm dazzled. So she is the one!

I take a deep breath and speak firmly but calmly while trying to hide the hot feeling rushing to my face.

> *"So you're the reason I have to explain rape to my eleven year old daughter? It's you that we forgave this morning while praying in our room, because you didn't know what you were doing."*

She tears up while I continue speaking. I explain to her that she is also a puppet in this puppet theatre. She thought she would expose the Puppet Master's perceived incompetence, but what she really did was to shatter the theatre box to expose a back-stage story that brought glory to His name. If it weren't for the first shocking article, the second would never have made it to page ten, let alone page one and three.

While she sips her cappuccino, I tell her the back-stage story — whether she wants to hear it or not — because she is now part of this story. I acknowledge our agenda, the one she wondered about. We are not trying to sell books or CDs, but we do want to use every possible platform to make sure people see more of a great God they maybe haven't met, and less of the small one they have created in their puny imagination. What we want to sell is the dream of a country that could change if everybody turned to Jesus.

Her cell phone rings. She looks at me oddly and utters a few inaudible words. Now it's her turn to confess something. It was another call by the same informant, phoning from the police station. They're hot on the trail of the four men and expect an arrest soon. She tells me about that night. The informant phoned her at five in the morning telling her to look out her window to where she would see blue lights flashing on the other side of the infamous creek where our fence had been washed away. She didn't get out of bed, but she probably could have seen our house from hers. The informant fed her the juiciest details from the dossier, and in turn she sold it to the newspaper's crime reporter. She seems sincerely sorry and vows to make sure I am the first to know if she hears anything else about our case.

The woman says she suspects that if they catch the guys, the police line-up might take place as soon as tonight. She asks if I will be able to handle it. Since I didn't see any of their faces, the line-up won't help much, but according to recently amended laws everyone's blood will be taken for HIV screening and their DNA compared to that found at the scene of the crime. Additionally, there was a pair of old worn-out shoes in my husband's closet where his good shoes had been, and there was even a jersey which had been left behind on our bed.

Immediately I think about the moment when I might have to face my rapist. If that moment ever comes I intend to tell him what I wanted to say that morning:

> *'What you did was wrong, but I forgive you, because I am forgiven. I wish you knew the Love that I know. If you did, you never would have done this. May I tell you about this Love?'*

Forgiveness is freedom. It is the reason I'm not carrying my rapist on my back. I'm not interested in carrying this beautiful woman around with me, either. I can't hate her. I like her. I'm making a new friend today. We walk to the nearest clothing store and record the interview in the dressing room. Because of the thick curtains it makes the ideal recording studio. It's understandable that the owner of the boutique looks at us suspiciously as we walk in ... and doesn't even make eye contact on our way out!

We spent so much time talking that I now need to hurry back home to meet my twin brother who has offered to come in from Johannesburg and sleep over for a few nights. Both of us still need to dress up in something red. Our whole cell group is coming together tonight, and we are going to dress in red to symbolically celebrate the blood of Jesus.

My brother and I arrive simultaneously. We rush upstairs to get dressed. My room! Everything is white! Everything is new! This is what Liza, the lady who did this beautiful thing, told me later upon my request for her side of the story:

> *The day I received a phone call from Michal (Michal and Liza are both on the Turn2God team that had prayed in our house the night before the burglary).*

I could hear his heart was heavy, and with his whole being he wished he didn't have to tell me what had happened. He was the one who broke the news of the rape to me. With his heart, soul and mind he dearly wished there was something else he could tell me. The media already knew and everybody needed to stand together. Many other beautiful people also jumped in to help, in their own ways. I was suddenly overcome by the reality. I became nauseous and collapsed on the spot. I vomited for two days.

The second evening when I got in bed, I suddenly experienced the most heavenly feeling. The sheets were soft, fresh and welcoming as they covered my body. While experiencing the luxury of the linen, it was as if the shock left my body. My spirit took over, and I received a clear message: ***"Get Hettie a new set of linen sheets."*** *First my carnal mind argued somewhat. Maybe this is just my own idea? Maybe she'll be offended. She's been through a lot.*

I decided that if it was a Godly command, I would hear His voice more clearly about this.

The following morning the message was stronger and more convincing than ever. In my mind's eye I saw her room covered in white linen, and I very clearly saw the logo of the familiar home ware store, @Home, as if I was walking through the shop's front door. Then I knew that I should drive to @Home and get everything I needed there.

As I walked through the doors of @Home, just like I had seen it in my mind, the reality struck me. Clearly it had been a command I should obey, but what about all the different possible sizes! Then I hear: "It should be fit for a Queen." I argued over and over: "I know Louis. He thinks big. It should be something like King size, extra length, double thick or something like that. Then twice I sensed it again: "It should be fit for a Queen." I should look for a Queen Size duvet set. As if to confirm it, they even have a snow white towel set with a silver tiara embroidered on it.

There were many different scatter cushions, but my heart was drawn to a snow white pair with grey embroidery.

When I arrived at Louis and Hettie's gated community, security was very tight. I was grateful that nobody from the family was at home. I just wanted to put everything together and disappear quietly.

Yet it wasn't as easy as quickly making a bed. It was as if I could not cross the threshold into their room. I stood there with everything in my arms, but I couldn't go in. It was someone else's room. It was private. Suddenly I became angry: "It stops me, but it didn't stop the enemy," I thought to myself. Then I walked straight into the room with a mission, and I prayed quietly nonstop while making the bed. Hettie's personal assistant was with me. I had never met her before, so I didn't pray out loud. I may have seemed very quiet, but my spirit was at war.

I couldn't believe it! And the scatter cushions I bought matched the couch next to the bed – both had the grey embroidery. I went downstairs and picked two white flower arrangements for the bedside tables. I put their wedding album in the middle of the bed between the pillows – a small reminder of the true covenant she and Louis have. Everything was done in white, and it almost looked like a honeymoon suite.

After leaving the house, I read the newspaper article which said that the word Hettie had held onto during that night was the affirmation that she was Jesus' bride. Now everything I felt I had to do made sense.

We serve a big, big God. He is present, even in the practical details. He does not leave us alone, whether we go through the valley of the shadow of death, or whether we are walking through something as commonplace as a shop's door. God Himself had ordered and orchestrated this new room for Louis and Hettie. From her testimony and my own story I realise one thing: nobody can argue with you about what you hear from God. His Spirit alone can open hearts to receive His words.

- Liza Wolfaard

I sit on the bed and marvel at the whole thing. How would anyone know that these flower arrangements are almost identical to the ones we had on our wedding day? The florist is no longer alive so it can't be him ... I page through our wedding album. I miss Louis. I wish he could see this. It says everything. It confirms everything. Even the towel set takes me back to the promises in Ezekiel 16 for the umpteenth time. I remember a reference to a diamond tiara and these white towels have silver tiara's embroidered on them ... God truly has done a complete work of restoration and has virtually set this silver crown on it as proof. I am overcome with love for Him and cry while getting dressed in red.

"I love you Jesus!"

My brother and I join the cell group. We share wonderful passages from Scripture with one another. My twin shares how the story of Jonah had confronted him two days ago. Jonah had a hard time coming to terms with the fact that God had mercy on the evil inhabitants of Nineveh. My brother, like most men would, nurtured thoughts of revenge and was enraged with the possibility that justice might never prevail against my rapist – at least not on this earth. As he mulled over the story of Nineveh, he had to make peace with the possibility that God may even do the unthinkable – grant grace and forgiveness to the robbers and my rapist if they, like the Ninevites, ever asked for it. Like Jonah under the wilted vine, we are tempted to cry "unfair!" We want to see revenge. Due judgement. Fair punishment. Behind our theatre is the God who has His hands on every living being and who challenges our Jonah-like claims and demands.

I try to explain in words how intact I feel despite everything that has happened. My cell group tries to believe me, but they suspect it is too soon to know whether I will really be okay. Someone asks if I plan on publishing everything, seeing as I have written books before. Before I can respond, someone interjects a few wise words:

"Now it's a chapter. A year from now it will be a book."

We debate back and forth about the possibility of being whole in the midst of attempted destruction like this. The cell leader's wife reads a passage as confirmation that it's indeed possible to be whole, because it's God's will for us:

> **May God Himself, the God who makes everything holy and whole, make you holy and whole, put together – spirit, soul, and body."**
>
> (1 Thessalonians 5:23, *The Message*).

We talk about the ways in which we sometimes live life – with our spirit lagging behind and our souls and bodies leading the way. In living life like that we can get hurt easily because our flesh sees and feels the pain, it hurts and bleeds and harbours revenge. A life with our spirit out front, however, is one wherein we don't perceive with natural eyes only, limited to viewing the puppet show. Spiritual eyes look straight through the curtains. The flesh life is our so-called reality, but it's also temporary. The spirit life is eternal and has already started for those who will look past this temporary concert we call life.

> **For instance, we know that when these bodies of ours are taken down like tents and folded away, they will be replaced by resurrection bodies in heaven – God-made, not handmade – and we'll never have to relocate our "tents" again. Sometimes we can hardly wait to move – and so we cry out in frustration. Compared to what's coming, living conditions around here seem like a stopover in an unfurnished shack, and we're tired of it! We've been given a glimpse of the real thing, our true home, our resurrection bodies! The Spirit of God whets our appetite by giving us a taste of what's ahead. He puts a little of heaven in our hearts so that we'll never settle for less. That's why we live with such good cheer. You won't see us drooping our heads or dragging our feet! Cramped conditions here don't get us down. They only remind us of the spacious living conditions ahead. It's what we trust in but don't yet see that keeps us going. Do you suppose a few ruts in the road or rocks in the path are going to stop us? When the time comes, we'll be plenty ready to exchange exile for homecoming."**
>
> (2 Corinthians 5:1-8, *The Message*)

The previous verse, 2 Corinthians 4:18 (*English Standard Version*), also reminds us of this truth:

> **... as we look not to the things that are seen but to the things that are unseen. For the things that are seen are transient, but the things that are unseen are eternal.**

It's a sad kind of poverty when we are only able to see up to the edge of the stage or even just to the curtains. Less than two days after my rape I'm experiencing a joy that can only be explained by what I saw in that foreboding place behind the theatre box.

New view

My eyes have seen such beauty
I have pictures of these views
of lakes and mountains framed in ferns all summer long
and then in snow when winter sweeps its crystal-whiteness there
and albums full of baby faces: smiling, sleeping, lashes long
for life has beauty everywhere
but all of these could not compare to what is finally in view

My pictures missed a colour never mixed on a palette
I missed a shape no bended branch has ever sketched
I've never seen this Depth or Height or sheer intensity of Light
or anything like this New Sky
Jesus, You have caught my eye

(Hettie Brittz, May 2010)

When we choose the spirit life, we will always be accused of being in denial, and sometimes even suspected of being mentally ill. But is it not the ultimate denial to believe only in the temporary? Which spirit is more disturbed than the one that denies the very Spirit from which it was born?

While talking to the cell group about the Lord's presence during traumatic events, a woman's name pops into my head. Then I hear the clear words:

> *"Phone her and tell her that I did the same for her, even though she didn't realise it."*

I stifle it. I'm starting to think I hear too many weird voices. I start rationalising: It would be so rude to say such a personal thing to someone I hardly know. She's old enough to be my mother. What would she think of such a phone call? What if I am way off base here? She'll be offended. She's probably already sleeping soundly. It's too late in the evening to call a stranger. I hear the Lord's reply:

> *"No, she's not asleep. She can't sleep tonight."*

I pretend I didn't hear a thing.

My new friend, the reporter, phones me. I slip out of the room to answer.

> *"Hettie, prepare yourself. They have the house surrounded with the robbers trapped inside."*

The police phone me an hour later with the same news. They will call to confirm the capture as soon as it is done. I am still with my church friends. I decide the ones who look the least angry can come with me; I'm not in the mood for Rambo nonsense. Now I really miss Louis.

We end the evening with a prayer for all the victims of violence in our country. While praying, the following words involuntarily come out of my mouth:

"You don't get to lay down palm branches on the ground for an earthly king to ride into the city on the back of a donkey. You get to lay down your very lives so that the King of Glory can enter the city on the back of martyrs. He will come in a glory you have not seen, but before He comes there will be a lot more blood."

I think to myself that this is what Jesus meant when He reminded me that I was His bride. It was never meant for my ears only. Two nights ago He did for me what He wants to do for His whole church in the last days. In her darkest days, He wants to be closer to her than ever before. There will be terribly hard times, but they're like the dark of night that comes before the glory of the new dawn. That's what the bride needs to know. She needs to know she will not bleed in vain. She needs to know that when she feels a great weight on her shoulders, it is Jesus who has chosen her to carry Him into the New Jerusalem. Louis's old song comes to mind:

It's when He comes again
When clouds cave in under the weight of His throne
When our King returns to bring us home
With a wedding ring
For His bride to sing
It's when He comes again

(Excerpt from "*It's when He comes again*" by Louis Brittz)

The police don't call back, and I realise tonight will not be the night. My twin brother and I return home to try and figure out the alarm system. I think I got it right, but I don't really care because I'm crawling into a white bed with my Bridegroom, who is closer to me than my own skin.

7 Angry letters and hot seats

Beep-beep.

Not again! An early text message:

> *Hets, because I love you, I want to urge you not to read the newspapers today.*

Letters from well-meaning people, but also from those who refuse to look at things with spiritual eyes and who hate spiritual realities, are going back and forth in the letter columns of several daily papers. A gall spitting contest. I had no idea this would happen. Like a shield, I lift up the verse one of the church members read and scribbled on a piece of paper for me the previous night. I'm not going to expose myself to this poison. I will read the letters in the newspapers later. I've been warned to lay low, haven't I?

> **And I'll be right there with her – GOD's decree – a wall of fire around unwalled Jerusalem and a radiant presence within.**
>
> (Zechariah 2:5, *The Message*)

Isn't it uncanny how people can spot their moments to attack when someone's walls are down and they are vulnerable? I realise the gift of God's radiant presence in me should be my focus and that it would not be wise to get involved in these pen wars. Everyone who knows me calls to warn me to stand down, because they know how prone I am to amassing firepower and retaliating with all I've got. They know me. There are few things I enjoy more than a war of words. This time around I surprisingly have no desire to enter the fray.

Later, on the second of April, I read these wise words by Charles Spurgeon and know with certainty that it would be foolish to hit back:

> **Calm endurance answers some questions infinitely more conclusively than the loftiest eloquence ... The anvil breaks a host of hammers by quietly bearing the blows.**

If we shout loudly at other people, it is so much harder to hear the Lord's voice inside of us. I find Him the quietest when I make the most noise, and His comfort is not easily felt when I try to break others down.

My big brother informs me that I can dare to read my Facebook messages, since most of them are constructive. Like the true engineer that he is, he has mathematically estimated that 80% of the messages are positive. He tells me a swimming coach wrote that he is predicting a good race time for me at the Midmar Mile because he notices that I adhere to the first principle he teaches all his swimmers: *don't look back*. I decide to read a few more messages.

That's when I discover a message from a very dear friend. The time and date shows that she sent the message while I had been at the hospital. The afternoon before the attack we had lunch together; we had deep conversations, some of which were about trauma and healing. Usually she is the strong one, giving me powerful encouragement and sometimes very poignant prophetic messages. This time she had a broken heart, and nothing I said brought her comfort. Still I kept insisting that with one word the Lord could strip down the sackcloth of her mourning, blow the ashes from her hair, and place her back in the land of joy. I saw how desperately she wanted to believe me.

That evening she tried to get in contact with me because she felt strangely concerned for me and had no idea why she couldn't find peace. I didn't take her concerned messages too seriously and texted back that she didn't need to worry – I really was quite fine! It was Monday night, our usual date night and the night before Louis's trip, so I ignored the rest of her calls and messages. Surely it couldn't be that important if we already talked for hours this afternoon, I thought.

Still troubled throughout the night of the attack, she stayed up and prayed for me. Early the next morning she tried to phone again and left a voice message on the stolen phone. After several attempts to get through to me, she settled for this message on my Facebook:

> *Hello Hettie,*
>
> *I've been looking for you the whole morning. Left text messages everywhere. Hope you are OK. Thank you again for yesterday. Last night I thought so much about you. I really hope you are OK. I feel very loving towards you today ...*
>
> *I see you standing before a large group of women. You have an intense message from woman to woman. It crosses the barriers of race and language. It is a new testimony and it comes at a price.*
>
> *So call me when you can, OK?*

I read another message, from an American friend with whom I had actually lost contact, except for the fact that she still lets us know from time to time that she is praying for us. The date is the date of the burglary. She's thinking of us and wants to know if everybody is well.

I think of Amos 3:3: *The Lord does nothing before announcing it to His prophets.* Sometimes we receive prophetic words from people that make no sense. For example, a month before the rape the secretary at the Department of Communication Pathology, where I had studied, tracked me down to tell me about a vision she had. She told me that she saw me running with a long, wavy white flag, and I was wearing a long white dress. She continued to say that everywhere the flag was flown people, especially women, were set free. I thanked her for the lovely idea, but it seemed so foreign. I don't generally enjoy women's ministry. I'm also not the flag-flying and banner-bearing type, and I don't wear dresses – ever.

Louis dubbed women's gatherings 'oestrogen fests.' We both avoided these, as well as the ever popular ladies' breakfasts, like the plague. My excuse was that I grew up with three brothers.

In 2008 I attended my first ever women's conference. I was very uncomfortable. There were women dressed in what looked like angel costumes with tiaras on their heads and flags to wave around during worship. They were sincere and what they did seemed lovely and all, but I felt out of place, like a triple cheese pizza in a health shop.

On the second day of that same Esther conference, Pastor Elza Meyer invited us to stand and ask the Lord out loud for the heritage that He was pressing on our hearts to ask of Him. She believed the Lord wanted to claim back every aspect and every corner of the country by restoring it to the custody of His men and women. We had to claim our piece of this in faith. The only thing I could think of to claim was the families of South Africa. They were the focus of my parenting ministry and of my books, and I didn't have much passion for other causes. As I stood there, the love for families turned into a consuming passion. I felt as though I were on fire. I vowed to stand up and ask out loud for the families of South Africa, provided that someone else went first. I did not want to be the first fool. A few moments later, somewhere in the front a woman yelled something unintelligible followed by the name of Jesus. I decided that it sounded too crazy to count and waited. No one else uttered a word. Elza dragged out the uncomfortable silence, insisting that we knew who we were and needed to get up out of our seats. I thought the chair's rising temperature was going to melt me, but I remained seated.

It was too much for me to ask for anyway, I thought. What would I do with all the families of South Africa? I was just one person with huge limitations. I felt I needed to talk with Elza privately, but then I started chatting with a few friends after the conference, allowing the opportunity to slip away.

From that day onward I had that uneasy feeling in my gut – the one you have when you know you've been disobedient. I needed to fix it. A few days later there would be a prayer conference at the same church. I felt like I needed to go and look for Elza and report to her like a soldier to a general for war duty. I would then claim the families, whatever that meant. She would hopefully explain what she had in mind. It was all new to me.

Louis and I went to the conference, and in an auditorium with more than six thousand seats Elza took a seat right next to us. With Louis seated between us, I hoped for a special opportunity and moment to present itself. The moment never came and Elza left to take her daughter somewhere. Now the uneasy feeling grew even stronger. It felt like such a difficult thing to do. It would sound so stupid! Elza probably already had 'groupies' lining up who wanted to attach themselves to her, like any other women's 'groupies' would do — those who recognised the mantle of authority on her shoulders and wanted to at least pull a corner of it over their own shoulders.

Afterwards Louis had to leave with a pastor from Dubai for a meeting about a possible visit, so I walked to the car alone. I turned the key in the ignition. Click. Nothing. I had one of those *everything keeps going right Toyotas*. What could be the matter? Some of the men in the parking lot fiddled under the hood, checked the battery and performed all the tricks of the trade. Still nothing. I phoned roadside assistance for the first time in my life, and then sat waiting in the car.

It became uncomfortable. Roadside assistance is not a speedy service by any means. I might as well go and sit inside, I thought. When I walked into the humongous foyer, only one person stood there – Elza. You couldn't miss her even if you had wanted to. In her bright green summer suit, she was my proverbial green light. I stumbled over my feet and my words and reported for duty. She looked me straight in the eye.

> *"So you are one of those disobedient ones at the conference who refused to stand up. God has called out a number of you already. So what do you want to stand for?"*

She asked this as if she was taking a casual order at McDonalds. To her it was a completely normal question. I thought I might as well respond in a 'completely normal' way and declare the unthinkable:

> *"I want to stand for the families of South Africa."*

She didn't flinch. She seemed satisfied, because according to her knowledge, there had been no one who had claimed that particular piece of South Africa. She said she hoped I could pay the price for it. I didn't know what she meant by that. To outsiders we would have sounded arrogant. Who did Elza think she was to have us report to her, and who did I think I was to claim anything on God's behalf? Did He really need us? The questions had no answers. Flushed, I turned around and walked back to the car ... not sure that I knew what I had just done. All I knew was that the uneasy feeling of the past few days was finally gone.

The car started on the first try and never acted like Balaam's donkey again. With a mixture of fear and relief I realised: God does not allow us to miss the good works – our callings – that He has prepared for us, even if He needs to make donkeys speak or cars choke ...

The more I thought about it, the more I realised that the families of our nation needed to be taken back with a fight. Most of the families I had dealt with were torn and trapped by the enemy's lies. A big team of people would be needed. They would need to be willing to step onto the battlefield. Where on earth would I get people like that?

Slowly but surely the strategy unfolded. The Lord sent people my way who made wise suggestions. I knew I had to train people and put a manual in their hands so they could help me all across the nation with this calling. The following year the Lord provided me with the strategy and resources for developing a parenting course with added training materials. He blessed the sales of my parenting books above and beyond what we had expected so that I could finance the course development. He sent more than 100 chosen warriors to be trained by our ministry, *Evergreen Parenting*. A team of leaders arose to help manage the ministry. They shared the passion for families. They fought the fight with me in dependence on the Lord for wisdom, power and breakthroughs in the spiritual realm. As the Israelites, who each repaired the piece of Jerusalem's wall that faced their own home – trowel in one hand, sword in the other – each of them did their small part to help rebuild South African families.

All of this floods back as I read my messages on Facebook. While remembering the prophecy of the white flag, I realise that my heart towards women has changed. When I now think of women's ministry, I realise it's something I pray will happen. I want to invite women to come and touch the hem of Jesus' garment, as I have. Many have been bleeding for too long. There are quacks who offer temporary healing at an exorbitant price, but only Jesus can touch the pain of a woman, however incurable it may seem to our human eyes. Fortunately there are wise helpers, who in partnership with God can show many people the way to healing. I realise that if women are not well, our families will stay in the ruins they are presently in. Damaged women raise damaged children.

I have a desire to fly the white flag with these words of Paul in 2 Corinthians 6:11-13:

> **The smallness you feel comes from within you. Your lives aren't small, but you're living them in a small way. I'm speaking as plainly as I can and with great affection. Open up your lives. Live openly and expansively!**
>
> (*The Message*)

For the first time I start to see the picture that had been taking shape behind the theatre box. For so many years my desire to make a difference in hurting families remained a mere wish. Before the rape, I would never have been able to touch the lives of women whose world is in ruins and who live with pain that I knew absolutely nothing about. Such women would not let me in, having locked those doors to live enclosed lives for fear of more hurt. Chances are ten to one that women with pain feel much safer sharing it with someone who has also seen a dark place. Now I can be that someone. Now, perhaps, women will share the sacred ground of their lives with me.

While reading more Facebook messages of women both in faith and despair, a desire lights up in me to see each one of them experience more of an expansive, wide-open, fearless life.

John 10:9-10 describes the small and big life in shrill contrast. It calls us sheep and portrays two very different ways that we as Christians can live. The small life is the life of fearful sheep cooped up in a confined pen – constantly afraid that a thief might scale the wall to come and kill, steal or destroy. Not knowing where he might try to enter next, sheep who live like this usually have their guard up 24/7. They feel the need to make a study of open doors where Satan may enter. They keep an eye on every possible entry point. They even have Christian jargon to accurately label these open doors. They run around closing doors behind them and other sheep as a full-time occupation.

These sheep are kept inside by their fear for the wolf that lurks outside. Therefore they have very little to eat and to drink. Their only nourishment is the trampled weeds that other sheep have sullied. And no stream of water has ever flowed through a sheep's pen...

Sheep living this small life have lost all trust because the previous shepherds were cowards who fled when the fold needed them most. They have turned their focus to the wolf instead of the Shepherd. They are too afraid to go out and find pasture, uncertain if there is still a shepherd they can follow and trust. They have doubts that a shepherd makes any difference. They figure out ways and formulas to fend for themselves. Christians in sheep pens often have little rituals and recitation without which they just don't feel safe. They are their own shepherd, their own watchman and their own doorkeeper. When they see a new danger, they figure out a new formula or a way to live even smaller in order to escape it.

In comparison, the abundant, free life is spacious and lush with green pastures. The sheep are of the same fold as those in the pen, but these sheep know that they have a Gate whose name is Jesus. Through Him they freely go in and out and find pasture. They know how defenceless they are – no canine teeth to bite with, no stingers to sting with, no claws to claw with, no strong hind legs to kick with ... Still they roam outside without fear of being caught by the thief because they trust their Shepherd. They believe He is the Good Shepherd who does not flee when the wolf comes. Rather, He lays down His life when we they need Him most ... They are not in denial about the wolf and the thief and their devices, but it can never again be their focus for they have become too enamoured with their Shepherd. They have discovered the secret of the open life – following the familiar voice. The comforting voice. The guiding voice. These sheep are fearless and free.

> **We find ourselves standing where we always hoped we might stand – out in the wide open spaces of God's grace and glory, standing tall and shouting our praise.**
>
> (Romans 5:2, *The Message*)

As I read more of the Facebook messages, words of comfort and questions, one woman's words, who had prayed for me that night, stand out above the rest.

I would bump into this woman at a ladies' tea a year later and learn how difficult it had been for her to post this message, because she hadn't understood how I would be able to experience green pastures and still waters. She had negotiated with the Lord and had asked Him for a more appropriate Bible verse, but in the end she was obedient and simply posted a seemingly inappropriate note on my Facebook page:

> *Hettie, read Psalm 23.*

Every word of the Psalm is true, and the view of the green pastures is best understood from the valley of the shadow of death.

While reading on further, I wonder when I will have the opportunity to wave the flag, knowing full well that the command still stands to keep clear of the stage for the remainder of the year. I resolve to share my experiences with women in one-on-one conversations only as our paths cross, to pray over which interviews to give, and to trust that the right moment will come when I will be able to speak about this louder and wider.

8 *Zoos and shattered glass*

It is Friday morning, three days after the robbery, and my parents are bringing the children home. The trauma expert and I had a few meaningful conversations, and she's ready to conduct my children's debriefing sessions so we can determine the impact the events had on them. They look forward to playing with the friendly lady. They are going to design zoos and play with animal stickers, they tell me. As the children begin their session with Marietjie, I finally have the opportunity to sit down to a cup of tea with my parents to hear how the past few days have been for them.

My parents had to put on brave faces for the children's sake while answering one emotional telephone call after the other. They found it especially painful that the whole thing had been made so public. *"I felt as though my liver was being surgically removed without anaesthetics,"* my mom summed it up. My parents use euphemisms such as *"expecting"* instead of pregnant and *"intercourse"* instead of sex. They have never to my knowledge uttered the word *"rape"*. Having to hear it, see it and say it in the same sentence as their daughter's name was just devastating to them.

My mom read all of the letters in the newspapers and on internet forums and battled through the onslaught of criticism. She even printed out every single one and filed them in a scrapbook. That was her way of coming to terms with the whole thing. At the same time she found great comfort in God's Word.

She is suddenly angry and using the voice I remember her using whenever we were really in trouble. She demands to know why nothing came of the police raid at the robbers' suspected hide-out. "I hope the reason you were never called for the line-up is because they have all been shot dead," she lets out her raw emotions. She immediately apologises for her cruel wish, but I know her and believe it's the immeasurable pain of a mother talking now, and an absolutely normal reaction at that. No hen could wish a fox well, knowing it came after one of her chicks, could it? In time she will return to her gentle self.

Like Louis and me, our parents are also carried by thousands of prayers and encouraging messages. My dad found peace in the most unlikely way: While a friend of my parents was typing a text message to send her condolences, she discovered something interesting. She called my dad and told him to go to his bedroom, sit down and key my name into his cell phone with the Afrikaans text prediction function switched on. My dad often used that dictionary function because it enabled his unsophisticated cell phone to guess the words he was typing, so that he only needed to punch each key once instead of two or three times. He went to his room and typed in my name. The Afrikaans word *getuie*, meaning witness, appeared on the screen. Tearfully he made his peace that I was never meant to keep quiet and that the Lord *wanted* to glorify His name on the front pages and in the letter columns of the newspapers through our testimony. I was meant to be His witness.

We are so afraid of shame, but hasn't God always turned nakedness, shame and weakness into glory for His name? Jesus' own death on the cross was everything but decent and private, yet its message still echoes forth loudly and boldly. If He puts us on display, it is often for the very reason that we are weak and ready to be set ablaze with *His* light since we don't have any light of our own. Not all Christians have to follow this route. Not everyone's vulnerable moment gets published. Neither is one's platform an indication of how spiritual one is. No Christian is more special than another. To be a Christian means that we each do the will of God, by His power, through the free gift of faith He gives us, by walking through doors only He can open and only He can give us the courage to walk through. It is all His work in us, His way, for His own reasons. It has very little to do with anything we have to offer.

I read Psalm 18 to my parents, assuring them that my peace about what happened does not mean for a single moment that I approve of it. Rape will always be unacceptable, as will robbery and kidnapping, death threats and housebreakings. My mother's anger is also not misplaced. In Psalm 18 verses seven to fifteen, it's very clear that God gets really angry when His children are attacked by the enemy. The earth trembles. Smoke, fire, thunder and hail stones come from the mouth and nose of God. It's a picture of anger. God rips open the underworld. He is furious.

Although many of the letters protested heavily against the idea that what happened to us was part of a spiritual battle (the writers of these letters preferred to view it as senseless violence in a hopeless world), the spiritual battle is an unmistakeable theme in the Old and New Testaments. The battle stories aren't there to give the adventurers in us a few moments of action in an otherwise uneventful history book. Surely it's there for a better reason – to show us the gravity of God's hatred for idols, injustice and sin. Amongst other names, God calls Himself the Lord of the angel armies. What use would He have for legions of angels if there was no battle to fight?

I tell my parents that I believe we would not become upset about the smaller battles we seem to have lost if only we could remain mindful that the war has already been won. I once heard a friend say to Christians who avoid reading the enigmatic last book of the New Testament: "You have to read the ending, people. We win!" The reason we will win in the end is because Jesus secured the victory nearly two millennia ago.

I tell my parents about an unusual dialogue I had with God about Psalm 18. I very rarely have the experience where God speaks and I answer, and then He comments on my answer. It is equally rare for me to ask the questions and to hear Him answer. But this was how I discussed Psalm 18 with God:

> *"Lord, I memorized large portions of this Psalm, but this part where You seem to be furious and ferocious, I did not even underline. I struggle to merge it with my image of You. Please tell me how I should understand it."*

"I do get that angry whenever Satan crosses the line and hurts My people. Injustice always makes Me that angry."

"What do You do when You're angry like this?"

"I take revenge."

"But on whom and how do You take revenge?"

"I take revenge on my enemy, who is also your enemy. He doesn't get away with it when he breaks spiritual laws. He doesn't have the right to lift a finger against My children. When he does, he pays heavily. He pays with souls, because that's what this war has always been about. I take souls in the same way as victorious nations of old took as plunder the women and children of the army they defeated. Souls are the only currency that counts in spiritual war. I take revenge by breaking down the door to the kingdom of darkness. I rush in and take for Myself lost souls – even souls that chose to be there – and I bring them out of the darkness into My Kingdom of Light."

"Lord, that's how I know you. You don't take revenge on people. That's not Your heart. You punish the one who's behind everything. Everything about You is beautiful. Even Your revenge is beautiful. Even in Your rage You rescue this world that You have loved so much and gave your life to save it."

"Remember the promise on your old Bible."

In 1991 a university friend of mine decorated a Bible that my big brother bought me as a birthday present. On the front cover she pasted a water colour painting of a rose along with a Bible verse and then covered everything with self-adhesive plastic. It was an odd verse from Scripture. She explained that it might not make sense now but would be significant later on in my life. I still have the Bible. The plastic wrap is wrinkled and deformed, and the rose has faded, but the Scripture from Isaiah 43:4-5 is still clearly legible:

Since you were precious in My sight, You have been honoured, and I have loved you; therefore I will give men for you; and people for your life. Fear not, for I am with you; I will bring your descendants from the east, and gather you from the west.

(*New King James Version*)

Inside the Bible's cover my brother had written Psalm 91:4:

He shall cover you with his feathers, and under his wings you shall take refuge.

Without thinking about it, I spontaneously said out loud:

"Lord, if I may truly ask for men in exchange for what happened to us ... take many! And will you start with my perpetrator?"

I tell my parents how I stood looking at these verses, feeling as though it all finally made a little sense. Still, initially I wondered if this idea was just fanciful theology, until I remembered a few things. Throughout the ages this is exactly what happened every time Christians were burned at the stake. It's written in the history books that the Christian persecutors stopped the executions in Rome because they couldn't afford the large number of conversions after every martyr's death. Tertullian, a teacher who died in 230 AD, reportedly recorded in his writings, *The Apology*:

> **The more you cut us down, the more in number we grow. The blood of Christians is seed.**

An unknown Roman leader wrote the following words about the persecuted Christians:

> **They dwell in their own countries simply as sojourners. They are in the flesh, but they do not live after the flesh. They pass their days on earth, but they are citizens of heaven. They obey the prescribed laws, and at the same time, they surpass the laws by their lives. Those who hate them are unable to give any reason for their hatred.**
>
> (*A letter to Diognetus*, Chapter 5)

After Stephen's unjust stoning in the book of Acts, God stuck His hand into the darkest corner of the enemy's camp, grabbed the chief persecutor of the church, Saul, by the collar and dragged him into the light without Saul ever asking for it. The new light was so blinding that Saul, later named Paul, took days to recover. He hadn't searched for God. He definitely hadn't chosen God. God chose him, and very likely as revenge on the enemy. Paul was loot.

God seems to collect the spoils of war in two different ways: He reacts when His children are taken away unjustly, and He releases those trapped in darkness even when they aren't looking for him. Isaiah says in the same chapter where my Bible cover verse is from: "To the north I will say: 'Give back!' and to the south: 'Don't hold back!' Bring sons from afar and my daughters from the corners of the earth, each one acknowledging me as God, who I made in my honour, who I created and formed ... bring out the nation with eyes that cannot see and ears that cannot hear."

Isaiah 65:1 says it even clearer:

> **I revealed myself to those who did not ask for me; I was found by those who did not seek me. To a nation that did not call on my name, I said, 'Here am I, here am I.'**

I strongly believe that many souls will be taken from Satan in return for what he did to Louis and me. Sons and daughters of God who've been carried far away from Him will also come back. Many of the letters we received in the months after the incident have testified of a return to God and His Word. People have written that they have found faith once again, and self-proclaimed unbelievers have written words similar to the following response to the crime:

> As an unbeliever, I think the way in which [they] handled it ... seems like a miracle to me. In a great way it has brought me back to a crossroads where I've started to think deeply about the purpose of life again.

And another said:

> I read the article [in the newspaper] yesterday. As an atheist, I was very impressed with what she said. My sister in law had a similar experience during which a voice had clearly spoken to her. She also believes it was her God's voice. I've started to wonder if there isn't a story behind the story. Maybe there is something out there I'm not aware of ...

It seems like a tug on the collar, doesn't it? I believe God does this every time His children suffer without cause. I believe that's what He means when He said He would come in glory, carried on the backs of the martyrs. I know that I wasn't raped because I confess the name of Jesus. The robbers had no idea whether I believed in Jesus, Buddha, a parallel universe, or pink crystals. I'm not elevating myself to the status of known Christian martyrs, but I know that because I confess the name of Jesus, my rape and the crimes against Louis weren't "free" and they weren't in vain. The Lord demands something from Satan for it, simply because we are His children.

I've heard many people claim that as European descendants, God sent us to Africa to bring the Gospel to the godless nations on the "Dark Continent". But when we get hurt in the process, it seems that suddenly this has nothing to do with our original calling. We want to be honoured for converting the "heathen of Africa," but we don't want to pay the price. Missionaries always bleed! People who think we can proclaim Jesus without paying a price are confusing evangelism with colonialism. It's about such people that Archbishop Emeritus Desmond Tutu said: "When the missionaries came to Africa they had the Bible and we had the land. They said, 'Let us pray.' We closed our eyes. When we opened our eyes, we had the Bible and they had the land."

A country does not change when those carrying the Gospel in one hand take something with the other. It did harm on every continent on the globe. People who do change a country are those who bring the Gospel in one hand and themselves and their rights on a platter in the other.

The biggest vengeance of all time was probably after Jesus' unjust crucifixion. It's the best example of the glaring contradictions of ugly, unlawful, bloody things written into the script of God's will. His illegal murder – because it was nothing less than a gross miscarriage of justice – was God the Father's will. I want to repeat it in case you did not hear the deafening kick against the theatre box: The horrible suffering of Jesus Christ was God's will. The prophets predicted it in detail. Jesus walked into the darkness of His death on a cross with His eyes wide open, sweating the blood that comes from such a terrible knowing.

Everything in the picture seems twisted, until we take a look behind the puppet theatre to see a completely different picture unfolding: The same Jesus who was tortured to death and has just breathed his last is not dead any more. He is walking through the gates of hell to take the keys from the same Satan who recently lied to Him and offered Him all the power and kingdoms of this world. It is almost ironic. To prove His power over death in a very literal way, He takes souls trapped in death, puts them back in their decomposed corpses, restores their putrid flesh, breaks open their old graves with earth shattering power, and makes them walk the streets of Jerusalem alive and restored for many to witness (Matthew 27:52-53).

I believe they were the first of many souls to be robbed from the kingdom of death because of Satan's wrongdoing. Each one of us who knows Jesus is now part of the spoils of war that He won on the cross. We are the fruit of His unlawful death. Because He died innocently, we are saved, though guilty. It is a Godly thing and therefore a privilege to be hurt unfairly in order for people who do not deserve it to receive the opportunity to see Jesus! The disciples knew exactly how it worked, and Paul wrote to the Corinthians along exactly these lines:

> **Yes, we live under constant danger of death because we serve Jesus, so that the life of Jesus will be evident in our dying bodies. So we live in the face of death, but this has resulted in eternal life for you ... All of this is for your benefit. And as God's grace reaches more and more people, there will be great thanksgiving, and God will receive more and more glory. That is why we never give up. Though our bodies are dying, our spirits are being renewed every day. For our present troubles are small and won't last very long. Yet they produce for us a glory that vastly outweighs them and will last forever! So we don't look at the troubles we can see now; rather, we fix our gaze on things that cannot be seen. For the things we see now will soon be gone, but the things we cannot see will last forever.**
>
> (2 Corinthians 4:11, 12, 15-18. *New Living Translation*)

We will never understand human suffering and the bloodiness of it all as long as we refuse to look at the invisible gain from such suffering. Moments of suffering can buy eternities of salvation. One death can save many lives. One murder can save many murderers. The smoke rising from a Christian burning at the stake can be the smoke signal showing a lost soul the way to life. If as Christians we've truly placed our lives as holy offerings upon the altar, how dare we complain about how the Lord decides to sacrifice us? Some Christians seem to have the idea that sacrifices are decorated and celebrated. No, they are burned.

During a sermon, Chip Ingram once reminded our congregation that we slip a blank cheque under the door of heaven when we give over our lives to Jesus. We acknowledge God's right to use us in this life as He sees fit in the interest of eternity – without terms, disclaimers or addendums. No Christian may give less than that. And no Christian may complain if God takes everything.

It's with this same conviction that my parents and I are sitting at the dining room table knowing God is not smiling over this. He's crying with my parents, because He knows how a Father's heart can be ripped out. He does, however, see the bigger picture, and even in His rage against these injustices, the Lord creates new life out of darkness and death.

My parents share about all the support and phone calls, the beautiful letters and emails. And then comes the bucket of ice water:

> *"Dear, you'd never guess who phoned late last night to wish you well?"*

I interrupt my mom before she can tell me.

> *"Mom, please tell me it isn't the woman whose name popped into my head last night at our cell group meeting!"*

Of course it was her. I start crying as my mom explains how this friend of hers was raped as a young girl and was still struggling to process the pain. That's probably why she couldn't sleep last night. She saw the newspaper article and recognised me. It must have triggered her pain. Maybe her nightmares had returned. I should have phoned her last night. Imagine the comfort it could have given her.

Why did I doubt the message God gave me for her? I'm overwhelmed with a mixture of guilt and joy. I heard Him correctly – this time it was not for my own comfort, but for someone else's. Then and there I decide never to be disobedient again. I now know what it sounds like. It is the sudden arrival of an idea coming from nowhere, totally illogical yet crystal clear. I hope I will hear it more often in the future, and that I will be courageous enough to be obedient. I will wave these words (the words I had been prompted to share with this woman) like a big white flag:

> *"Jesus did the same for you, even though you didn't realise it!"*

I have to do it, even if it sounds hollow and silly in my head. It's not my place to decide which messages I will leave out and which ones I will convey.

I decide to go in the other room and join the children's play therapy session. They are drawing pictures of cages for the animals in their zoo and sticking animal stickers inside the cages. They make rules for the zoo. Marietjie gets them to talk about their own boundaries, in order for her to discern whether the thieves had broken through their "boundaries" in such a way that it makes them feel vulnerable or exposed. It's so creatively done. Even in my ignorance I can clearly see how each one is in control of their own zoo with strong bars between the wild and tame animals. There are no antelopes in the lion cage, no tigers with the baboons. They charge exorbitant entry fees for visitors and make up logical, strict zoo regulations. They feel safe and in control.

Marietjie helps them to understand that they can always make plans in bad situations and can always say "yes" or "no". She teaches them in a way they can understand: how to draw boundaries and how to handle it if someone tries to get through them. They talk about people who are so strong that they can break through our boundaries, but even then we still have choices. Marietjie guides this conversation to set the stage for what we still have to tell them.

My son wants to make plans to protect us against the thieves: He's going to set traps all over the yard. My oldest daughter gratefully realises that the Lord had said "no" to a few things that night:

"They couldn't steal my gift – my music – because the Lord didn't allow them to steal my piano or my radio."

My youngest daughter still has her favourite blanket and her teddy, Pumpkin, and the thieves weren't even in her room. She seems pleased with that.

Instead of telling the children we were tied up, Marietjie allows them to discover all the facts in a non-threatening way:

"So, if you were the crook and you were going to steal people's stuff, what would you do to them?"

"I would tie them up tightly."

"Is it a good idea?"

"Yes"

"Is it right?"

"No, but it's a good plan!"

"That's exactly the same plan the crooks made with Mommy and Daddy."

"It was clever, but it was wrong."

"Yes, it was."

The children work through the burglary and the kidnapping, make their own plans and decide that it was the right thing to say "yes" to the robbers for everything they wanted to steal. They were armed and we weren't. The kids come up with a conclusion that it would have been stupid to say *"no"*.

Marietjie keeps to our agreement not to talk about the rape yet. We have a plan: The kids and I will drive to Natal first along with my assistant and her son. I will participate in the Midmar Mile open water race. The kids will see that their mommy is strong and healthy, and then we will tell them the bad news in the best possible way. We will find a pretty ribbon to tie around the putrid parcel. We still have a few days to think and pray about how to do it.

Marietjie's feedback is that the children look calm and peaceful but that I need to be on the lookout for any signs of trauma that may appear later. Following everyone's recommendations, we are trying to keep the routine as normal as possible. So, next we will go to my eldest's music lesson, after which we will pack the van and head off to Natal.

We leave for the piano lesson. Just to make sure one last time, I ask my daughter:

"Sweetie, did you understand everything we talked about or is anything still bothering you?"

"Mom, I understand everything, except why you had to talk to the police at the hospital."

From experience I know that if we avoid questions about sex, drugs, divorce or any other "adult talk," our children can create suspicious notes in the back of their minds about the subject. They flag the topic as forbidden, and the channel to talk to our children open-heartedly about that subject is closed in future. I won't be able to use delay tactics now. *'Marietjie, where are you now? Lord, give me the right words!'*

A man is walking on the other side of the three-way intersection. The idea of a smash-and-grab comes to mind. The children who live in South Africa, especially in the crime capital province of Gauteng, know very well how it works. Someone leaps out of nowhere, smashes the car window, dives over you, and nabs your handbag and other valuables. You almost die of fright and struggle to shake the effects of the trauma. I learned from Marietjie today how to use defusing terminology, so I ask my daughter what plan she would make if she knew beforehand that the man over there was about to commit a smash-and-grab.

> *"I would roll down the window and give him my purse, because then I wouldn't get frightened or hurt. And then he wouldn't even have to break my window."*
>
> *"That's what happened on Tuesday night. By God's grace Mom was ready beforehand and knew the man in the room wanted to do something like a smash and grab."*
>
> *"Did he want your purse, Mom?"*
>
> *"No, Sweetie, he wanted my body as if I were his wife."*
>
> *"Is he one of those people who only know Hollywood love, Mom?*
>
> *"Yes, exactly. He only knows lust and power. I didn't want to get hurt, and I didn't want to make the man angry because I was afraid he would hurt you all or Dad. Even though it's usually the wrong thing to do, because he is not my husband, I could not stop it from happening. My 'no' wouldn't have made any difference. It was awful, but Jesus really helped me and held me close through it all."*
>
> *"Yes, Mommy, it was the right plan because he was stronger and the men were armed."*

We park in front of the piano teacher's house. She hops out, then sticks her head back through the window just as I start pulling away.

> *"Mom, that's why there's no broken glass in your hair."*

I think to myself: *If I could really predict a smash and grab, I would take out my driver's license and ID book before I gave them the handbag.* Again I gratefully realise that I did have time to make sure everything that was precious to me was out of my 'purse', in order that the rapist couldn't take anything that couldn't be replaced. Here I am only three days later, and I still have my identity as a beloved child of God firmly in my hands. I have power, love and a sound mind. I have peace and joy. What a miracle!

On top of all of this, I can see in my mind's eye how the enemy, defeated and perplexed, is forced to roll down his window and give back souls that are no longer rightfully his. I know he is already being robbed in revenge. I want to shout it out:

> *"Take them Lord; take back lots of lost souls!"*

9 Blood and water

We pack the van with everything we think we may need for this weekend in the Midlands Meander, a picturesque region with green rolling hills and the well-known inland lake where the Midmar Mile race will take place. I make sure I have my goggles and swimwear. The adrenalin pumps through me at the mere thought of the hundreds of bodies at once in the water, spray flying everywhere. I can't wait. I'm looking forward to being in nature and to three days away from the phone. My friend who is going with us has been manning the phone for the last three days, and she is probably just as relieved as I am to be able to get away.

As we leave, we meet a neighbour at the gate who lives near the end of our street. She is bringing us her famous tuna pie and a bouquet of flowers. She is petite and feminine and very pretty. I'm so glad that she was not the victim. These emotions towards her catch me by surprise. I've always been intimidated by seemingly perfect women like her. I've never felt compassion for them, since I was either jealous, suspicious or judgemental. I always assumed vanity and shallowness in such women. Something has changed. I now assume great value and deep worth. I want to put my arms around her and tell her how everything about her is beautiful. And I want to encourage her to celebrate her femininity and purity. I want to convince her not to be afraid, even though her sense of security has also been shaken by what happened on her street. But all that comes out of my mouth is a sincere thank you.

We load our wonderful, timely gift in the back of the van, very happy that we'll have food to eat upon our arrival. The road feels long after the last few short nights. It's narrow with tricky bends and unclear signs, made even worse by the rain that is now coming down in buckets. I hope this doesn't predict bad weather for the swim. The organisers have to call off the whole thing when it rains, because poor visibility makes it impossible to see and save swimmers in distress. All of my hard hours of training in the swimming pool and our long drive down to Natal will then have been in vain.

By the time we reach our quaint little cottage it's past midnight. As I get out of the car, something feels wrong. I notice a bloodstain on the seat – a really big one. Luckily for me it's pitch-dark. We carry the four sleeping children to their beds, and I go back to try and clean the seat. I'm not sure what to do. The doctor didn't say to expect this.

After a virtually sleepless night that consisted of trying to manage heavy bleeding without the necessary sanitary ware and while trying to sleep without making a mess, I wake up worried. I probably shouldn't swim tomorrow if I keep on bleeding like this, should I?

With the unending phone calls of the past week and all the people visiting, I still haven't caught up the night's sleep I lost during the burglary. I haven't exercised for more than a week, and now with this bleeding I'm going to lose even more energy. What if I faint and drown ... As my mind files through the options, I realize I must register for the race today if I'm still going to do it, but I need advice from my doctor in order to make the right decision.

I phone the gynaecologist who gave me her number. It's several hours before I get a hold of her. She explains that although she can prescribe something, it usually takes more than a day to start working. I doubt this countryside pharmacy will have something in stock that will solve my problem. Apparently, the medication I was given at the hospital can sometimes cause bleeding if a woman takes it just before ovulation, but such bleeding is rare and usually not substantial. I was at the very end of a cycle, which makes such an amount of bleeding very unusual.

I suspect that this might be more spiritual than physical, so I phone Pastor Elza and her prayer team who are on a retreat praying for the Turn2God event. I lie down on the grass in front of the house with one hand stretched to heaven and the other holding my phone against my ear. I can just imagine how strange I must look. I hope my children don't see me, because they might think I'm waiting to be beamed up by a spaceship. But, then again, everything has been a little strange for the past few days.

The women take turns praying for me. *"It's like an abortion,"* one of the ladies explains, *"The Lord is destroying what Satan planted. The Lord is making you spotlessly clean. The Lord is going to make the enemy pay for this."*

I'm convinced that this is the truth, even though the whole thing is a bit bizarre to me. I've heard of deliverance sessions in which people bleed more blood than a human body can hold, or vomit enough to cover the whole floor in inches of it. I've also seen people's heart rates and breathing stop, people go mute, turn bright red, and even turn deathly pale during deliverance sessions, so I know such manifestations can also come from Satan from time to time. I also know his goal is always the same – to lie and spread fear. It's a facade to try and divert our attention from the truth, namely that he has been defeated and disarmed. Maybe that's his goal with this unnatural bleeding. I decide to phone a friend who works in deliverance, and she prays earnestly that I will be free from all that the enemy wanted to transfer onto me via the rapist. She prays to make sure there are no ties left between us.

Sex with anybody, whether consensual or forced, makes us one with them. Sex is a blood covenant. Unfortunately there is an exchange, like the exchange of pieces of clothing or weapons between covenant parties in ancient times. During intercourse people exchange their sexual, emotional and spiritual baggage. God isn't just trying to spoil our fun when He says an emphatic "no" to casual sex. He is trying to protect us from soul ties during which we might receive nasty "gifts" we did not bargain on. All that is theirs becomes ours; all that is ours becomes theirs. Our fates and faults become linked.

This is why people who live promiscuously often experience increasing bondage to destructive habits and thoughts. They are carrying around their sexual partners' perverted baggage inside of them like a morbid collection of bones. Even after one sexual experience with a promiscuous man, a former virgin can suddenly become like a magnet attracting other equally promiscuous men. I've heard girls cry:

> *"I was raped when I was still very young, and it seems as if 'rape me' is written on my forehead because it keeps happening to me over and over again. What is wrong with me?"*

Spiritual things are so difficult to explain, but I sometimes put it to them like this: *"A spirit has a smell to it that another spirit can recognise. That is why Paul calls us a stench to unbelievers and a lovely smell to those that God has chosen. We smell of what is inside of us. The smell will repulse some and attract others, depending on whether our spirit clashes or resonates with that smell. Dirty things stink and attract flies. Unless the dirt from the souls of molesters or rapists gets cleaned out, more flies and pests will come ...*

It's like two strings resonating. While your spirit is vibrating with the lust carried over onto you, you strum the strings of those who have the same spirit or emotional baggage – unless you identify and reject the spirit of lust that was handed to you in the covenant. The stronghold of a spirit of lust can be broken when you forgive your offender, repent of your own sin if you were a party to sexual sin, and to make a conscious choice to follow Jesus. Someone can pray with you or you can simply say this sincerely:

> "I forgive ______________ for the sin that he/she committed against me, and I proclaim him/her free in the Name of Jesus. In the name of Jesus I cancel the covenant or soul tie that formed when ____________ and I became one in body. In the name of Jesus I choose against a spirit of lust [and any other spirit that came in with the sexual transfer]. I choose purity. I reject the enemy's plans to keep a hold on me through lies, shame or guilt, because I accept that Jesus' blood also paid for my forgiveness and healing. I accept that I'm washed spotlessly clean with his blood. He carried my curse so that I can be blessed."

Of course this prayer is for those who really have been washed in the blood of Jesus. We waste our time when we try to get rid of dirt in our lives by our own power. It is like sweeping out a house only to have the dust blown back in. Jesus needs to clean our house — and it starts with Him moving in and taking over.

Meanwhile, everyone else is now awake in the cottage, so I decide to pray for and anoint all of them before I go to the dam to register for the race. It feels a little strange to anoint them. I've never done it before. I am not convinced that it is entirely necessary, but at the same time I understand the meaning of it in the spiritual world. It's a testimony and a declaration that we are covered in the blood of Jesus. All I have to anoint them with is sunflower oil that we brought along for cooking. I don't want to upset or confuse the children so I explain it in terms I hope they understand:

> *"What I am now doing is called anointing someone. When we do that, we mark them for Jesus. Jesus can see the mark and His angels can also see the mark. Even the bad angels can see it. It shows them whose side we're on. We are on*

the winning team. It's like war paint. Do you remember the blood the Israelites smeared on their door posts in Egypt to show that they belonged to God? It's the same thing when I anoint you."

After this explanation, the boys are especially proud of their invisible war paint and excited to know that the angels now realize they are on their team.

While driving to the dam, I pray and phone a few people to ask for their advice about whether or not I should swim. It's probably simple – if I bleed or if it rains, I should drop everything; if the weather is fair, I will swim, but only slowly – in case I get a cramp from the blood loss ... Everyone I phone cautions against the dirty dam water and possible infection that would do real harm to my weakened body in combination with the antiretroviral drugs.

I phone my twin brother. He's staying at our house while we're away. From the sound of his voice I can tell that something is seriously wrong. He sounds pale. If you've ever talked with someone over the phone right after they've been scared half to death, you will know what pale sounds like. He gives me the reason: Earlier this morning he tried to cook some eggs and thought the smoked glass cover of our gas stove was a fire-proof cooking surface. He switched on the gas burner underneath the cover and put the frying pan on top. After a minute or so he thought he heard someone at the front door. As he stepped out of the kitchen, the whole cover exploded into what looked like thousands of black diamonds. It covered the whole kitchen in a layer of glass. A few seconds after the explosion it was still raining pieces of glass from the ceiling and cupboard doors where the tiny shards were temporarily lodged due to the impact.

He feels very bad about the damage, but I'm just glad he is alive! My vivid imagination immediately shows me how the flying glass could have stripped every piece of skin from his body. It could have and lodged in his eyes. He realises that he is with us in this battle. I warn him that He needs to pray and be alert. I tell him to anoint himself with oil from the kitchen cupboard, for a moment not too concerned about the Biblical justification for it. I don't believe there is any power in the oil itself, but that the power is in our testimony and our declaration. In Revelation 12:11, the apostle John writes that the victory of overcomers can be attributed to three things: the blood of Jesus, the word of their testimony, and the fact that they did not love their temporary lives. This anointing with oil is a testimony to the spiritual world. Through it, we all declare that we want to fight this battle from the position of the finished work and victory of Jesus.

I phone my oldest brother. His family and my parents are at an athletics event at their children's school. My brother shares with me his conviction that the whole family is doing battle with us. An hour later he phones me back and we laugh at the comical picture he paints. The vendor at the Chip 'n Dip stand next to the athletics field had most definitely never seen anything like it – a grandpa, grandma, dad, mom and three kids all anointed with his cooled-down deep frying oil.

I still have a ways to go to get to the dam, so I dig in the glove compartment for some music. I find a Third Day CD and pop it into the CD player. The lyrics and notes resonate with me:

After all that I've been through
Now I realize the truth
That I must go through the valley
To stand upon the mountain of God (From *Mountain of God*).

I stop at the shop to buy something to get this bleeding under control and to pick up some bananas – just the right energy food for tomorrow's race. Unable to hold back, I tell the woman who is weighing the bananas about Jesus. I explain to her that she never needs to be afraid. As I leave the store I walk straight into a couple who are covered with more ink than skin. The tattoo marks, Goth clothes, and piercings in their eyebrow, chins and noses scream: *'Stay far away from us, we cannot be loved!'*

Usually I stay away from people like that, but somehow this girl's empty gaze is like a super strong magnet. I decide I have nothing to lose.

"May I hug you?"

"Why?"

"Because God wants you to know how much He loves you – unconditionally."

"I don't believe in that."

"What don't you believe in?"

"In God and in love."

"You are one of His exquisite works of art and He loves you. Even though you do not believe in Him, He believes in you and in your future. He has great plans for you."

"I don't believe in that either."

"That's okay. I pray that in your sleep, when you're unable to push Him away, He will, even tonight, come and gently give you the hug you couldn't receive from me today."

There's no response. The look she gives me is not a gentle, pitiful look. I'm okay with that; it's not about me anymore.

I laugh at myself as I'm driving off. Am I turning into one of those people who would try to convert even the lampposts? I've always wondered what it would feel like to love people so much that you didn't care whether or not they received your love. For the first time in my life I think I now know.

The atmosphere at the dam is electrifying. Thousands of people are here. I'm inwardly smiling at my own joke: *If a thousand men in Speedos don't trigger hyper-vigilance in me, nothing will!* My t-shirt with the Turn2God logo is not made for this sweltering heat and high humidity. I decide to change, knowing that I will be forgiven for opting for 'cooler' methods to be a witness than wearing a thick, black witness-wear t-shirt.

I meet up with a few swim buddies and we stand next to the dam, chatting. The sun is very hot, and the glimmering waves on the dam's surface make my mouth water. I talk to a young man who wants to know why I look so chirpy. I explain to him that I was privileged enough to be given a second chance in life this week. I'm chirpy because I can fully live out my second chance with less fear and more joy.

I ride the shuttle to the other side of the dam where the starting point and registration tents are. There is a yellow swimming cap in my envelope. Hooray, I don't have to swim in cattle-class again! It's terrible when you have to swim with a white cap; it means you're in the largest group of unranked swimmers. It's a flurry of flailing limbs. In my first race in cattle class a man swam right over me doing backstroke. He hit me right on the head. I swallowed so much water I thought I'd never stop coughing and was sure I would drown. I was kept down by his strength and could not come up for air. It has many similarities with rape, I realize now. Lots of chaos, lots of aggression and deep waters that could very well swallow you. That day, however, I finally found my rhythm again and ultimately stood on the opposite shore, safely, just like I'm doing now.

It reminds me of the most beautiful part of Psalm 18, the promise I held onto four nights ago:

> **But me He caught – reached all the way**
> **from sky to sea; He pulled me out**
> **of that ocean of hate, that enemy chaos,**
> **the void in which I was drowning.**
> **They hit me when I was down,**
> **but GOD stuck by me.**
> **He stood me up on a wide-open field;**
> **I stood there saved – surprised to be loved!**
>
> (*The Message*)

I remind myself that I don't have to live a small penned-in life out of fear of the thief. I'm living in a wide open field. The bleeding and the exploding stove are all ways to try and get me to forget how strong my God is. For years fear had been my silent partner, and I'm not going back into that unholy covenant. I *want* to swim. I'm not going to allow fear to take that away from me.

The drive back to the house along the winding roads is breathtakingly beautiful. Out of the blue I hear that beautiful Voice that has now become unmistakeable:

> *"My girl, will you be swimming with Me tomorrow?"*
>
> *"Jesus, if You are going, I'm definitely coming along!"*

All the uncertainty is gone. I feel like a teenager invited to a dance. The bleeding will stop even without medication. I just know it. It's already getting dark; there are no signs that the situation will improve, but it just has to.

I walk into the chalet and find my oldest lying on the bed crying. She has realized something: There might be shattered glass in my hair after all.

"Mommy, are you going to die of AIDS?"

Our late employee's death is still very fresh in her memory. She knows how women contract AIDS. I should have known that she would put two and two together to figure out the health risk the rape holds for me. I show her my antiretroviral tablets.

> *"The doctors and I are doing our best to ensure that I stay healthy. Every morning and every evening Auntie Elna sends me a text message so I won't forget to take my pills. Do you want to pray with me and ask Jesus to make the medication super effective?"*

We pray. I hold her for a few moments. I wish I could give her a guarantee, but I don't have one myself. She immediately reminds me to take tonight's dose. She was going to watch me like a hawk every day. We eat the delicious tuna dish. I'm glad we even brought the flowers along; it lightens the mood standing there all bright and colourful.

I struggle to sleep in this strange single bed, constantly concerned about the bleeding. I dream that I'm late and miss the race. I don't know if I slept one hour or six hours, but when I wake up I feel set and ready for the day's swim. I go to the bathroom. There is no sign of any bleeding – absolutely none. It stopped sometime during the night – as abruptly as it had started.

I get everyone else out of bed. There will be great entertainment for the children at the dam, and I would love for them to wait at the finish line. We leave right after they all gulp down their chocolate cereal and I my medication.

The fog is thick in the valleys, and I can barely see a thing on the road. It can't be. If the fog is this dense and hovering just above the water as it often does, it will be unsafe for the swimmers. Today every swimmer has a dream, and each one of them would like to see that their preparations are rewarded with a medal and a bottle of energy drink from the sponsors. My dream is to keep my appointment with Jesus on this Valentine's Day.

The children help me to write my registration number on my shoulder and thigh with a permanent marker. I don the unflattering swim cap, put my goggles around my neck, strip down to my swim suit, and then put on the traditional Midmar wear – a black trash bag with three slits for the head and arms. My friend drops me off at the starting point and drives back around the dam to where the spectators are getting ready for a fun day.

My race will be the first of the morning. It's bitterly cold and drizzling lightly, but the fog is slowly lifting. The race is going to start a bit later, but at least we are going to swim. I stand barefoot under the gazebo with my black trash bag on as the red and blue capped swimmers start the race. Yellow is next. The black bag is unsightly but it keeps the cold wind out. Last year I was too vain to wear one, only to discover that blue skin with goose bumps that nullify the morning's shaving effort is even less attractive. The idea of the black bag is that as soon as your cap colour is announced, you unceremoniously rip off your wind-proof cover-up and throw it into the nearest trash can on your way to the water. Today I'm planning on stripping it off along with every morsel of residual disgrace. Today I enter the water for a fresh start.

I've eaten two bananas. I forgot my concentrated energy drink in my car. They call us closer to the water. The mud feels cool and slippery between my toes. There are more swimmers than I thought there would be. I realize that it's going to be a stampede anyway, but I'm not in a fighting mood today. I'm going to let everyone get going, and then I'll swim in my own space and hopefully pass one or two swimmers on the way. I'm just going to enjoy it.

After a few minutes in the water I find my rhythm. I practiced with a song in the pool so I could keep a constant tempo. I sing my song. The words and the water wash over me with a comforting tranquillity: *You raise me up so I can stand on mountains, You raise me up to walk on stormy seas. I am strong when I am on your shoulders. You raise me up to more than I can be.* I chose the Josh Groban song months ago because of its easy rhythm. I have a long stroke (read: I'm not fast). When I chose the song the words were incidental, but right now they mean the world to me, however corny they may seem.

The opposite bank approaches faster than I expected, and there are no signs of my usual side stitches at the half-mile mark or cramps just before the last quarter mile. I have enough left to sprint the last few hundred metres. On all of my previous swim photos, I look like an injured seal trying to pull her hindquarters out of the water. Today's photo will show a contented smile. I am standing up straight instead of slumping forward. My time is much better than last year and only two minutes slower than my personal best at the Platinum Mile just two days before the rape.

With a chill down my spine I remember my own words from a week ago. I was at the qualifying race with a friend who had lost an arm in high school when their yacht's mast touched on high voltage cables. His brother lost an arm and a leg and he lost one arm. He regularly shares his testimony at men's breakfasts and is a successful Paralympics track athlete. Last week, as he got out of the water after successfully completing his mile swim, everyone applauded him for the courage it took to overcome his physical disability in such an amazing way. Someone shoved a microphone in his face to let him tell his story. Afterwards we had a conversation.

> *"Niël, your external scar gives you so many opportunities to bring honour to God by telling your story."*
>
> *"It's true. People see it and usually ask questions. It gives me the opportunity to tell what Jesus did for me."*
>
> *"Have you ever thought of it as a privilege? People don't come up to those of us without visible scars to ask us what God means to us."*
>
> *"It might be true Hettie, but you really don't need scars to be able to testify. It remains a choice whether you want to speak up about Jesus or not."*

But now I am scarred, and my refusal to cover it up disgusts some people. For a while longer, reporters will shove the proverbial microphone in my face. But because I don't carry any external scars, my testimony will soon depend again on whether I truly want to proclaim the glory of God. I don't mind becoming old news, but God and what He has done for me is not a story that can get old.

We take the children to the amusement park to play for a while before making the long drive home. Early in the evening we arrive back home. It's the children's first night back in their familiar place. They all crawl contentedly into their own beds. No one even asks for a bedtime story. No nightmares, no child sneaking into my room. They all feel safe. I feel safe.

At one in the morning the security alarm goes off. Before I have time to be afraid, I see in my mind's eye my youngest standing on the staircase. It's confirmed when I see the alarm panel indicating an alarm in the zone called "stairs". I forgot to inform my children about the alarm. My youngest is used to going downstairs to the kitchen by herself for a glass of water, and she's standing there looking at the flickering red lights, stunned and fingers plugged into her ears.

Three hours later the alarm goes off again. The panel reads "alarm in garage." I remember our gardener asked if he could sleep over in the garage, since he wanted to work an extra day. We made him a bed there. Unsuspectingly, he was probably just turning over in his sleep. I don't know how to bypass a zone yet, so I switch off the alarm completely. It's bothering us more than it's helping us, I decide. I realise the fearlessness which I'm experiencing tonight while sleeping in my white bed is a precious gift, and I pray that I will never lose it.

Hopefully Louis is also experiencing peace and rest tonight on the other side of the world.

10 *A feast and jewels*

The next day I receive a call from Louis in Dubai. The tour is going very well, and they're experiencing a special blessing on their work. Of course I also want to know how he's doing emotionally; we tried to organise a trauma counsellor to debrief him on his way to the airport the day after the burglary. I was worried that my reserved husband would bury the trauma of death threats and kidnapping very deep down and that it would live somewhere inside of him where I would not be able to access it. Like many men, Louis doesn't talk about his emotions easily and rarely shows them. To reach his heart is already like a treasure hunt ... I do not want to have to hunt for buried trauma years from now.

Everybody is worried about me because rape sounds so much more traumatic than kidnapping and having a revolver lodged in your ribs. But I realize that the separate attacks on us have two different lies associated with them, and those lies determine how much hurt there is. The lie behind the attack on me is: *'I'm going to damage you.'* Louis was pounded repeatedly with a worse threat for hours on end: *'I'm going to kill you!'*

What a relief when Louis tells me what the Lord did for him. He had to redo the video backdrops and lyric slides that accompany his performances because they were on the laptop that was stolen. He used the flight time from Johannesburg to Dubai to do it on his new laptop because he would have to start performing just a few hours after his arrival. The first song to type up was his own rendition of Psalm 23:

You make me lie down In Your green pasture
You guide my feet along Your way
I'm still a seeker, who found Your favour
The greatest gift of all must be
The home You made in me

Should I blindly run through darkness
Through the fury of the fire
I'll find my refuge near
Find freedom from my fears
Should the deathly shadows reach me
And cover me with cold
Should I stumble when I flee
Your love will salvage me

You lead me to a quiet stream
Where You whisper to my soul

And if I should go astray
By Your voice I'll find my way
You set the table for a feast
In the face of my enemies
Oh Shepherd-Friend who heals me
Come stay – eternally!

The words written so long ago encouraged and healed him. The dam wall broke, and he cried like a baby in view of the air hostesses and other passengers. As he continued typing each of the lyrics he'd written in years past and sung many times over, the songs acquired a new and richer meaning. The Lord strengthened his soul and spirit. Although Louis was physically tired, he felt strong enough and ready to minister to others when he landed.

He continues to share with me how his testimony struck a chord with the audience, especially because so many of them had left South Africa because of their fear of crime. He centred his message on the value of forgiveness, the truth that God is present when bad things happen, and that He is capable of carrying us through such times. He encouraged people to choose against fear so that they could experience the advantage of supernatural power, love and a sound mind. After his performances, people came up to him and shared intense pain and their struggles to escape from the bitterness trap.

One woman, who had lost a son, testified: *"Tonight, after all the years of resentment, I forgave God. The weight has been lifted off my shoulders."* Another woman shared the pain of having a missing child who has still not been found after many years. Louis's heart broke for her, and he felt a new compassion for people whose healing doesn't come quick and easy. He realised that we still know little of true suffering and trauma.

I agree. We end the expensive long-distance call.

My phone rings again, but since it is now mid-morning I don't mind. It is my good friend – the one who was troubled that night of the robbery and spent the night praying. She calls to announce she is bringing a sports masseuse to our house to massage out the tension and stiffness of the Midmar Mile. She is completely convinced that I need it, and her friend is said to be one of the best.

On the way to our home she tells the masseuse what had happened to me. Suddenly the masseuse refuses to continue driving. She says there is no way she can do it. She was a hostage in a bank robbery a few years earlier and was a twisted ball of spasms for a long time afterwards. There is no way she can handle feeling the damage and tension in my body under her fingers. It's simply too close for comfort. Luckily my friend convinces her in the end and assures her that I won't fall apart under her hands.

We spread an old beach towel over my white bed, and I share the testimony of how I it had come to be so fresh and beautiful. She starts rubbing my back. It feels wonderful, and I start getting sleepy. She's good! But very quiet. She whispers something to my friend and then starts crying. Baffled, she mutters:

"It's as if there are no muscles."

At first I feel a little offended, but then I realise what she means. She expected to find knots and stiffness, but instead my body is telling her fingers a story of peace and healing. The three of us talk about how one's spirit should rule over one's soul and body, and that healing in our spirit can flow over and literally command our soul and body to be healed. King David understood these principles; in a number of Psalms he referred to the relationship between his spiritual battles and sicknesses and his spiritual recovery and the healing of his body. He knew one's spirit could command one's soul to hope in God. This hope, he knew, is magnificently restorative just as hopelessness breaks down the very fibres in our body.

With the time zone difference, Louis and I are struggling to get in touch with one another. International roaming doesn't want to work on his Blackberry because, unbeknownst to us, the thieves had made a duplicate of his SIM card, and we are busy running up a bull of a bill to the tune of thousands of rand. The mobile phone client services also don't realise what happened, so they keep insisting that their system shows the cell phone is working and being used for international calls. But the international calls that they think Louis is making from overseas to me turn out to be calls from South Africa to Zimbabwe and Botswana. The thieves must have set up a little phone booth and rented out Louis's phone. Very entrepreneurial of them!

So Louis calls me from someone else's cell phone. He wants to know what to do with all of the gifts people are sending to me, because there are too many and they are too heavy for his baggage restrictions. He can't possibly bring all of it home. He says they are interesting gifts – jewellery, including bracelets, necklaces and earrings, body lotions and such.

> *"Honey, it is Ezekiel 16! It contains this promise that after washing off my old blood, God would put jewellery on me. It also promises the delicacies of foreign nations: honey and oil."*
>
> *"Exactly! Women gave me treats unique to Dubai, Australia and New Zealand – and I see this hand lotion says 'with honey and olive oil'. One lady even removed her necklace while speaking to me about something else and told me to give it to you. 'Hettie will understand,' she said."*

I do understand. The Lord is confirming to me that I had heard Him correctly and that it was Him talking to me all the time. I won't allow the mocking letter writers to make me doubt who He really is. I'm not going crazy.

> **I adorned you with jewellery: I placed bracelets on your wrists, fitted you out with a necklace, emerald rings, sapphire earrings, and a diamond tiara. You were provided with everything precious and beautiful: with exquisite clothes and elegant food (some translations call it 'the delicacies of the nations'), garnished with honey and oil.**
>
> (Ezekiel 16: 11-13, *The Message*)

Many theologians and church people believe one can never interpret the Bible the way I do. They claim it wasn't the Lord speaking to me and the quoted Scripture was for someone else, anyway. The literal context indicates that it's a message from God through

Ezekiel to the Jerusalem of that day. According to the Old Testament experts, I don't have the right or grounds to apply this Scripture to myself, nor should I imagine that it could also be true for me.

I've pondered this many times before. How do I know if a Bible verse I read here or there is meant for me? How can I claim that the Lord speaks to me from His Word? This is an important question, isn't it? Because, as we all know, some people have committed abominable acts in the name of the Lord based on Bible verses they took out of context. Apartheid is a good example of the danger of taking from the Bible ideas that suit you without knowing the One whose ideas they were in the first place ...

Paul, the top Pharisee in his day, says in Romans 15 verse 4 with reference to the Old Testament writings of Moses and the prophets:

> **Such things were written in the Scriptures long ago to teach us. And the Scriptures give us hope and encouragement as we wait patiently for God's promises to be fulfilled.**
>
> (*New Living Translation*)

How can we learn from, be strengthened by, or be given hope through something if it's irrelevant to our situation? How can the Word encourage us if we are only allowed to apply it to the person or people who heard it first? If we have an undying hope and promise that the Word of God wants to encourage us with, then we have the right to claim that for ourselves. To me, nothing else makes sense.

The Word wasn't written for us to look at, but to take part in! Would God prepare a mouth-watering feast and then expect us to sit at the table salivating as we watch the privileged ones eat it — privileged just because they were lucky enough to be living in Jerusalem at just the right moment thousands of years ago? I believe not. The Lord prepares an eternal feast of Living Words, which He's been doing through the ages. Everyone is welcome to sit and eat and be satisfied. This very idea upset Jesus' casual followers of the time – the comment that they couldn't live unless they ate or drank of Him. Even today it upsets so-called followers of Jesus who turn their backs on Him because the Bible has become to them as outdated and inferior as a meal of only bread and wine ... In looking for more, they miss everything.

Someone even advised me once to remove the Bible verses from my parenting course so it would appeal to a wider audience. More people would attend my courses if they didn't have to look at a Bible verse on every other page. As if God wanted to answer on my behalf, I realised something I'd never thought about: *He who is offended by the Word of God is offended with Christ Himself.*

For those who realise there is only one place to find the Bread of Life, and for those who aren't ashamed to say that their lives depend on it, the Word is a cupboard stocked with an endless choice of nourishing food. It's a source of wisdom for all who acknowledge that they actually understand little of life. That's why David's longest song, Psalm 119, is about the Word of God. Singing this Psalm, he sounds like a businessman going on and on about his best strategy – a salesman sharing the secret advantage he has because of the wisdom of God's words (verse 98, 130). He sounds like a deep sea diver elaborating about his newly discovered treasure (verse 162) and a starving man stumbling unexpectedly upon a feast (verse 47, 103).

Psalm 119:111 gives us the key that unlocks satisfaction, enlightenment, wisdom, and protection:

> **I inherited your book on living; it's mine forever – what a gift! And how happy it makes me!**
>
> (*The Message*).

David calls this book his heritage. He claims it as his own, even though it was also meant for someone else earlier in history and for millions since. Inherited items belong to the heir just as much as they once belonged to the original owner. David ate the Word — he didn't only look and listen to it. It was his all-weather torch, his bulletproof vest, his *Google Maps*, his *Nine Steps and Seven Habits*, his chicken soup, his *Happiness for Dummies*, and his favourite diner. He put knowing more of God's Word at the top of his bucket list. Simply by choosing not to only read it sometimes ... but to *always* make it his own.

In the church and in Christians' lives today our saddest deficiency is this: we analyse the feast, argue about who is invited to the feast and which sins or preferences would ban us from the table and send us instead into the fiery kitchen. We categorise the food. Is it real food, the history of food, poetry about food, scientifically correct or incorrect, creationist or evolutionary, cultural or cross-cultural? Should one eat a whole book at a time, a chapter at a time, or are you allowed to eat daily devotional snacks? Shouldn't one understand the science behind the food before it will nourish you, or are you allowed to eat it even if you don't know if it's starch or vegetables? If we would only taste and eat! We're seated at the table with Christ, dressed up like lords in His righteous robes, we know the names of all the dishes thanks to Sunday school and sermons galore, but we abstain. It's probably not for us ... I see David in heaven being held back by angels as he screams in desperation, *"Just taste and see that the LORD is good, will you?!"* (Psalm 34:8).

A number of the most vehement letters among the hundreds were reactions to the fact that I had so childishly gulped down the delicacies of the feast. The fact that I took delight in phrases like the Lord being my rescuing Knight and I His bride was an indulgent act of gluttony that disgusted them. How dare I distinguish myself like that? How dare I sing Bible verses when other peoples' sheet music has been blown away in their storm? I truly do have empathy with them, but at the same time I want to defend my exuberance in loosely the same words Jesus used when He and the disciples were called gluttons:

> *"While the Bridegroom is here, it's time for a feast. There will be times when I live off crumbs, but now I celebrate."*

To see me enjoying the feast hopefully intensifies a different grouping of people's hunger. I pray they put down their newspapers, reach for their Bibles and soon forget about me. I pray they're too busy digging in to be concerned about my interpretation of Scripture.

Unfortunately others shy away from the feast even more, because they believe the lies of the enemy:

> *"It's only for people like her. Her husband is a Gospel singer. They are professional Christians. You are not."*

They think I've always had the assurance, joy, power and courage I now have. They don't even know me. They don't realise how painfully aware I was of my own spiritual weakness when the rape took place. They don't know how powerless I felt – vulnerable and flapping around in the wind. They don't know that I still fight temptation and seduction. So they are probably right in a way. The feast is only for people like me: broken ones. It's only for those who realise how exposed, covered in old blood and powerless they really are without Jesus.

For those like me, there is even more than a feast. There is jewellery. New clothes. New wine.

The year off stage is not yet over, but God sends so many women into my life. Sometimes when I share the story, I mention the jewellery, but mostly I'm afraid that the women in the audience might say to themselves:

> *"Wow, she's privileged that Jesus spoiled her so much. He wouldn't do that for me, of course."*

I'm on my way to participate in an appreciation day for women from Danville, the neighbourhood that I once refused to live in. These women were trained to be care workers, and I was asked to just come along and affirm them and perhaps share a few points about parenting and education. On the way there, I heard the Lord saying:

> *"You can give them your parenting CD's to listen to. Today, instead, talk to them about how valuable they are to Me."*

The organisers have no problem with the change of plans. The event is very informal. The ladies are sitting on plastic chairs in a circle against the wall of a cramped room. Some are standing so they can rock their screaming babies on the hip. I look at them – some are HIV positive, yet God tells me to tell them that He sees them pure. Some are addicted and in debt, but I must tell them God sees them free. Many are too ashamed to make eye contact, until I tell them what God says: "You are My brides."

The community workers behind this beautiful morning manicure the ladies' nails, colour and cut their hair, wash their feet and paint their toe nails pink. The women blossom with a new freshness. One can hardly distinguish between those from Danville and those from the higher end of town. Clearly restoring a woman's outer beauty has an impact on how she perceives herself. In tatters, she struggles to see the bride in herself. Putting jewels on her makes her one.

> **"They shall be Mine," says the LORD of hosts, "On the day that I make them My jewels. And I will spare them as a man spares his own son who serves him."**
>
> (Malachi 3:17, *New King James Version*).

One of the organisers hands me an envelope.

> *"I apologise for not getting you a gift. I prayed about what to give everyone who participated today. This is what I felt the Lord told me to give you. Please don't be offended by it. It is not a hint in any way."*

I smile and thank her, puzzled. Being as inquisitive as I am, I open the envelope while driving home and nearly lose control over my car. The thank you note says:

> *"God said to dress you in fine linen."*

In the envelope is her business card. She is a fashion designer and dressmaker. I let out a scream in disbelief. Only this morning I stood in front of the mirror staring at the accumulating tummy flab – one of the side effects of the antiretroviral drugs.

> *"Lord, I have too much jewellery now. But really, I have nothing that fits my ever growing curves!"*

Now my 'I have nothing to wear' moment seems so ridiculous!

I am asked again to share my testimony with a different group of women from Danville. They have a ladies camp – one of those I swore never to attend, let alone minister at. I firmly decide not to mention the jewellery I received as presents, because it feels like bragging. As I stand in the hall in front of women who already feel inferior, it confirms my decision. It would be insulting. As I talk about how God wants to restore their lives, it just slips out that He wants to adorn them with jewels. In the back of the hall I notice the camp leader wiping tears off her face. I fear I might have hurt everybody.

We end the evening with a hot drink and delicious rusks. I am relieved to slip into my bed in the tented camp among the thorn trees. The short night is ended by some Bushveld birds I have not learned to identify. They go off like an alarm. The thin tent flap makes them sound like they're standing on my bed. I must get ready for the morning and afternoon session of teaching and am praying that I will be more sensitive this time around. I am still convinced that the mentioning of the jewellery was insensitive.

After the last session we are called to line up for a surprise. There is a baobab tree made of wire out on the veranda. The branches of the tree are heavy with small pink and silver satin pouches, and each woman has to take a turn to pick one from the tree. Inside each pouch is Miglio jewellery. A Miglio agent sponsored everything: necklaces, bracelets and all types of jewellery to the value of thousands of Rand. Expensive jewellery for hurting but precious women. Life may have pushed them out, but Jesus, their Bridegroom, had sent someone to adorn them. The camp leader knew about this surprise. Her tears of yesterday make sense to me now.

I will always associate jewellery with the restoration of women's purity and worth in the eyes of the Lord. At a number of events, even without mentioning anything about jewellery, women gave me everything from bracelets to heart-shaped earrings and a jewelled handbag hook, always with the same words:

> *"I'm not sure why I need to give it to you, but the Lord told me to."*

[I'm in my bedroom typing this page. It's Saturday, March 12, 2011. My husband has just returned from another 'Esther' conference where he led worship. I have just completed the above two paragraphs. He enters the room with two organza pouches – each with a bracelet inside. In the red pouch is a note: *You are My bride.* It's written on a page torn from someone's diary. The date at the top is 9 February 2010 – the date of the rape. An anonymous woman from the conference sent it with Louis to give to me.]

I can only but smile, like one who knows a wonderful secret: Women were healed today, and the words that healed them were the truth about who Jesus really is … and the truth about who they really are in Him. These truths always bring healing – without exception.

11 *Honey, I'm home!*

It's the 24th of February. Someone phones to inform me that she just heard on the radio that the police have caught the robbers. That's strange, I think. Nobody told me. I sit in my car and wait for a news bulletin. She is right, they did catch them. An hour later the detective arrives at our home to share the news with me. One of the robbers is the infamous leader of a notorious gang that is associated with break-ins spanning a wide territory including our neighbourhood. They caught him with a new gang hanging out near a train station. These men had break-in equipment with them including some wire cutters and poisoned meat, which would probably have been used to poison guard dogs.

The decisive piece of evidence that links them with our case is the odd looking revolver that appeared to be the same one we had described to the police. It looked handmade, had an angular barrel, and appeared to have been sanded with steel wool. The detective explains that each of these men would be subjected to DNA tests in order to compare the results with the evidence in the rape kit taken during the forensic process. He will let me know if one of them is my rapist.

A reporter phones to ask me to give a statement. How do I feel about the arrest? I'm happy they've been caught, because even though I have forgiven them, I know they are dangerous and could become even more dangerous. Who knows? Maybe when they're behind bars I might even talk to them one day. Maybe behind bars they will come to their senses. I so wish this will turn out as it did in the nightmares I used to have where I lead the attempted rapists to the Lord. But I realise life doesn't always turn out like a dream.

In an unguarded moment I say to the reporter that I would love to see some sort of reconciliation. It would be my desire that the rapist repent of his sin, and carry the torch with me at the Turn2God march in two weeks; especially since the movement is all about moving away from our past and overcoming crime by turning back to God.

Unfortunately my statement is dished up a few days later in a very sensational article. I can't blame her. It was completely unrealistic of me to expect the police to let me talk with someone who is awaiting trial. Besides, the DNA-test backlog in our legal system is stacked up in labs like piles of dirty laundry in a boarding house. There would be no conclusive identification of my rapist in time for the march. Perhaps not for years. The legal process will take years to resolve, anyway, and no criminal will be allowed to carry any torches in the meantime.

I meet with more psychologists and therapists at my home and in coffee shops. Every week. Almost every day. It takes up so much time that I don't get anything else done. Each one of them wants to personally look me in the eyes. They probe here and try to trigger something there. According to them, someone needs to do the necessary to help me out of my denial. They can't find the cracks they are looking for, and so one by one they come to the conclusion that the Lord really must have done something extraordinary. One day one of them phones and says:

> *"Hettie, yesterday I realised that I've been phoning you every day, even though I've known for a long time that you're OK. The truth is, I'm the one that's not OK. I'm struggling to accept what has happened to you."*
>
> *"That's OK, I realise the people around us are more traumatised than we are. I have done more counselling and have comforted more people in the past month than all the previous years combined."*

I share with her a sweet story I heard from a friend in our cell group: One day a distressed Corrie ten Boom (author of *The Hiding Place*) mentioned to her dad that she couldn't stand to see people suffering so horribly. Her dad reportedly replied:

> *"If you need to board a departing train, Daddy will give you a ticket to ride the train. In the same way people who need to survive tough times will receive a ticket from their heavenly Dad. You can't carry their suffering, because you don't have a ticket for that train."*

Louis and I received tickets for this train, but the people mourning and agonizing on the platform haven't.

The newspapers are not letting go of the story and snide comments. Some reporters comment on my "unsettling smile." I respond by saying that I've heard of many people like me who have come through trauma unscathed, but they are quick to stop and remind me that the biggest test to prove I'm healed is yet on its way:

> *"Just wait till your husband wants to touch you again ..."*

Well, the moment has arrived: Louis's three week tour has come to an end and he's landing this afternoon. His deodorant was confiscated in Perth, and he flew back via Dubai, so by the time he arrives home he heads straight for the shower. I stand in the bathroom doorway like a naughty teenager, admiring his body through the curtain of water running down the shower door. I've missed him. I decide to get in the shower with him. Why should I believe the prophets of doom?

The water washes over us. I think of being pure and clean and realise there is only one possible thing that could still come between us. I had told Louis previously about the man occasionally standing on the periphery of our puppet theatre. Louis knows how intensely I fear the Lord, and he knows how black and white my perspective is on marriage and sexual purity. I tell him again, hoping he will somehow blow it all away for me. I confess that I still occasionally have a wandering heart. Louis assures me my heart is not in danger. But I feel I have to tell him again that I'm still fighting this fight. I don't want to leave any secret between us for the enemy to toy with. Louis smiles dismissingly; he knows he is my only prince:

> *"I know you are crazy about me aren't you? You would never be able to shut a bedroom door behind yourself and another man."*

I pray that he is right; I'm glad that he trusts me, but I also know that none of us is exempt from making fatal mistakes. I could make this mistake I fear the most. I know I could.

He gently washes my back.

> *"Am I supposed to feel differently about you? Should I be cautious in the way I touch you?"*
>
> *"I don't know. I don't feel any different."*

We step out of the shower together. Nothing feels different. We are still who we've always been. Everything is as beautiful as before. Everything I had learned in December about intimacy is true in these moments: no other loves, no fear, no shame, no lies, no demands, and now – no more secrets.

While he gets dressed I cry in my pillow, thankful and relieved, because I know this could have been so different.

The enemy, of course, had a different agenda in mind. He is always trying to edit God's script. It's easy to see the damage he could have caused. Could there have been a more devastating way to attack our faith, mock our trust in the Lord's protective hand, hurt our children, or threaten our marriage than by planting death in my body and soul in this cruel way? Could there have been a more effective way to shut a woman's mouth and to break her spirit?

But on the night of the 9th of February 2010, my loving Father didn't frantically grope around for a pen to scribble a few lines to see if He could save our story. He does not try to make all things work together for good after the fact by picking up the pieces in the way one makes arty mosaics out of broken crockery. He works *in* circumstances in real time. Even in advance. He started with this story long ago. He long ago recorded our days in His book and wrote the necessary resilience into our story. He also wrote lessons in intimacy into my storyline, knowing that true intimacy has healing power and would heal me even before the attack. True intimacy would be the impenetrable, protective shield ... a safe place where I would hide when trauma came.

Our reactions to the burglary, kidnapping and especially the rape should be seen in context. I'm not prescribing how all Christian women should react after they are raped, because I would never have the arrogance to think that I could stand on anyone's holy ground in my high heels. I want to stand barefoot before every broken person, knowing their trauma is holy ground. We truly cannot ever really stand in another person's shoes. Nobody can copy and paste from another's story and expect everything to work the same way.

Our past journey and our history play a defining role in how we handle the present.

Apricots are my favourite fruit. As a child I probably ate hundreds of them in my grandmother's backyard. She used to puree them and spread them on wax paper and then make them into the most delicious dried apricot rolls. Her jam was celebrated in the most delicious little tarts and on top of warm buttered toast. My favourite, though, was fresh apricots, oozing with those shiny nectar drops that appear when you squeeze out the seed. If I ever did eat a rotten one or one with worms in it, I don't remember it amongst all the sweet memories of one perfectly ripe fruit after the other. If I regularly found worms in the apricots, though, my favourite fruit would have fallen from grace and I would have avoided apricots at all costs.

Sexual experiences are similar to eating fruit. The rape was the first bitter, rotten apricot of my sexual life.

There was one other worm I remember from long ago. One night, during a large family gathering, we stood in my apricot-grandma's kitchen, when my mom's cousin offered to put me to bed to save my mother the trouble. I was probably four or five years old at the time. Once in the guest room and out of sight, he slipped his hand down my panties for a brief moment, explaining that he needed to check whether I had changed into my pyjamas yet. I didn't understand that the action, which lasted only about two seconds, amounted to sexual molestation. It was so fleeting and he didn't threaten me or hurt me. Such behaviour was like an unexpected little worm in a sweet fruit. "Stupid man who checks for pyjama's in such a dumb way," was all I thought of it then. I was used to my dad dressing and undressing me from time to time, so I wasn't warned that it was inappropriate for other people to get that close. I never saw this family member again and never had any other experiences with other "stupid men" who had inappropriate ways of checking what one was and was not wearing.

My entire life before that moment, as well as all the years afterward, have effectively erased this experience since it didn't resonate with anything else in my life. I never suppressed the memory. I thought about it from time to time, but never knew if and how I should tell someone. Years later I told my mother but still did not know exactly how to describe the incident. Now that I'm a little wiser, I realise what that man did was exactly what paedophiles do to groom their victims for future acts of molestation. One can only hope that this person never tried it with another child, but the odds are he has done worse. I'm thankful that our paths never crossed again, because my innocence and naïveté probably would have made me a soft target.

Many men and women have been scarred by similar experiences, but they were left with much more pain simply because their lives before and after this experience were filled with other bitter fruit experiences. So, compared to me, they have gone through much worse pain. Their pain is real, their stories are different, and they naturally have to resolve their pain in a way that will differ from mine. Their healing will require the healing of a string of painful memories, not of only one, like mine.

Random associations can torment injured people by reminding them of traumatic moments they had in the past. They can be triggered unexpectedly by a range of things: a smell, an image, hearing a song on the radio, or a swiftly moving shadow coming from behind – anything that triggers what their offenders may have done. These triggers may be unpleasant, but they serve a good purpose. *They can be like a flashing red light that warns us: there is deeper healing needed here – it's not over yet!* Those heeding the red light will get help until healing comes. But, they can also cause us to believe certain lies about ourselves: *'You see, you will never be healed. Certain things will always haunt you. You're permanently damaged!''* The pace and depth of our healing depend on whether or not we listen to these lies. It depends on what we choose to believe when these emotions from the past well up inside of us.

One night, about a year before the burglary, I was driving home after a speaking engagement. It was eleven at night, and I was alone in the car. The children's choir music that was playing on the radio carried me away to the nostalgic memories of childhood and my own choir days. Consequently, I forgot to do my usual 360 degree safety check as I stopped at the red light. Suddenly my car jolted sideways. When I looked up, a man's nose was pressed flat against my window. Both his hands were on my door handle, yanking wildly in an attempt to open the door. He was peering into the car to see what he could steal. I started yelling at him and honked the horn hoping that it would prompt the driver in front of me to go through the red light so I could get away.

It didn't faze the prospective thief one bit. He pressed his nose against all the other windows of my car in turn, presumably looking for valuables that would make it worth his while to shatter a window. The car behind me had stopped too close for me to back over the guy, as I always imagined I would do in this situation. As he yanked in vain on the front passenger door, the driver in front of me finally realised what was happening. In unison, all three of us ran the red light, leaning on our car horns as we drove off. It took me several hours to stop shaking.

About a month later I stopped at that same traffic light, this time in broad daylight. The next moment, a flower vendor approached me quickly with his bouquet of apricot coloured roses and leaned in close to my car window. The shape of his nose just triggered something in me. My whole body started shaking spontaneously. The aggressive Hettie jumped up in me. I rolled down my window and screamed like a demented woman at the poor innocent entrepreneur:

> *"I know what you do on this corner at night under the cover of darkness! It was you, wasn't it?!"*

I did exactly what the traumatised residents of our security complex had done to the innocent security guard the day after my rape. Driving away from that corner for the second time, I was trembling just as much as the night when my car was almost broken into. My response to a bouquet of roses was the same as to a real and present danger, all because of a nose! Having let out my fear and anger, I was not a bit better. My response did not in any way heal me. I had unresolved trauma, for sure.

Through that experience I know what the after-effects of trauma can feel like. I understand the random triggers that could have sent us all the way back to the dark night. After the screaming incident, I realised that unless I could find a truth that would set me free, I wouldn't be able to drive around alone without the threat of another random panic attack. I prayed and was reminded of the promise in Matthew 6 that not a hair will fall from my head without my Father knowing and that I could not by worrying add a single day to my own life. Since the wannabe thief wasn't armed and couldn't have caused permanent damage, the worst thing he could have done was to steal something which was temporary and earthly – nothing of eternal value. That truth settled in my heart and the terror left me for good.

Some people's attackers don't appear only once on an obscure street corner or in a dark room, but instead they are constantly there – living or working close by. Repeated exposure to one's perpetrator is pure torture. Others never see their offenders again but are harassed by flashbacks. I have experienced that. The person wasn't a molester or a criminal, but he was someone who had too much power over my emotions. For a long time my memories of him were accompanied with intense pain. To break free, I had to accurately interpret the pain's message. My emotions radiated from a dangerous lie: *He will always have a painful hold on your heart!* I even wrote a poem declaring this impossible situation. What a waste of my soul!

Memories

Through knot-thick bark the bore worm burrows
Gnaw-crawling tunnels into soft sapwood
Yet *you* creep even deeper in
Through layered stone of my intentional ignore
You bore

The earwig drums on tender tympanums
Squirming, scratching, utterly maddening
Yet triggers fewer nerve endings
Than a single flicker-fleeting déjà vu
Of you

As octopus ink quickly blurs to blackness
Crystal clear water that sparkled before
I try in vain to clear your cloud
That pours out over my delight
Your blight

(*Hettie Brittz, June 2010*)

I needed liberating truth. One beautiful day I realised the truth: I am the one reminding myself of this pain. I can stop looking back. The pain had become like a garment that I frequently dressed myself in ... and it started to fit comfortably. But, as with the black trash bag I wore at the Midmar Mile, I could decide to rip off the painful memories. Today the pain of the memory doesn't fit me any longer. I never even try it on anymore. I keep rejecting the lie that a person can forever hold my heart captive in pain. It is not and will never be true.

Trauma often echoes into the past and into the future. Every painful experience strengthens and confirms the things you already believe. Trauma can discolour your memories as well as your outlook on the future and can frequently steal the joy you have in the present, as well. Suppose as a child I had been molested repeatedly and as a woman had been treated disrespectfully, convincing me that God didn't even know my name. Then, when I was raped, it would only have confirmed my worthlessness in the eyes of God and men, and for the rest of my life I would have had to live with the echo of that lie-affirming trauma.

But with my past experiences taken into account, this was not a logical outcome in my case. I had stored up a memory bank full of experiences of love and nurturing that bring with them buffer-beliefs or protective truths that make up my views and convictions. I've only been intimate with one man – my own husband. Our marriage is one full of respect, warmth and humour, which means there is nothing in my personal history – no rejection, abuse, loneliness, humiliation, bitterness, perversion or fear – that could have resonated with the rape. It sank away in the sea of positive experiences. There was no echo. It was one rotten apricot in a basket full of luscious fruit.

A marriage this secure does not come easily or automatically. And ours was not always so. Years ago, right before going on a long tour overseas, someone warned us that there were lots of cracks in our marriage. She had seen a spiritual picture of it. It looked like an island hut – leaves and reeds strung together with large gaps in the walls. Around us in the bushes were dark figures, lurking behind the trees – a bow and arrow in hand. We were a soft target, and she warned us to close the gaps. We had no idea how.

By the fourth month of the tour, the few leaves and reeds that had been our marriage were blown away to such an extent that one morning we found ourselves in someone's basement, on opposite ends of a double bed, saying to one another: "I don't like you anymore." For the sake of our kids we had no intention of doing anything drastic about it, and for the sake of the tour we would keep our pious poses until we got to Nashville, where we would be staying in our own apartment. Then there would be all-out war.

When we arrived in Nashville we had no idea what to do with each other. No amount of screaming, crying, arguing, begging or accusing had been effective over the preceding months. How would we get ourselves to see eye to eye on even a single issue? We had unlearned how to speak to one another. We wanted to be away from each other, but we had one car and were stranded. We made a strange pact. Two nights a week we would sit on our double bed, like shipwrecked survivors on an island, and would talk until we had a few leaves and reeds strung back together again.

At first we just screamed. Later the screaming became less and the crying became more. Then the tears made way for adamant accusations. Slowly we made our way from the little things to the deeper desires of our hearts. We admitted our failures, shared disappointments, and dared to speak our dreams. After a few sessions, we were talking less and praying more. In prayer we sacrificed our own dreams and desires so that, together with the Lord, we could start looking for a new dream. By the time we had finished, our marriage hut had become a fortress. It had only taken three weeks.

That healthy habit of two nights per week on Intimacy Island was swallowed up by real life once we returned to South Africa. A few years later we came to a similar point and realised we would never again have a healthy marriage without fighting for it. We started to put Monday evenings aside for each other. Monday after Monday we unknowingly gathered treasures that would help to carry us in times to come. Those investments into our marriage helped us to pray with unity during the burglary, to support one another and to accept one another's actions under pressure. We had to give each other the benefit of the doubt, not knowing if either of us could have done things better or differently that night and thereafter. That trust in the other's best intentions had matured in us over time like good wine. We had become one in spirit during those Monday evenings, and it allowed us to have one perspective of the Lord's character, one testimony about His goodness, one dream to build His kingdom, and one confession: He is always good.

I remember clearly one such Monday evening. We were lying in bed and I said:

> *"Honey, it's so easy to thank the Lord for His goodness every day. Look at our marriage, our children, our house, our ministries and our health! I just hope we have the kind of faith that would enable us to praise the Lord even if we should lose everything. Otherwise we are serving Mammon – the god of good times."*

Louis answered:

> *"I agree; an untested faith is worth nothing."*

I never made notes during that time of the things that had pulled us closer together. I did, however, make notes during this year of a different rebuilding – the rebuilding of the marriage between Jesus and me. Those warnings to sit at His feet were similar to the vision of the dilapidated hut. I knew it needed urgent work, but I did not know about the arrows that were already pointed at my spiritual shelter and, once again, at my marriage hut.

Both of these homes were under attack. I had to fight daily temptations that threatened to tear apart my relationship with Jesus and my marriage to Louis. Both homes were in need of stronger roofs and thicker walls. I'm thankful that the Lord planned it in such a way that the reparations began months in advance. That is probably the main reason both homes are still standing after the robbery and rape.

This is also why Louis could step through the front door only three weeks after the incident and call with anticipation:

> *"Honey, I'm home!"*

12 *Lost paradise*

Intimacy is not something we build; it's something we win back. Intimacy is the paradise we have all lost. We were created to be intimate – to be fearlessly connected with one another and our Creator like Adam and Eve were before the fall: naked, but unashamed. They strolled with God in the garden in the cool evening breeze, without the urge to cover themselves with fig leaves. That's the intimacy we need to win back.

And to win back intimacy, we needn't add anything. All we need to do is rid ourselves of the things that eroded our intimacy in the first place.

Through my own struggles with temptation, God taught me the importance of one of the pillars of intimacy – its exclusivity. There can be no other loves. This is true for our relationship with God and for our relationship with our spouse. I didn't learn this simply in theory – I had to feel what it felt like: Jesus had paraded before me all my other loves. He made them sing to me. Every cell in my body resonated with their songs, but then He asked me to turn my back on their music and walk away from their allure by choosing only Him.

The first turning point came on the first of January when I remembered the warning that if I did not sit surrendered at the feet of Jesus I would get hurt. I knew it was time to place the unauthorized love, the illegal infatuation, before Jesus' feet. I cried while praying:

> *"Take it Lord. I'm allowed to love only You. But will You please fill the void this will leave? Will You woo me instead of this person I've grown so attached to? Will You charm me?"*

He seemed to answer:

> *"Like Mary you have poured something precious, something that made you feel special, on My feet. You anointed My feet to walk in new places in your life, on new places in your heart."*

That's when He gave me Psalm 18 as my Scripture for the year. Looking back, I can see that the prerequisite for experiencing healing intimacy with Jesus was to pour out all my loves on His feet. I believe it is true for all of us. Only when Jesus is our first love, will we be healed by Love.

On the 5th of January I wrote down Psalm 45:10-12 in my journal. The passion of this declaration of love struck me, and I had to think about it for a while. Could Jesus, the perfect and pure Son of God, truly love me like this? I was sure He could and that such a love had to be answered by loving Him only.

> **Now listen, daughter, don't miss a word: forget your country, put your home behind you. Be here – the King is wild for you. Since He's your Lord, adore Him! Wedding gifts pour in from Tyre; rich guests shower you with presents.**
>
> (*The Message*)

The message is clear: forsake all and choose only Him. He is worthy of that exclusive devotion and adoration.

On the 7th of January, my daily devotional reminded me that to live for any other purpose than to live for Jesus was to commit spiritual adultery. Two days later I wrote down Spurgeon's words in my diary again.

> **Desire is as insatiable as death, but He who fills 'all in all' can fill it. Who can measure the capacity of our wishes? But the immeasurable wealth of God can more than overflow it.**

The prayer that I had prayed asking Jesus to fill the hole that an ended relationship would leave now stood in pathetic contrast to this abundant promise. Not only could He fill every void – He could flood it!

On the 12th of January I wrote down in borrowed words my intentions, should there ever be competition for my heart again:

> *"When the siren song of pleasure would tempt you from the path of right, reply, 'Your music cannot charm me; I am Christ's.'"*
>
> (C.H. Spurgeon)

In the weeks and months that followed, I repeatedly prayed these words out loud. Crying, sometimes sobbing. Determined to know no greater love than Jesus, I whispered constantly: Your music cannot charm me anymore. *Your music cannot charm me anymore. Your music cannot charm me anymore ..."* The temptations kept on coming, but now I felt as though I knew what was at stake. Most of the time I could walk away, but at other times I gave in to the charm of the old music ...

One morning I woke up with the voice of Jesus ringing in my ears:

> *"Do you love Me?"*
>
> *"Oh Jesus, please don't ask three times like you did Simon Peter. I know I also betrayed You, but please know that I love You as much as my flesh will permit me to."*
>
> *"You love Me. But do you prefer me?*

Dagger in gut. It felt worse than being asked three times if I loved Him. I had to answer honestly:

"No Jesus, I prefer sleep above resting on Your lap; I prefer the words of a charmer above Your Word; I prefer the advice of colleagues above Yours; I prefer to get fit in the swimming pool rather than in the gymnasium of life where I have to constantly bench press against temptations. I love You, yes, but I have other preferences as well."

The Lord seemed to keep wrestling with me until He had pried my fingers open from the strong grip I had on my other loves. It took several months before and after the rape. In May I wrote a poem about this in my journal, when I once again had to bring the same sacrifice that I had brought on the 1st of January. The sacrifice had crawled off the altar and back into my heart, I suppose.

Preferring You

Lord, what a wandering heart I have
so prone to roam away from You
so easily enticed and swayed
so loosely anchored to Your way
I beg You to arrest my soul
to chain it closely to Your heart
then shall I shackle willingly
my passions to Your feet
I'll sit, or even lie down still
and wait
until my heart is trained to stay
Then shall I walk faithfully with You
no longer wild, but true
Then shall I stand unwaveringly
forevermore preferring You

(*Hettie Brittz, May 2010*)

God insists that we love nothing but Him. He is jealous of His beloved. It's not because He wants to withhold pleasure from us but because He knows that no other love can complete us like He can. All other loves are idols, and they need to be smashed and burned. They represent all of the people and things in which we find more self-worth than in the simple knowledge that we are children of the only living God (2 Samuel 24:10, Matthew 6:19-24). Idols are all the things that fulfil us more than God does (Psalm 16:5-8) and everything in which we hope to find joy besides in Him (Psalm 4:6-8). If we look at something or someone else for comfort and security, the Bible calls us prostitutes (the whole book of Hosea deals with this). Everything we gather for ourselves without trusting God will be destroyed anyway (Isaiah 33:4-6, Jeremiah 51:58).

I believe I could have definitely experienced more heartache had I not already grown closer to Jesus as my first Love. I wouldn't have been able to get back in my husband's arms with someone else between us. The fact that it had been the first danger of its kind in seventeen years of marriage hadn't been a coincidence. This idol could have caused more damage than the rape, because intimacy is not only dependent on loving someone.

It is dependent on choosing someone above all others. It is about preferring only one.

The second intruder that can destroy intimacy is fear. After being raped, one of the saddest losses for the victim can be her inability to discern between safe and unsafe arms. She tries to flee from all embraces, and unintentionally her body can react and even flee from the arms of those who desire to comfort her. Intimacy and safety are very closely interwoven. The enemy of safety is fear.

Often, when God approached people – in person or through angels – the first words spoken were: *'Fear not.'* Why? Fear makes it impossible to receive what we need the most. Whoever fears cannot receive love, because we can't love the person we fear (1 John 4:18). Whoever fears cannot receive the truth, because fear spreads lies. Whoever fears cannot experience freedom, because fear is a claustrophobic jail cell made of cold, hard walls with no windows to heaven. Whoever fears cannot hope, because fear expects the worst. Hope expects the best. In summary – whoever fears cannot receive the healing that is locked up in the security of true intimacy.

Fear is unacceptable to God, and in His word He opposes it strongly. His biggest concern, it seems to me, is that the spirit of fear is a spirit of slavery that robs us of the blessing of Fatherhood. If we fear that God will punish us, reject us, or keep us bound in the slavery of what we owe Him, then we can't call out *Abba, Father* with confidence and claim all the benefits that being His children offers us (Romans 5:18). Fear can lead us to believe we are outsiders and orphans. This sort of fear is the fear of rejection.

God is not only opposed to our fear of rejection but also to our fear of pain and our fear of falling short. He accuses us of having little faith when we fear that He won't provide everything we need (Matthew 6). We're also not allowed to fear men (Isaiah 8:11-15 and Proverbs 29:25). When we fear men rather than finding our security in God, it reveals how small we have made God in our minds. Our images of Him are shamefully small if we think that the threats of men can compare with the saving power of the One who can calm a storm with one word.

Fear is a distortion. Fear makes us look at life through a telescope – all the small and distant people are suddenly horrifyingly close and dangerously big. Then fear hands us a pair of binoculars and makes us look at God through the wrong end of it. He becomes ever so distant and small. In believing this disproportionate representation of the threat versus our God, we find ourselves fearfully doubting where we really stand. We feel suddenly unsafe. In commanding us not to fear, God is in effect saying: *'Let Me turn around those looking glasses for you so that I can correct your perspective; I am closer than your own skin and indescribably powerful.'* In comparison to Him everyone and everything else is a powerless speck on the horizon.

Fear reveals more than a distorted image of God. It also reveals a warped image of reality.

Shortly after the burglary I was driving past our local grocery store and doing what I had been doing for days: examining the memories of that night in the way a doctor would examine a body that had fallen from a three storey building. I was systematically making sure I was still OK. I did it by going through the memories of the attack from the moment I woke up to the moment I stepped out of the hospital the next morning. I did it to check for discomfort, a tightening of my chest, possible memory fractures, signs of trouble. Everything was clear and intact. I could recall all of the night's happenings chronologically. My pulse was calm and constant. There was one exception. The recall of the very first memory of that night: the three dark figures standing behind my husband at the foot of our bed and one standing to my left with the gun to my head. This picture was so menacing that I didn't ever want to recall it again. It made my pulse race. Recalling the rape had no such effect on me, but this memory disturbed me – why? I realised that the lie of the rape had been dispelled: I was not destroyed and I knew it. This other threatening image was still lying to me, and the message it was still screaming was: *'They can come again at any time, and you will be helpless again!'*

It has been my belief for years that for healing to occur, images such as these would need to be rewritten. I'm not talking about a pop psych swindle or guided visualisation. Images such as these can't be adjusted by meditating to the tune of dolphin sounds or by losing oneself in a peaceful seaside fantasy world. The only way to extract the sting of death from this image was to ask Jesus what He had seen. If He, standing behind the puppet theatre, could give me His eternal and all seeing perspective, then I, like the toddlers at the puppet show, would be able to sigh with relief, discovering that the dragon puppets couldn't really breathe fire after all ...

I pulled my car over to the side of the road. I closed my eyes. Reluctantly I recalled the picture of that scary moment. Before I could even try to manipulate it or build an imaginary new frame around it, I instantly saw it differently. The three men behind Louis were in black suits. They looked like FBI agents with earpieces in their ears. They were huddled protectively around Louis like body guards. God seemed to say:

> *"I commanded them to make sure that not a hair would fall from Louis's head.'"*

The man next to me looked like an eight foot tall angel. I was about to argue with the Lord about this picture, because I was convinced none of these men were angels, when He seemed to say:

> *"That man with the revolver was the same man who told the others not to harm you after the rape and to put you back under the bed. When they were fighting over what to do to you, he had the instruction to save your life."*

I could look at the picture now without my heart racing, because now the picture told the truth: Not a hair on our heads gets touched without the Lord knowing all about it. As in so many stories in the Bible when God used evil people to protect His children, to provide them with everything they needed, and to give them back what they had lost, there was nothing preventing God from also handing Louis and me something beautiful and gracious through a dirty hand. An absolutely demonic Egyptian Pharaoh had to let God's people go, loading them with gifts, even when he actually wanted to kill them all ... He was not in control. He did not have a will as free as he would have loved to believe!

This new image challenged me. Why had I so readily believed that these men had been completely under the control of Satan and outside the control of God? Why did I assume that they could always come and go as they pleased and could do us any harm they intended? Were we truly at their mercy? Was this kind of thinking even Biblical?

This new image told a different story. It told of an enemy who had exercised some limited power within time and space, but who was in no way in control of our lives, our death or our destiny. Since the image was now revealing the truth, all the fear evaporated from it instantly so that I could and still can recall it without any discomfort. It did not lie anymore. It proclaimed: *'Satan has never given life. Where would he have gotten the right to take a life? He is not almighty. Where would he get the ability to do what God forbids? He is the destroyer but has not been given weapons without limits.'*

Satan lied to Jesus when he promised Him the kingdoms of the world, and he still lies every time he pretends that he can rule over those of us on this earth who belong to Jesus. Through Jesus, we have conquered all evil, and because of His victory over the grave, we too, are no longer victims (1 John 2:14).

Satan uses fear in a plethora of ways but always with one primary purpose: to destroy our intimacy with one another and with Jesus. He convinces us not to confess sin to our spouse by scaring us into thinking about how negatively our spouse will react. In the same way he advises us not to grow closer to God, because he tries to convince us that God is angry with us or will be put off by who we really are. He throws a black shroud over certain threats and marks them with a skull and crossbones, hissing at us through his teeth: *'Those things are simply too dark or too scary. Your God is not there. If those things should ever happen to you, you would never recover from them. Walking there, you'd be walking alone!'*

For some, the shroud is ominously cast over cancer, the loss of a child or parent, unemployment, homelessness, the unfaithfulness of a spouse ... For me it was rape. I had always believed it would be the one place too deep, too dark and too devastating. Several times I thought how I would prefer a rapist to just cut my throat, thinking I would prefer death to living with memories of a rape. Surprisingly, Jesus came and used that very black shroud as a backdrop. On it He painted the clearest picture of His face I have ever seen. The event that should have destroyed me became the most love-affirming experience with my God.

I suspect many people have in similar fashion met God in the very place Satan said they would be abandoned by Him. The black shroud is a lie. God is Light – everywhere.

Whenever I pray with women about hurt in their past, they have the same excuses: *'I don't want to 'go there.' It will swallow me whole. It is a can of worms I cannot afford to open. It will destroy me. It will destroy others to find out about this ...* 'The list is endless but very predictable. It is Satan's skull and crossbones. But to me it is like the little flags pushed into the ground on an archaeologist's site. It screams, *'Dig here!'* And when we go back there together with the loving Christ, the shroud gets lifted and freedom comes.

If we want intimacy with God and with our spouse, it will require of us to choose against other loves and to choose against fear. And there is also another intruder we have to fight against: shame. Intimacy crumbles when unhealthy shame enters the relationship. The feeling of scandal and humiliation drives away any intimacy that could be between people or people and their God.

We absolutely have to be unashamed. It is not the same as being shameless. Think of a seductive pole dancer dancing for another woman's husband. She is shameless. She would do well to have a little shame. A healthy amount of shame can bring us closer to God's righteousness, but shamefulness always drives a wedge between us and God. True guilt leads to repentance, but false shame leads to a break in relationships.

Leviticus 16 distinguishes between the two as it describes the sacrifices on the Day of Atonement. Two animals were involved – one was slaughtered to pay for the true guilt of sin, and the other was used to pay for the shame of a guilty conscience. The first goat was slain and the blood sprinkled on the altar. The offering took care of the guilt. The second goat received the shame on its head and was sent into the desert as a symbol of that shame needing to depart from everyone's sight. It proclaimed what God says so many times – the removal of our sins as far as the east is from the west, the drowning of our sin in the sea of His grace, the kind forgetfulness of a merciful God who promises not to think about it again ...

It is tragic when we sacrifice the sin goat, and accept forgiveness for our sin, but then we chain the shame goat to a stake in our backyard. Every day we look at it, we blush a shameful blush all over again and beat ourselves up. W feed that goat our peace and joy. Many Christians still live with their goats of shame, thinking God is reserving judgement for them. This naturally destroys all intimacy and hope for a shame-free relationship. The goats' constant bleating in the backyard makes it impossible to look into God the Father's face.

If my relationship with Jesus had been full of shame and disgrace, He would still have been able to help me during the rape, but I wouldn't have been able to lift my head, call out to Him and take His helping hand, because people suffering from shame are always staring down at the ground around their feet.

Unfortunately many marriages are full of shame and disgrace. It happens when couples rub one another's noses in their past mistakes, the way I would have liked to rub our naughty dachshund's nose in the puddles he made on my carpet. It brings humiliation. It undermines trust, and it makes intimacy completely impossible. We're not allowed to go after their shame goats after having forgiven our spouse for a misstep against us. We should never go after the goats of shame, bringing them back into remembrance and into our backyard. Who could ever be intimate with their spouse while goats bleat in the background? Some of us keep these goats so that when someone who had wronged us dares to ask us a favour, we can kick the goat in the ribs, making it bleat on our behalf: *'Actually you have no right because you still owe me!'*

Forgiveness is the opposite. It is taking the bleating goats from you who wronged me and walking them off into the wilderness for you, helping you forgive yourself and helping all of us to forget in the way God forgets. We stop telling the story that makes the other person hang his head. We make peace with the fact that the guilty person may one day forget what he did to us. We are OK with him forgetting that he owes us. We stop insisting on a constant apology or grovelling. We say: *'Never say you are sorry about this again. Once is enough, because the guilt goat has stopped bleating. Now give me that shame goat and I will take it into the desert for you.'*

Shame can also enter our marriages when we try and force one another to act against our own healthy shyness. Sometimes marriage counsellors have wild, hot ideas of how to spice up our nights in the bedroom, but some couples blush at the very thought of them. When some women (and men) try out the counsellor's tricks at home, it leaves them with even more shame, because when people give up their healthy shyness, or when they force others to give up theirs, this induces shame.

Some of us feel ashamed more readily than others. If we put the very shy married person who gets dressed in the closest on one end of the scale, and the person who shamelessly walks around naked in the house on the other end, then most of us are somewhere in the middle. We need to respect the boundaries of our spouses and not expect everything that happens in the bedroom to be equally comfortable for both people. Intimacy means both parties feel safe.

Of course there are unnatural forms of shyness that call for healing. When the slightest thing makes us feel exposed, we should seek help and healing.

In my marriage there has never been any pressure to cross shameful boundaries. We prefer a spontaneous intimacy where we both feel free and safe and no one has to cross his or her own boundaries in order to put a smile on the other person's face. That would almost be like rape and sexual slavery, wouldn't it? Rape, unless perpetrated purely to hurt another or as a hate crime, is misusing someone else's body for your own pleasure. This is why some women may feel dirty instead of sexy after dancing around a pole on their husband's insistence. These same women might feel differently if it were their idea, and they had gone for pole dancing classes without feeling forced. A woman with no dignity feels ugly, cheap and dirty. A man who tries to push her across her own boundaries of shyness will soon discover the repercussions of such actions. She will respond to him as though he were a rapist.

I'm convinced that if I had ever felt forced, felt shame or felt lust during my intimate moments with my husband, it would have resonated with my rape. I believe I would have struggled after the rape to accept his arms as a safe place. If he had ever looked at me as a chunk of flesh as the rapist did, I would have felt an urge to flee. If he had ever thought that it was okay to mumble *I want* and then take what he wanted from me because he considered it his married right as a husband, I would never have been able to separate him from the rapist in my head. If he had been the kind of man who hastily rips off my underwear like an animal, I would have seen the beastliness of the rapist in him and would probably have never been able to erase that image. There is nothing wrong with enthusiasm, but a woman shouldn't feel like helpless prey. I praise the Lord for a marriage that had and still has true intimacy without that kind of shame.

Force and demands also have no place in our relationship with God. This intimate relationship shouldn't rest on preconditions or demands. We read in Psalm 78:18 how the people of God angered Him because they stubbornly demanded the food they desired. They tested God, and He punished them for it.

One of Jesus' temptations in the desert was this same temptation – the temptation to test God. Satan told Jesus to jump off the temple roof and make God catch Him. He was tempted to force God's hand into doing an unnecessary miracle. Jesus discerned this, and His response was: "You shall not test the Lord your God."

Even in our relationship with God, we are tempted at times to involve God in a game in which we try to force God's hand. Some people pray like this: *'Lord, please make this business deal fall through if it is not Your will'* or *'stop me from marrying the wrong man.'* And then they jump off the temple roof by signing the contract or wearing the ring. God now has to catch them if He does not like their decision. It is a sin. In a mature and intimate relationship, we don't manipulate the other person in such a way.

To be expectant in a relationship is not the same as having fixed expectations. We're allowed to have full confidence in God's character and in His intentions. In fact, God welcomes it when we expect the impossible from Him. He encourages this through Paul's words in Ephesians 3:20 where we are reminded that He can do much more than we could ever hope, dream or imagine. A list of expectations, on the other hand, turns the intimate relationship into a calculated game, a business deal, or a hostage situation where a ransom demand is made. An intimate relationship will be destroyed very effectively by the words: *'If you love me, you will ...'*

Many couples may feel that they've gotten rid of their other loves, their fears, their shame and every unfair demand in their marriage, but they still experience that something is hindering them from living in fearless intimacy. Oftentimes the barrier is secrets. Nothing destroys intimacy like keeping a secret. And yet, few things can tie hearts together in deeper intimacy than the sharing of a secret. A secret concealed alone in one heart is dangerous and introduces division. The secret a spouse shares with a third party of the marriage is like a poisonous spider in the marriage bed. It can harm either or both, and it is never quite sure who will get bitten and when. It is always just a matter of time. The fact that you know it's there does not make you immune to the venom.

We can learn a lot from God about secrets. God eagerly shares His secrets with those who love Him; He also expects us to completely open up our hearts to Him (Psalm 25:14, 32:2-5). Even though He knows everything about us, something wonderful happens in our relationship when we sit at His feet and honestly share the secrets of our hearts with Him. We can share secret fears with Him: "Lord, today I feel especially weak and discouraged. I know I should remember how You have picked me up from this place in the past, but today I just wonder what would become of me if You don't intervene quickly and miraculously." We can share secret wishes with Him: "Lord, every now and then I catch myself fantasizing about a quaint little cottage in the countryside with fig trees in the backyard and a swing on the porch ... Could such a peaceful retirement be awaiting me?" We can voice secret disappointments: "Lord, I know it was by my own choosing, but this job that I'm telling everybody I love is not actually enjoyable. I'm too proud to admit it to my friends, but I'm going to tell You the truth: I think I made a mistake. I should never have resigned from my old job."

When the doors of our hearts are swung open wide like this, we discover the doors of God's heart are also wide open. At this vulnerable, intimate, secret place many people hear God's voice for the first time. They hear Him in a unique way. This unique language between God and a person develops over a period of time. This secret place is the place of true worship. It is comparable to the marriage bed. What happens there will be magnificently personal and sacred and unlike the relationship God has with anyone else.

In the same way that a couple in love often have their own theme song which becomes a part of their love story, we can also develop theme songs with the Lord because of the secrets we share. Instead of all the flashing memories of pain, there are moments that make us smile because we see or hear something only we and the Lord know about.

I have a friend who loves feathers and who firmly believes that the Lord speaks to her by sending beautiful bird feathers her way. While telling me this, she was at a particularly tough place in her life and desperate for encouragement from God. We were seated in a tea garden and a magnificent feather was just on the other side of the fence. A forbidding sign in large print stood between her and the feather. A few minutes later a baby accidently tossed its pacifier over the fence. The dad, knowing that naptime without the precious item would be like slow suicide with a cap gun, hopped over the fence in defiance of the sign, picked up the treasure, then spun around:

"Anything I can do for you ladies while I'm on this side of the fence?"

What are the chances this was coincidence? This man could not possibly have known what a feather would mean to my friend. But God knew, and Jesus showed up prince-like with a feather for His beloved in one hand and a pacifier for a baby in the other ... or would you say I'm reading too much into it?

In Jeremiah 33:3 God promises to share secrets with us that no one else knows about. We often see the exchange of secrets between God and His good friends. God confides in Abraham before He destroys Sodom and Gomorrah (Genesis 18); He sends Gabriel to tell Daniel all that will happen with the city – including its destruction (Daniel 9:20-27). I find it very moving to read how the angel tells Daniel that God loves him passionately before he tells him the secret plans of God (v 23). Secrets are for lovers. Even dark secrets.

That, I suppose, is why I felt such intimacy with Jesus when He reminded me of His love just minutes before the rape. He reminded me that it was the love a bridegroom has for his bride. This secret message helped me realise what was about to happen next. It is as though Jesus was carrying the secret. He knew what was written into my life's story because He is all-knowing. I didn't know because I'm human. By telling me just in time for me to prepare myself, He strengthened my relationship with Him and our intimacy. We shared a secret. I experienced special love with the sharing of that secret, even though it was a painful one. Daniel's secrets, delivered by God with such a declaration of love, were equally dark and foreboding — actually much worse.

People are very upset when I talk about this. They feel that a loving God who could see it coming should have stopped it. Some think it strange that He would warn me with such short notice and leave me no time to escape. Others refuse to believe that God would give bad news ahead of time unless He intends to give, along with it, a key for escape. These people must not have read through the prophetic books of the Bible. God continually warned His people – against both avoidable and unavoidable events. Even Jesus agonized in the garden of Gethsemane because He was warned. His Father shared with Him the death that He was about to die. Jesus was terrified. The warning doesn't always take away the fear, but it does help us to remember that God knows everything before it happens. When horrible events start playing themselves out on the stage of our puppet theatre, we are comforted by the knowledge that the script comes as no surprise to our Almighty God who loves us enough to talk to us through it all.

Someone used the image once of a man burning his hand on a hot stove and experiencing pain. It's not traumatic, just painful, because he could see it coming. Imagine if the stove had crawled down the passage in the middle of the night and burned him full of blisters in bed ... now that would have been traumatic! That's the difference between pain and trauma. You see pain coming. Trauma catches you by surprise. Jesus experienced tremendous pain on the cross – but not the shock of trauma, because He knew what was coming. It's because of this knowing, however, that He sweated great drops of blood!

I don't like surprises. Sometimes surprises can be traumatic for me. God knows this, because He made me like this. My love language is advance notice. He merely spoke my love language to me. My intimacy with Him would have been damaged if I had felt that He hadn't prepared or warned me at all. If we had talked about all the things in my life except the rape, then what type of a relationship would we have had? The secrets that He shared with me in the months before the rape (even though I did not know at the time that all the Bible references to being washed and picked up and rescued would pertain to me on this specific night) were written down in my journal as grounds for this assurance: If God knew and spoke beforehand and was with me and spoke in the moment, won't He also be my God all the way to the end? My declarations of trust in Him, which were also written down in my journal, stand as proof of our intimate relationship ... the relationship in which I, the sheep, had heard and am still hearing His voice.

While heading up the community upliftment project in Proclamation Hill, I prayed often with children who were being sexually abused by family members. I had to watch them walk home in the afternoon to drunk, abusive fathers. I had to watch them being picked up for a weekend at Grandma and Grandpa's house, remembering the little prayer notes they had mailed into the prayer post box: *'Jesus, I don't want to go to Grandpa's house anymore because he hurts me.'* The social workers that I reported this to were too tired, too hardened or too caught up in red tape to stop this from happening. It seemed like no-one could help or even wanted to try. All I could do was pray with them and hug them and be a pair of safe arms.

I will never forget one little girl. She was a challenge. Her violent outbursts were such that one had to suspect some kind of abuse. She was seven years old at the time, but when she lost her temper we could not hold her down. I called in the help of an experienced counsellor. She asked the little girl if she wanted to hear a Bible story. She picked the story about David and Goliath. She explained her choice:

> *"There is a giant in my life, too. And he hurts me."*

After reading the story they prayed and the counsellor asked her about the giant. She flinched and recalled those scary nights of abuse by her stepdad. She closed her eyes, sat quietly, then suddenly her face lit up:

"Jesus says the giant will only come one more time and Jesus will be with me. Then the giant will be gone and never come back."

I was so worried about this. What if Jesus didn't take the stepdad away? What would happen with this little girl's faith? What if Jesus was only there in her imagination and hadn't really spoken to her? Why did the counsellor allow her to go home with such false hope?

But that weekend things unfolded just as she had said: Her stepdad came again. She held onto Jesus' words. She believed Him. She did not feel fearful and abandoned. She believed that the secret Jesus told her was true. She woke up the next morning to hear that her mother had no idea where the stepdad had gone. His belongings were missing, too. He wasn't coming back.

Three years later, the last time I saw her, he was still missing. The rage with which she had struggled was gone. The truth, namely that Jesus had known everything and told her the truth directly, had washed over her like a shower of purifying water. This washing had coloured all of her horrific memories with a new colour, because she had gotten to know a God who told her the truth. She trusted and loved Jesus. She felt safe and saved.

We shout and rebel against a story like this. *"It's not good enough,"* we say. *"It shouldn't have happened to this little girl even once. It should have been prevented the first time."* If we can forget about how we would have run her life if we were God and look into her eyes, we would see that she is far from bitter and upset. She is living with joy, freedom and healing. In the midst of the most horrifying abuse of intimacy, she experienced true intimacy with Jesus. This kind of intimacy is restorative. This is paradise spilling over into the hell of real life, transforming it forever. If someday later in her life she finds an echo of the old pain, she won't approach it with despair but with expectancy that Jesus will speak to her again and will come to her as He did before.

Of course lies also destroy intimacy, and as long as they are around, we will have no Eden. In Isaiah 30:12 God warned His people because they had silenced the prophets who had brought bad news, which prohibited them from speaking the painful truth. They had commanded the prophets to bring only comforting news. That's why their lives had been built on lies, Those walls slowly cracked and were now tumbling in, destroying everything and everyone that had built on falsehood as a foundation. Lies are always like that. They create illusions of safety, and eventually the very things that are supposed to protect us fall in on us and crush us.

The most dangerous lies are the ones we believe about God. We believe things that He never said in His Word. Things He did say, we often refuse to believe. We also find for ourselves modern-day prophets to soothe our ears with sweet-sounding messages that paint God in our own image. In this way, we build a theology for ourselves that will not withstand the shaking of a life and death crisis.

Jeremiah 9:3 warns us that when we start loving lies, our tongues start speaking them, too. Before long, we won't be able to speak the truth about God anymore. When we lie long enough, we lose the ability to recognise the truth and to know God. He is the Truth.

We all know people like this: deluded people who have lost touch with reality, having chosen to believe their own lies. There is an alternative – the truth that sets us free (John 8:31) – the truth that tells us who God really is and who we really are:

> **It's in Christ that you, once you heard the truth and believed it (this message of your salvation), found yourselves home free — signed, sealed, and delivered by the Holy Spirit. This signet from God is the first instalment on what's coming, a reminder that we'll get everything God has planned for us, a praising and glorious life.**
>
> (Ephesians 1:13, *The Message*)

That night in my room, God spoke the truth to me. It set me free from all the lies the situation could have told me. The fact that He lovingly warned me, dissolved all the lies that I could have believed – lies that could have said He hadn't noticed me, He hadn't been there or even cared.

That last lie – the lie that no-one cares – is a primary destroyer of intimacy in marriage. Often it's due to a misunderstanding, ignorance, emotional immaturity, or maybe just some divided attention that makes us feel unloved. The pain makes us rock hard, aggressive, and cold. It becomes more and more difficult for someone else to love us – all because we so readily believed the lie. Feeling unloved becomes being unlovable.

In our relationship with the Lord, this lie is the slyest of them all, because it questions the very essence of God. If He is not Love, as He claims to be in 1 John 4:8, where does that put you and me? What could be more terrifying than to be in the hands of a loveless God? I think J.I. Packer said he could think of only one thing: to be in the hands of a loveless God with endless power. Many people live with such a distorted image of God. He is God. He is Almighty, but He is not personal, they believe. As long as they experience God as cold and distant, they will unfortunately never experience intimacy with God despite their best efforts. And without intimacy, there will be no healing.

I once met a man who had been molested by his tennis coach over a long period of time. He had walked with secret shame and rage until he was in his mid-forties, because the lie that God hadn't been there, and that He didn't care, can often be just the beginning. If one first starts doubting God's character and ones' own self-worth, then the other lies start streaming in: *'It was your fault because you never screamed for help. Nobody wants to hear this story – it is too terrible. The coach is a respected man; nobody will believe you. It happened so long ago – let sleeping dogs lie. Don't open up the can of worms.'* The result is pain heaped upon the injury and feelings of powerlessness and of shame.

This man told me about one special day when he was reading God's Word, praying and journaling. He recalled his painful history and everything boiled over onto the page in his journal. He saw himself scribbling the words that must have been screaming inside him all those years but that he didn't even dare to pray:

> *"Where the hell were You?!"*

In the blink of an eye, he felt himself lying pinned down under the heavy body of the tennis coach. He felt as trapped and powerless as all those years ago. It was as though

God was taking him back to that moment to rewrite it. His head was turned away from the coach's face, and he could see a cross planted right next to him in the ground. Jesus was nailed to the cross. He was bleeding. Jesus was so close that he could have stretched out his hand and touch Him. Jesus didn't say a word, but the way He was looking at this hurting man made him see that Jesus saw – really *saw* – everything. He cared. He was bleeding for it right at that moment.

Many people still live with a distorted image of God like this man had lived with for years. They believe Jesus is strong but not necessarily on their side. He is all-powerful but not all-loving. When this man saw the pain Jesus felt for Him and saw that the cross was meant for that moment, his life changed forever.

Lies that we believe about God and pains that we carry from our past are like strips of Velcro stitched onto us. None of us can afford to walk around like that. It gets caught on everything. It collects fluff and pet hair ... It prevents us from progressing, from forgiving, from becoming whole and from dislodging our pain. It attaches itself to so many heavy things, that later we struggle to get close to other people and they struggle to get close to us. It robs us of all hope of true intimacy. It damages our relationship with God by causing something very small but destructive – a sense of separation.

If we don't effectively fight against these (other loves, fear, shame, secrets and lies), we can get robbed by these intimacy eaters until we are doomed to resort to a life of counterfeits of intimacy – like cheap sex, virtual relationships, or each married partner doing their own thing. If we are secretly filled with fear, shame, keeping damaging secrets, or believing lies, we can sit in church for years and never experience first-hand the reality of God. It's a lot like the fig leaves that Adam and Eve once wove together: at least we don't feel naked. But like real leaves, these too will shrivel up and shrink until finally our shame won't be covered anymore. Living like this can never return lost paradise to us.

It's worth fighting for true intimacy with each other and with God, because it's the place where we can be effectively prepared – even for a rape, where we can rest – even during a rape, and where we can return safely – even after a rape. This is true paradise.

13 To hear God speak

It's the morning of the Turn2God event. The municipality has decided that a torch would be a fire hazard, so I will be carrying a flag with flames on it, instead, leading a procession of runners and cyclists who have come from the four corners of the country to meet at the Union Buildings – all bearing flags and the Turn2God logo as a symbol of the entire country's return to God.

In South Africa, God is not always acknowledged as the final authority. We suffer dearly for that and the day will be all about praying for this to change. The organisers have asked me to represent the thousands of victims of crime in South Africa who also need to turn to God for healing, as those behind the crime and corruption need to turn to God for forgiveness. Besides this proclamation I also want to proclaim this message: Even if there would be no noticeable change in our crime statistics and in the godlessness of many in government, yet we will turn our hearts to God in expectation and praise. By God's grace we won't be embittered and will pray incessantly against the darkness that threatens daily to envelop our country. We will intercede for our government as we continue to implore them to bend their knees before Jesus, but we will not revolt, knowing that God's Word is clearly against it. We will declare that the Bride of Christ will not be destroyed by the evil in our country. We pray she will rise again after every setback to walk uprightly and fearlessly, declaring that Jesus is the only hope for South Africa.

I strike up a conversation with my fellow flag bearer before the start of the ceremony. He tells me how his wife has been in a deep coma for the past two years, how the two of them had always run races together, and of the many adventures they had experienced before a mishap during minor surgery rendered her comatose and irresponsive. He tells how the Lord Jesus had turned his life around during the accident. In shock and anger in an ominous hospital hallway, he had a meeting with Love. Talking with someone who had experienced the same thing I have – life changing Love in the pitch black darkness – refreshes me.

We talk fast and excitedly, sharing our understanding of what it means to us to live a Spirit-led life. We both found it hard to explain to people who had not experienced a supernatural encounter with a God who breaks human laws of logic. People won't take my word for it that a healthy spirit in a raped body can spill wellness into one's entire being, simply because God has designed us all along to be led and ruled primarily from the spiritual core of our being. This new friend gets it and has been living with this realisation and conviction for much longer than I have.

His wife, a beautiful sleeping princess, is still alive without the aid of machines – which means her spirit isn't with God yet, but still with him and their children at home. Hopeful and beaming with visible love for her, he does everything for her at home. Her body has lost the ability to love him and their girls affectionately although her soul can no longer shine through her eyes or speak through her lips. Yet my friend tells me he is convinced her spirit hears everything he tells her. I'm equally convinced it's true, since it was with my spirit that I heard God's love that night in the midst of all the voices – the threats, the noises of the robbers ransacking our home, my own heartbeat and breathing, and Louis's intermittent prayers. My physical ears could only hear these things. Spirit words from God's Spirit to mine, however, were what called me to life and joy and gratitude on the inside.

This young man's sacrificial love, choosing not to leave his bride to waste away in an institution, but rather to spend the prime of his life caring for her, lifting her into the bath every morning, washing her, combing her hair ... reminds me of Jesus' love for His bride. In many ways we are all like this precious woman – incapable of doing anything without Jesus, our Bridegroom, unable to love Him or really do anything for Him in our own power. Our very existence rests on the fact that He chose not to leave us but to love us. He nurtures us, washes us clean from the filth we lived in before we knew Him and has hope that we will one day wake up from our slumber. He sees past our wilted souls and dying bodies and calls our immortal spirit to come alive and to love Him.

To wave a flag with this brave man, who lives very literally not by what is seen but what is unseen, is an honour.

Pastor Elza Meyer, founder and visionary leader of the Turn2God movement, is on stage to share the vision for Turn2God that the Lord has given her. The leader of the Democratic Alliance, Helen Zille, sits to the front and left of the stage under a little gazebo that is not quite up to the onslaught of the African sun. Someone hands her and other dignitaries chilled bottled water every hour or so. She is the leader of our country's strongest opposition party and one of the very few government leaders who accepted the invitation to commit South Africa to God with us on this day. Being in government, she probably sees the need for restoration, justice, truth and forgiveness more clearly than many of us normal citizens.

Between speeches and fervent prayers, Louis, along with a few other artists and a choir, sings the songs he had completed recording in his studio just minutes before the robbers tied him up. I remember how Louis told me that they cleaned out the studio, taking every piece of sound equipment and every computer, except this hard drive with the completed CD recording on it. As if commanded to do so, they unplugged it and left it on the floor. Today we have these Turn2God CD's with their powerful message as another testimony to the wonderful truth that evil and crime in South Africa will never get the better of the Good News of Jesus Christ.

While in the refreshment tent behind the stage, I start a conversation with Retief Burger, one of our dear friends and a wonderful worship pastor. He expresses the shock he felt as he heard the news of our robbery.

"Hettie, I felt physically sick. I told God: 'It can't be. It's too much. I can't accept it!' Do you know what God showed me? He showed me the rapist on top of you and asked me: 'Retief, of these two people, who do I love the most?'"

The shock at his own words is still evident on his face. I reassure him that this question and it's answer don't upset me. In fact, it is precisely what I experienced in the room that night. God's ultimate act of love in the form of Jesus' sacrificial death was reaching out equally to two broken people – to the rapist, with a willingness to redeem, and to me with a willingness to restore. Whether we embrace it or not is a different story. God has never been repulsed by any person's impurity. In fact, Jesus seems repulsed by the religious and instead attracted to sinners and those ostracized. He touches and is touched by prostitutes, lepers, tax collectors, poor fishermen, the demon possessed, and adulterers. He is unimpressed with any person's attempt to become "holy" on their own terms.

God's undiscriminating love did not distinguish between the rapist and me. The difference between us is that I have accepted with great thankfulness that which Jesus held out to me – salvation and healing – but my rapist is probably still in the same broken state he had been in when he entered my home half-drunk. He is the one that needs a love revelation the most.

Pastor Elza's daughter joins us in the refreshment tent. She notices me taking my antiretroviral drugs on the hour as I have to do every twelve hours. She has had to take the same medication after an accidental needle prick during her internship as a medical doctor. She smiles sympathetically.

"I bet those make you feel really sick?"

"Actually I have noticed only a slight light-headedness. No nausea or head-aches so far!"

"You are extremely fortunate! I actually came to tell you that Helen Zille wants to speak with you. She saw the newspaper reports and wants to know how you and Louis are doing."

What a privilege! How humble of her to want to speak to me. It's another opportunity that I would never have had under different circumstances. Who would have thought a rape would unlock the door to such an opportunity? For a while now I had secretly dreamt of an opportunity to speak with someone in our government, to have a face to face meeting with these decision makers. I believed it would make it easier to pray, support and vote in an informed way.

I rush to the little gazebo and take a seat on the available white plastic chair next to Me Zille. The introduction is surprisingly comfortable. It must be her humility. She gracefully asks a few safe, empathetic questions and gives me the opportunity to tell her what the Lord had done for us. I can see she wants to believe me and that my testimony is cemented onto a spiritual foundation that has already been laid in her heart. I realise she is present at this event for more than a politically correct public appearance. She wants to be here. She wants to acknowledge the higher government that we all have to submit to. I can hear it as she explains her desire to see this country change. She wishes me well, and I leave shaking my head with the cliché ringing in my mind: *God works in mysterious ways.*

A young Christian entrepreneur, the one serving us with the wonderful water, brings me two ice cold bottles. Immediately I recognize him. He was in his senior year of high school when Louis and I led a youth camp at his church. We were newlyweds and probably too young for this responsibility. Yet, during that camp a number of young men gave their lives to the Lord. If I remember correctly he was one of the few who already knew and loved the Lord and who passionately prayed with us for the salvation of his friends. He celebrated with us when the ringleader of the tough guys responded first, jumped to his feet and dared the others to stand up in surrender to Jesus.

> *"Hettie, I have to tell you something about the night of the robbery. I was tossing and turning in my bed – wide awake. Usually I interpret that as a call to intercede for someone. Your name and Louis's were in my mind but having lost touch so long ago I did not know what or how to pray for you. I heard the Lord say that I should go to the gas station and buy a newspaper. I got dressed and did just that. It was filled with crime reports. I prayed along the lines of protection for you and your children and then fell asleep in the early morning hours."*

Getting up at that hour, driving to the gas station, praying for hours ... I'm astounded by such obedience. I'll drive to the shop at night for a yummy chocolate, but not that easily for prayer tips. I am once again so grateful for his sacrifice and prayer, which, along with the prayers of many other faithful prayer warriors, made a very real difference for us.

Thousands of people are still sitting in the sun, sharing the gravity of this day. At Pastor Meyer's request they stand in unison, stretch out their hands in the direction of our government buildings, pray together, sing together, and declare together that Jesus will rule in South Africa. Underneath those very government buildings, in that very soil is the innocent blood of many. Underground chambers once echoed with the cries of torture and despair in the era of Apartheid. Inside those buildings are the ones walking with the sceptre that could be pointed in one of two directions: the path that could bring an end to the intolerable level of injustice in our country or the path that could take us back to the dark place where people fall into cycles of vengeance upon vengeance.

For years we've been standing on this line between two possibilities: reconciliation or destruction. Today we pray that we will all give up our apathetic, defensive positions and do everything in our power to create momentum in the direction of reconciliation. The first step will always be to cultivate a forgiving heart. Anyone hoping to help heal this land must start there.

We go home after a long, intense day, thankful and convinced that God had, through His grace, blessed our insufficient, human efforts to change something in our country.

It has been more than a month since the burglary. The messages are still streaming in, and there is no sign of life returning to normal, at least not yet. I just want to get through all of this and continue on with my life, because if I am not able to do my work, then it may drive me off my rocker more than any trauma could. For someone like me, work is therapeutic.

An old childhood friend sends me a message on Facebook and asks me to phone her so she can give me some good advice concerning my antiretroviral medicine. She is an HIV specialist. I phone her, and during our conversation she suggests that I take an extra antiretroviral drug. It's still a few weeks before my next blood test and, according to her, we can do even better than the standard medication. She gives me more good news. According to her understanding, HIV is more treatable than diabetes. HIV medicine is so advanced, she says, that they can now treat people who have tested positive to such an extent that the virus count can drop so low that subsequent tests start showing negative results even though the virus is still present. Because of this effective suppression of the virus, transfer becomes unlikely. Accounts have been recorded of HIV-positive people not infecting their spouses after five years of treatment, and without using condoms, since the virus had been effectively brought under control. Of course these patients and their spouses were monitored and religiously faithful to the administration of the medication. Naturally this is not realistic in most of Africa, which is the reason why the pandemic still claims hundreds of lives on the continent every day.

I am very glad to hear that even an unfavourable outcome in this respect would still not be a death sentence. I share my excitement as I pick up the prescribed tablets from our local pharmacy. The pharmacist agrees. Treatment for HIV & AIDS has made huge leaps. Up until now nausea hasn't been a problem, so I expect it to stay that way. I have also been through three and a half pregnancies without feeling any nausea, so this has left me bravely optimistic. In fact, my appetite is very healthy, and I am excited to be invited to dinner with friends from church. I add half a pizza and most of a can of sweetened condensed milk to the first dose of the new tablet combination.

It turns out to have been a bad idea. Now I know how the rest of the people on antiretroviral medication feel. It takes me several minutes every morning to scrape together the courage to move. Whenever I tilt my head forward or back so that I can wash my hair, nausea washes over my like a tsunami. I also discover that my hair is falling out in big handfuls, which apparently is a known side-effect. Unfortunately any sideways motion immediately triggers vomiting, so my movement options are limited. It must look pathetic to see me sitting in the bathtub, balls of frothing shampoo in my face, taking aim at the toilet which is of course out of reach. This morning it took a whole hour to finish bathing; I felt like I had bathed a hundred unruly two-year-olds, I was so exhausted. Picking up the hair dryer was enough to send me running back to the bathroom. I did it twice and then gave up, letting the dreary locks dry in droopy dullness. Fortunately, I only have to take these pills for one week and then must stop for two weeks so that the blood test will be accurate.

There is also something else bugging me: strange, anonymous text messages that began about a week ago. First, they were blank, and later there were just three kisses. No words, no name, just "XXX". Then came outrageous suggestions to meet this person somewhere. Initially I thought it was just teenage nonsense – a naughty boy who had gotten hold of his mother's spare SIM card, which happened to have my number on it, or something to that effect.

Today the content of the text message is simply vulgar and almost threatening. I'm not so sure that it is just teenager nonsense. The frequency of the messages isn't one or two per day anymore. There were twenty the other night. It makes no difference whether I ask to be left alone or don't respond at all – the messages keep coming. My phone automatically displays at least the first six or seven words of every text message that comes through, making it impossible to delete it without seeing at least a part of it.

One by one I contact all of the cell phone companies. The only way they will help me block this sick person's number is if I have a case number from the police. At the same time all of the companies claim that the number is not registered on their networks. How is that possible? He must be using one of their networks. This man is clever, I realise, and maybe even dangerous. He speaks Afrikaans, which rules out the suspects from the burglary.

Louis and I warn him that he should stop since our calls are monitored by the police (who are trying to locate our duplicate SIM cards). He promises to stop. With a lame apology and fake sympathy he is back in full swing a day or two later. We try to call him in order to be more persuasive, but the phone keeps ringing without going to voicemail or an engaged beep. It is highly unusual.

A relatively uneventful week has passed, and I am off the awful cocktail of antiretroviral drugs. I can even stomach coffee again, which I have with a really good friend. Just as I leave the mall and open the car door, my phone beeps again for the tenth time today.

> *"You look cute."*

I did go through a bit of extra trouble with my appearance this morning, seeing as I can finally do the necessary without running to the bathroom every other minute. Is he watching me? Then why would the other text messages ask me who I am, where I live, whether I like pearls and what I look like?

Sometimes this cyber stalker's messages are incoherent as if he's drunk and confused. He is grateful for what happened the previous evening. *What?!* As if I should know what he is referring to! It makes me really mad. I could ignore all the crazy questions, but this is too much. I decide to respond by texting him a question:

> *"Who are you?"*

His response sent chills up my spine:

> "Satan travelling through Africa."

What if my phone should lie around and someone would come across these suspicious messages? The combination of people's predictions that my trauma would start showing somewhere, my confession of an emotional tie with another man, and messages like "thank you for last night", might eventually start eroding Louis's trust in me as a spouse. It's difficult to believe that only a few months ago my life had been characterized by innocence, purity and naivety. Now it's full of all sorts of ugliness.

I'm trying to hear the Lord's voice, but it's getting more and more difficult. There are too many other voices. I need wisdom, but the vilest and most unwise words I have ever heard stream to my own phone like a deafening buzz. I need to get away from everything. The text messages are not the only noise. The phone calls are still coming in, too. At least most of the calls are friendly. People are inviting us to go to the coast. People with holiday homes from the Kruger National Park all the way to Cape Town are offering them to us for a break-away. It's not the right time, we feel, simply because we will continue to fall even further behind with our work which has already begun piling up. But our family really needs a break. We are struggling to regain our normal routine and yearning for quiet.

Some good friends offer us their holiday club points for a week in the Drakensberg Mountains, spanning over my birthday. We decide to accept this gracious gift. While there, both of our mobile phones are cut off. When trying to make a call, we hear: *'Your service has been suspended. Your account is over the credit limit.'* After figuring out how to contact client services, we get a simple explanation:

> *"You have both made thousands of rand worth of calls that exceed the limit. Many are international calls."*

We explain once again the situation with the duplicate SIM cards after the robbery, and they switch our phones back on again, effective twelve hours later. Within an hour of our phones being switched back on, the system detects the same huge debt on our account and we are automatically cut off again. It continues like this for days. Of course we feel very disconnected. Pun intended.

It takes me a while before I realise how wonderful it is and that this is exactly what I need. I make peace with the phonelessness and recalibrate my spirit to a frequency at which God's voice will be more audible.

Each day my son chooses a new hiking route. We climb every hill in the area. Every minute I spend with him is precious, because we now know how quickly it could have been taken away from us. The children ride horses, drive a few golf balls with Louis, and all complete a junior wall climbing certificate programme with the resort's local adventure centre. I train for a two mile swim that is due to take place on the day after our return. At night, Louis and I talk about everything going on in our hearts. We read, we recover long lost sleep, and we have special times together.

Our stay extends over a long weekend which means accommodation is fully booked everywhere, so we need to look for another place to stay overnight for our last day – my birthday. We stumble across an idyllic little place with a typical English veranda on which they serve flavoured teas and scones with cream and jam at tea time. We feel very young amongst the guests here, as we are the only ones swimming and playing table tennis. The other guests gaze longingly at the youthfulness that radiates from our children who never stop moving.

Louis knows me well and has my birthday present figured out in a jiffy – a single voucher to do the Canopy Tours in the Drakensberg. The heights as well as the speed with which one shoots in your harness across dizzying ravines is exactly what the doctor ordered. While zipping between the tree tops from platform to platform, the women in front of and behind me – probably now acutely aware of all their fears – start talking about the violence and crime in our country. The conversation heads in the direction of the wave of recent killing sprees in the province of Gauteng. They are all thankful they don't live there.

They ask me what it's like for me, being from the crime capital. I share my experience of feeling safe in the midst of extreme danger that night. At each new platform in between the trees, while hooking and unhooking our harnesses, they ask me more questions about fear, faith, bitterness and forgiveness. One of the men on the technical team asks me whether or not I feel uncomfortable when he stands so close to adjust the straps around my chest and legs. He is stronger than me and is black like my attacker. Don't I get anxious around him? He answers his own question before I can say a word:

> *"I can see that you don't."*

At the end of our treetop adventure, one lady says goodbye with these words:

> *"My biggest fear is gone. I suppose seeing you alive and joyful despite all that has happened to you has taken it away. It convinced me that I would also be able to survive if something horrible like being raped should ever happen to me."*

Excitedly I think that it's not that difficult to wave the white flag that can free people. All you have to do is tell the truth and the truth will set people free.

Evening arrives. The waiters decorate our table with rose petals and candles. Our children are in the children's dining room around the corner. After our romantic four-course meal, a neat, elderly man walks in the door. He walks straight to our table and asks us if we are celebrating an anniversary. We explain that it's my birthday, and with that he turns to me. With a slight German accent and a straight, penetrative look in his eyes, he says in a fatherly voice:

> *"God knew you when you were just a baby in your mommy's tummy and He called you. He has great plans for you. The best is yet to come."*

He turns to Louis and repeats the words:

> *"Yes, the best is yet to come. I see open doors."*

He excuses himself and walks away as if he did something completely normal like placing serviettes on our table.

I can't help myself. I must go and explain to him how meaningful and encouraging his words are to us; I need to ask why on earth he brought such a message to our table. Was it his standard "Hallmark card quote" for all those who are celebrating a birthday or anniversary?

I approach him and ask if I may join him and his sons at the table. He looks defensive, as though he is prepared for a negative reaction from me. He quickly explains:

> *"I was in bed in my pyjamas when the Lord clearly gave me a command to get up, get dressed, and go to the dining room. I was to look for the celebration table, and to give the message He would give me to the woman at the table. I negotiated with God, because He often asks me to do this, and at times He gives messages that are offensive to the hearers. I've told the Lord many times that I don't want to live out such a bombastic prophetic calling, since I receive many guests that don't appreciate such messages! The Lord had answered my*

prayers by sending more Christians to stay over here to whom He wanted to give messages of encouragement. They don't get as upset. Tonight He wanted to remind you that what is coming will be better than all you've experienced so far."

What a special gift to hear God as clearly as this man does! Later that night in my room I think about it. It strengthened my faith when I heard God speak to me that night of the rape, that evening at the cell group, and that day at the Midmar Dam, but this man's words have stirred me so deeply that I can't sleep. I desire this gift with all that is in me. I want to be able to give other people accurate messages that will encourage them the way this message encouraged us tonight. I can hear God for my own sake. Now I want to hear Him for the sake of those who can't.

Some people believe this gift died out with the apostles. In Acts 22 one of these apostles, Paul, preached to a Jewish crowd about how a messenger had given him his calling with the words:

The God of our forefathers chose you to know His will, to see the Righteous one and to hear Him speak (v 14).

Imagine someone announcing to you: You will know God's will, you will see Him and hear Him speak! According to Paul it wasn't just a gift given to certain people during a certain time period. He called the prophetic gift a spiritual gift that can unlock the hearts of seekers (1 Corinthians 14:24-25) – since it can reveal secrets. If someone prophetically spoke to you about things only you and God knew about, it would prove something and would be difficult to deny. Paul says in verse 31 and 32 that each one in the congregation can prophesy in order for all to learn and be encouraged, but he also advised that one should always judge or test prophetic messages carefully.

Many people with whom I have shared my testimony have expressed that they feel inferior or even cheated out of a believer's privilege because they don't believe they can hear God. They don't know what He sounds like. They've only known the voices of criticizing moms and dads, demanding teachers, and grumpy grandfathers. They always suspected that His voice was similar. But we shouldn't listen to people to find out what God sounds like. Not even good, friendly preachers can teach us the sound of God's voice.

God's voice contains vibrations that have life-giving power. God's voice, the Word, is Jesus. What does Jesus sound like? There is no way to learn what He sounds like without reading the Word. We need to especially read Jesus' words in the gospels and the words that His best friends, the apostles, wrote about Him.

When I ask people if they read the Word of God and how they read it, I often discover they do one of three things: They read books *about* the Bible, or they lose themselves in Christian fiction, or they read the Bible out of habit. Few people read the Bible as a love letter written personally to them. Very few have ever read attentively through the whole Bible. It's almost like they don't expect the Bible to be tasty and sweet. It's as if they expect tough, tasteless meat or celery stalks: nutritious, but full of unappetising fibres. They attend a feast with a notepad and wait for corrections and instructions.

Suppose your toddler comes strolling into the living room. You are happy to see her. You're looking forward to playing with her or feeding her some juicy fruit slices. But instead of coming straight to your lap, she seats herself across from you in a business-like manner and asks: What did I do wrong and what do you want me to do next?

That's how we act with God. Maybe He didn't want to give you any commands today, maybe you were already fragile and bruised enough, maybe He didn't want to talk about your recent outburst, or maybe He just wanted to serve you refreshing fruit from His Word. In fact Jesus was described like this:

> **When someone's life is broken like a snapped reed, He will not break it off and where it's weak like smoking flax, He will not extinguish it.**
>
> (Isaiah 42:3a, *The Living Bible*)

I believe we sometimes struggle to hear God because we are suspicious of His character. We have difficulty believing He wants to, and is able to, utter kind words to us. He's not Santa Clause, which does justify our reverence for Him. And yes, it's true, He does have laws and He is just. But do you know the core of His justice? He will not trick you as His child by punishing you for the same sin His Son already died for. He does not collect debt payments in double. He also does not hold back from those who believe the rewards Jesus was crowned with because of His obedience until death. That obedience shows as credit on every believer's balance sheet, entitling us to our own free share of the reward. He won't keep you at arm's length when He already removed all that was ever between you and Him. You are welcome to lean on His shoulder, close enough to talk with Him and hear Him speak, even when He whispers.

Why do we approach the Lord with such caution as if we think we will somehow slip through one of the technical cracks of grace? Why do we fear that God will show us the fine print stipulating that Jesus' contract of reconciliation somehow does not apply to us, that it was all too good to be true after all?

With such a low expectation of grace, how can we expect to hear God's voice clearly, either with personal messages to us, or with encouragements for others?

I lie awake and think of 39 years with less than one personal message from God per year. Can one call this a relationship? A new overwhelming desire is growing inside of me: to hear His voice so clearly that I will know if I need to go and buy a newspaper one night ... to hear the Lord Himself declare that He loves me and a rapist equally ... to hear when to call on a whole nation to turn back to God and to declare it in front of the government buildings ... to get out of bed and get dressed again, just to tell someone that the Lord knew them when they were in their mother's womb ... Perhaps the rarity of this is due to the incessant noise of life. The competing messages vary from empty and troublesome to vile and blasphemous. If I can't switch them off or block them out, those ugly words will completely clash with the music of God's voice in my life.

We are back home after the refreshing time in the mountains. There is a parcel waiting for me from East London. It's a necklace. A friend sent it with these words (condensed version):

15 March 2010

> *Hello Hettie,*
>
> *This is an early birthday wish, confession, and testimony all in one. Last year at a Prophetic Beading Workshop I made a necklace with a prophetic meaning. When you wear it, you declare that you are Jesus' bride and you are preparing yourself for His arrival.*
>
> *In January (a month before the rape) when you were with us here in East London, I had, throughout the weekend, experienced an urgency to give you the necklace. I couldn't understand why. I knew you didn't like being made a fuss of. The enemy convinced me that it would be over the top to give it to you – really childish of me. I was disobedient to the Holy Spirit and didn't give you the necklace.*
>
> *I think the biggest shock I suffered during your ordeal in February was when I read in your testimony that Jesus had told you that you were His bride. Then I knew I had heard Him correctly and that I had been disobedient. I had failed to deliver you a direct message.*
>
> *I then decided to make you a new necklace and talked with the woman presenting the workshops. She had goose bumps because during the week of your attack she received the command to make a new necklace – with the name 'Mary-an Honourable Woman'. She made it and wrote down the meaning of every component. It's included in the package, and I trust it will mean a lot to you.*

In the explanation of the symbolism of each bead and element of the necklace, one of the things written was:

> *The small, medium and large turquoise balls represent a journey of growth. Some of them are big and some of them small – one right after the other. One might be heavier to carry than another. God is saying to you again: 'Do not be afraid.' It's in those times, especially when He promises to shelter you under His wings – the wings of the Most High.*
>
> *Just as Mary was willing, God wants you to be willing and say: 'Let it be done to me according to what YOU have said ...' God will supply in all your needs on your journey of life. He already has a design for you – one that He dreamed up for you – even before you were born."*

14 Blood tests, candles, and choices

It's the 25th of March, the date of my first ELISA blood test. It should have already happened a few days ago, but as usual I'm running away from the needles. My assistant knows me well, so she phoned a good friend to come and kidnap me to the clinic.

I think back to the day I first drove to the hospital, praying about whether or not I was HIV positive. The Lord answered other questions, didn't He? Maybe He would clearly tell me if I was sick or not? In my mind's eye I saw myself walking on a catwalk wearing a royal blue evening gown. When I reached the edge of the catwalk, I turned around. HIV+ was embroidered on the back of my dress in bright, metallic thread. The + looked like a cross, not a plus sign. I asked Jesus if it meant that He had carried it for me on the cross or if I would have to carry it? There was no answer.

The doctors are friendly when I arrive at the exam room which I have come to know so well. I don't recognise any of them from the night of the rape. I realise they have probably read the newspapers anyway and have seen the photos and have put two and two together to reach their own conclusions about the reason for my visit as well as my state of mental health. Some are very friendly while others avoid eye contact altogether. I'm very thankful when a senior nurse walks in. She looks experienced enough to be able to find my needle-shy veins with even a dull needle, blindfolded. She does exactly that, except for the part about the blindfold. I stop just short of hugging her.

The following day Louis accompanies me to the hospital for the results. Nowadays one can get everything from pizza to a home loan and a new bride over the phone, but not blood test results like these. You have to be there in person. Once again the doctor on duty is a new face. Her cherry red hair is styled artistically around her delicate face. She has the results with her. She doesn't even try to compose herself as she flings her arms around my neck and blurts out the very good but premature news,

"You're clean!"

She trusts that the later tests will simply confirm it.

Oddly enough, I struggle to process the result. I think I was ready for bad news, not for good news. A part of me started to believe the prophets of doom who predicted that my strong tower of wellness would crumble sooner or later. They foretold that everything would overwhelm me at some point and could not wait to see if I would still 'wear the battle scars with pride' if the scars included the blight of HIV. According to their predictions I would test positive, then I would realise that God didn't actually protect me from the worst of it all and then the whole deluded faith thing would implode on itself. Then Louis and I would have to deal with the rage and bitterness that so many other victims of violence and rape have to deal with. We would finally react 'normally', they hoped.

When we arrive home, the children are confused. We tell them it's good news, but they are wondering why mommy is crying in her bedroom for a little while.

I try to analyse my strange reaction to the news, and then I remember the words I had spoken to my youngest brother: "The most difficult thing for me to process is that I don't have normal trauma to process." It's as if I'm following an unfamiliar route, like driving to Cape Town with no map and no road signs. Everybody could tell me how to grieve or deal with anger, if only I had grief and anger. But nobody seems able to tell me how to rejoice without feeling guilty that my road is so much easier than the road of so many other women. I received so much backlash to my remarks about being emotionally and spiritually unharmed and about the rape having been less violent than they think, that I thought everyone would feel better if I were at least infected by the AIDS virus. The spectators of our story aren't the only ones struggling to handle my trauma-less recovery. I'm also in the dark as to how to correctly tell people, and how to accept the fact that I'm now also physically healthy. If I had been sick it would have been easier for everybody, however strange that might sound. Then no one would have to believe that a complete miracle had taken place.

The dispute between us and the cell phone company has been sorted out, and our cell phones are finally working again. They have agreed to repay the thousands of rand they had automatically deducted from Louis's bank account. Unfortunately, repaired communication is also good news for my cyber stalker.

Another month has passed by. It's now the 18th of April. Louis is away for the weekend. The cyber stalker seems to have taken a break, but I am caught up again in frequent contact with the man I should not be talking to. I fight against the temptation to choose conversation with him above conversations with Jesus. Why is this so hard? All he did was invite me for an innocent cup of coffee somewhere in public, and yet I know he has no role to play in my puppet theatre. I start rationalising again: *The conversation is good for both of us. We understand each other. We won't do anything wrong. It is just coffee.* Then I scold myself: *How can you be victorious over a rape and yet still struggle so much with this stupid emotional addiction?*

I thought I decided not to go, but I am already in my car. My grip on the steering wheel is so tight that my knuckles are turning white. I do what I've never done before –'I scream at God at the top of my voice:

"It's too hard! You promised not to tempt us and to give us a way out of every temptation, but You aren't doing it!"

For the first time in a number of weeks I clearly hear the Lord speak to my heart:

"Do you want Me to give your legacy to someone else?"

It doesn't sound like one of those rhetorical questions parents sometimes ask, like: *'Do you want me to send your bike to the poor kids in Africa?'* This question is different. There is compassion mixed with urgency. I sense that I actually have a choice. I need to choose what it is that I want to leave behind for my children and for a generation of fragile families. It's a very difficult test that I could either pass with flying colours or like one snatched from the fire. It's my choice. If I chose the tough test, I'd leave a rich legacy. On the other hand, if I barely passed this test I probably wouldn't lose my salvation, but there would most definitely be heart-breaking losses in other areas. Even if I failed completely, I know His grace would be more than enough for me, but I would never get to know the primary course in life that the Lord originally mapped out for me.

The idea that God would take away what has been put before me and give it to someone else, has me in tears. Never before have I done such a bad job that my work had to be assigned to others. I definitely don't want to disappoint the Lord in this way. I beg for forgiveness for my rebellion, and I ask for a second chance to mop up the mud in my life ... My head slumps forward on the steering wheel and I cry my heart out. I let go of the steering wheel and start walking back into the house where my three precious children – my primary legacy – are playing games, completely unaware of the snake their mother had almost let loose in their home.

I'm still not catching on to the fact that I'm fighting this the wrong way. From my experience during the rape, I should have learned that there comes a time when you have to declare your total dependence on the Lord, and fight on your knees. I'm still trying to conquer my weaknesses with brute willpower and by standing tall. It worked in the past, but this test is the most difficult one I've ever faced. What has worked in the past is not going to work for me now.

The sum total of all the powers of our soul – our willpower, mind and emotions – is not strong enough to overcome spiritual tests.

(Zechariah 4:6, *The Message*)

I had a troubled night, and the words by Thomas Watson at the bottom of the page in my diary shed more light on what I am feeling:

The devil enjoys it when we stay in the deep waters of remorse until we get into trouble, and later completely drown in the depths of despair.

Underneath his quote I write: "I refuse!" If I commit the biggest mistake of my life, and wilfully become an adulteress, I will definitely drown in despair. How will I be able to proclaim hope to the families of South Africa if I destroy my own? I could easily explain having a cup of coffee with another man in public, but what will I do if it doesn't end there?

I flex my strong mind muscles, I ignore my phone, and I stay off the internet and bite my nails. I drink too much coffee and swim a mile or two at the gym every other day. I'm bent on breaking out of this cycle. I have been successful for about two days now. I am exhausted. Louis is back, but I am not really here. I fall asleep earlier than usual and wake up from a terrible nightmare. I am praying in tongues, and there are tears on my cheeks. My whole being is shaken. I remember the reason now. It is the dream I just had.

A grey man dressed in a long grey garment was standing in front of me, holding two candles, one in each hand. The candles looked dull, just like the man and his robe. He expectantly held out one candle to me, presented in the manner that a schoolboy would present a carnation to the girl of his dreams on Valentine's Day. I got the impression that if I accepted this candle, I would in some way have committed myself to this unimpressive man. I didn't want to. I wanted to look around for possible brighter prospects. I lied politely so I wouldn't offend him:

> *"Thank you for the offer; I'll be back soon. Keep my candle in the meantime. I quickly have to do something."*

There was no reply, but the grave disappointment showed in his body language as he pulled back the hand that held my candle and allowed me to leave.

I walked away in search of someone more colourful, I suppose, and immediately just such a person caught my eye. His attractiveness was evident even as he sat with his back to me. There was an empty chair across from the handsome man. This chair must be saved for me, I thought. I sat down and started chatting to him, but before I could complete my first sentence I realised that something was not right. He looked disturbed. He warned me with his crazy eyes:

> *"You can't choose me!"*

He lifted a revolver to his head, but I tried to stop him. A shot was fired, but I could not be sure who had pulled the trigger. In the confusion that ensued, he shot himself again and again and fell off his chair. I tried to catch him and he bled to death in my arms, leaving me with the nauseating realisation that I had made the mistake of my life. One word came to mind: self-destruction. I buried him, tried to wipe the blood off my hands and clothes, and then ran back to the place where I first met the grey man.

It was now dark, and on the edge of a table I saw what was left of my candle. It had burned down. All that was left was a flameless black wick sticking out of a shallow stump of cooled wax.

I now realise the obvious meaning of my dream. God is the Grey Man. I made a mistake thinking the candle was a dull offer. That candle was grace. Stanley Wood once said: *Grace is free, but when once you take it, you are bound forever to the Giver.* I realise that the Lord wanted to save me from my dare-devil self, but I was too proud, independent and ungrateful to accept it. I was still weighing options. All this time I didn't realise that there aren't really any options here. There is only one way, and if I fail to take it, there will only be death and destruction before me. My flame would be extinguished. The dream felt real. The urgency is real. This feels like a clear warning that my decision time is up.

My candle is in jeopardy. Coupled with the event a few days ago, I get the message clearly now. I need to grab hold of that dull candle with both hands and walk with the wise Man. It is not a choice between my husband and another man. It is a choice to follow Jesus wholeheartedly or to follow my own deceptive heart. I never considered leaving Louis. He is everything but dull and truly the love of my life. I was merely being wilful, infatuated and flattered, of course. The final choice I needed to make now was between Jesus and the same idol I let go of once before – the idol of human approval.

I get a call from a sweet lady friend who offers to let me stay in her wooden cottage in the bush. I gratefully accept, knowing that I really need the weekend to pray and work on a book that stubbornly would not write itself. There is no mobile phone or internet reception there in the bush. It will be good to get away from the major portals of trouble.

It's the morning I'm supposed to leave, and I wake up with an eye infection. It feels as if a corkscrew is screwed into the back of my eyeball and someone is pulling on it. There are so many tears streaming from my eye that I can't see a thing, and I can't find my car keys anyway. My chances of going away this weekend are looking slim. My laptop's power cable is also missing. It's an impossible situation. I need it in order to work on my book. I look everywhere in the house before I phone Louis to hear whether or not he accidentally took it with him. He didn't, so I start phoning others. Finally, I discover that my assistant's young son, who simply wanted to help his mom pack her stuff, accidentally packed it in her bag yesterday afternoon. It still feels like a crisis, since she lives on the other side of Pretoria, and I am already running very late.

I send a text message to my friend who offered me the cottage to thank her for the offer. I tell her that although I really want to go, either the devil or God or both are keeping me at home. She replies with this prayer:

> *"We come against you Satan in the Name of Jesus Christ. We trample you under our feet and say to you in the Name of Jesus Christ our Lord: Flee and be gone with your evil plans. Satan, you will not let Hettie's candle burn out, in Jesus' Name."*

I said nothing about a candle! I only said that my eye was hurting and that my car keys and laptop cable were missing. Through her text message I realise that these obstacles might be meant to keep me at home where I can easily forget to take up that candle ... I agree with her prayer and continue looking for the car keys. In the meantime my assistant is driving through peak time traffic to bring the power cable, even though I still can't see well enough to drive.

Our domestic helper suddenly receives Godly inspiration and searches for my keys in our children's bathroom closet where she finds them nestled between the two bottom towels! My youngest daughter apparently played 'treasure hunt' with them. We would have spent months looking for those keys, since that closet is full of our old towels and the children usually only work their way through the top half of the stack before it is laundry day again. My eye is also tearing less and the pain medication has kicked in.

Half an hour later I'm on the way to the bush where I hope to talk with the Grey Man, the Grace-giver, about my only option. After arriving, I clear my head, write a few chapters in my book, and read a few long excerpts from the Word of the Lord.

I make my final decision.

15 A shortcut to truth

A congregation asks Louis and me to share our testimonies with them as part of a Sunday morning service aiming to answer some questions surrounding violence and fear. We agree, even though my orders had been to stay off the stage for the whole year. This congregation is not my audience, but my family and I reason they dearly need some resolution to their distress. They also want Louis to share his thoughts about forgiveness and the truth of God's Word.

After the service, a man, whom I respect immensely, jumps in line in front of a row of crying women waiting to pray with me. He wants to correct me. According to him my testimony leaves others feeling inferior, and it's way too soon to claim that I have escaped the trauma of the robbery and rape. It's irresponsible of me to share my testimony in such a way. In the future I have to be clearer about the fact that I was the exception to the rule. I need to choose my words more carefully when I claim to be OK, and I should reiterate that I'm still on the road to healing.

I'm instantly ablaze with anger and struggling to conceal it. Written on the flyer that was handed out this morning are his own words: Pray that the victims of violence and crime won't have psychological damage, and that their trauma will be healed.

I blurt it out:

> *"Haven't I just testified that those prayers were answered? Rejoice with me that all the prayers that had gone up on the first night were powerful. Rejoice with me, don't scold me. It's as if you want to tell the lame man who can now walk to go back and lie down out of respect for the other lame people, and not to proclaim what Jesus had freely and undeservedly done for him. I feel as if my eyes that were blind can now see, but you want me to keep them shut for now, because the miracle might only be temporary. I should share my testimony differently so it's easier for some to swallow. Well, unfortunately my testimony is the simple truth, and I'm not going to lie and in so doing rob God of the glory that He deserves for what He has done for us!"*

I think to myself: Should I then, through diluting my testimony, give other people permission to be trapped in fear, anger, loss and bitterness for longer than I was? Why? Shouldn't I acknowledge that I, like the rest, didn't know that this sort of healing was possible? Shouldn't I be rejoicing with people in the hope that this gives all of us? Shouldn't I be able to draw courage from this miracle to sustain me in possible future difficulties that could cross my path? Why not draw strength from this part of my story to attain victories that I'm still asking God for?

I also want to cry out that Louis and I are not that unique. In the past few months I've met countless men and women who experienced similar stories and have not gone through long periods of trauma. They, like us, are normal people. These people have come through very difficult circumstances and, in a short time, come out whole, happy and filled with forgiveness and gratitude – losing parents, seeing a spouse shot dead, losing a child through a tragic drowning, being gang raped as a teenager, and causing someone else's death due to foolish negligence. All of these men and women had worked through their traumas in a matter of days and weeks, as opposed to months and years. One of them, like me, had experienced healing from her trauma within minutes. While her dad was bleeding to death from a gunshot wound, she ran after the murderer crying out Jesus' forgiveness over him, and every day after that she has prayed for his soul. Two of these people were women at the church who told me their stories. They comforted me with these words: "Many won't understand, but we understand, because we have experienced the same thing." So I'm not special. That is what I want to say: If it happened to me, it can happen to you! What Jesus paid for on the cross for me, He also made available to you, and He made healing available to all of us!

On the way home from church I fight through these thoughts to the point of tears. Louis is quiet, but his facial expression says that I'm being a little too intense. Any word could add fuel to a fire that is this hot. He decides not to utter a single word. At home I walk straight to my desk where I had put the scrapbook my mom had made of all the letters people wrote to her personally but also on blogs and in the papers. It is time to read these letters. I need to understand why our testimony and particularly my words are upsetting and triggering so many people. What would cause someone who has seen many miracles in his own lifetime to try and force me to keep quiet about the one true miracle I have experienced? Maybe one of these scores of letters would hold the answer.

The writers, like the man at the church, are upset about the fact that I claim to be fine. They also mention spiritual pride, disrespect for hurting people, self-righteousness, delusion, falsehood, and denial when referring to my testimony.

I don't understand this. Is it wrong to be healed and happy about it? I read Isaiah 53 again and am reminded that it speaks of the healing Jesus made possible for us by suffering such pain and anguish. Interestingly, the sentence it starts with echoes the emotions I'm feeling now:

> **Who has believed our message? To whom has the LORD revealed his powerful arm?**
>
> (Isaiah 53:1, *New Living Translation*)

It seems that people have always been struggling to believe in the wonders of God. One of the reasons for this comes only a few verses later:

> **There was nothing beautiful or majestic about his appearance, nothing to attract us to him. He was despised and rejected – a man of sorrows,**

> **acquainted with deepest grief. We turned our backs on him and looked the other way. He was despised, and we did not care. Yet it was our weaknesses he carried; it was our sorrows that weighed him down. And we thought his troubles were a punishment from God, a punishment for his own sins! But he was pierced for our rebellion, crushed for our sins. He was beaten so we could be whole. He was whipped so we could be healed. All of us, like sheep, have strayed away. We have left God's paths to follow our own. Yet the LORD laid on him the sins of us all.**
>
> (Isaiah 53:2b-6, *New Living Translation*).

People look at people and struggle to look beyond the first judgment or impression. Perhaps something external about us is offensive already, even before we start speaking. Jesus, the Servant of God, was not described as a very attractive person. He is called a rock of offence elsewhere in the Bible. People could not see past his persona either.

It's clear throughout this whole chapter that healing and salvation are not just metaphors or exclusive to an elite cream of the Christian crop. Inner healing has been paid for any who would have it, and peace and joy are already available just as the angels and many other prophets promised throughout the Old Testament and New. Because I believed it, I took hold of it. I wish I could tell each and every person who wrote these letters:

> *"Believe that Jesus' wounds brought you healing, then take it for yourself. It's exactly the right dose of medicine for your specific wounds. Don't allow my testimony to hinder you from receiving your healing. And I don't want to force my healing down your throat. Mine won't work for you. Yours won't work for me. Don't get angry with me because I'm already healed. I didn't steal your medicine. Yours is right there on the Healer's shelf, with your name on it. It may be a dose strong enough to heal you in an instant. It may be a long course of remedies you will have to complete like a course of antibiotics. In the end it doesn't matter how long it takes. It proves nothing either way. What matters is that Jesus does not play favourites and that no one needs to stay sick at heart."*

My natural inclination to argue, which has been dormant for the past few months, is now wide awake. I argue out loud with the letters:

> *"People, don't we have a choice in how we look at trauma? Can't we decide what we believe in? Everywhere in the Bible we are commanded to renew our minds, to think straight, to capture our thoughts and make them obedient to Jesus, to think only about what is pure and good. I choose to focus my thoughts on life-giving words, on freedom, healing, power and above all – love. Each one of you can also choose how you think. You are thinking too much about us. Think about where you stand, instead!"*
>
> *The choices I made were not because I'm a special breed of Christian. I think it's well stated in the words of the book, The Shack, where God is said to tell a particular person: 'I am especially fond of you.' Later on in the book it becomes clear that He says this to everybody. He is especially fond of all of us. His love has a quality that makes us feel unique and set apart. A friend's young daughter said*

> *it well: God does not count people 'one ... two ... three ...' He counts them 'one ... one ... one...' I believe the Lord is especially fond of me, and also of those of you who might still be trapped in trauma. I believe He is willing to fight up a storm for you until you are free from all the lies entangling you."*

I remember a time in my life when some Christians' testimonies offended me, too. No matter how they phrased it, it seemed spiritually boastful to me. I didn't want to be like them, but I dearly wanted to personally experience the Lord doing things in my life. I had been unsure of how to cross the great divide between the outsiders' court and the inner circle. Metaphorically speaking I felt like I was outside in the spiritual cold peering into the house where other people were contentedly spending time with Jesus huddled around the warm fireplace. Shivering out in the cold I could only hear their distant voices when the wind was blowing in the right direction. These people seemed to be close to Jesus; they listened to Him and they spoke with Him. I was jealous and at the same time convinced that the people in the inner circle were experiencing one of two things: a strong delusion or an unattainable level of holiness to which normal people like me could never progress.

At a youth camp where Louis led the worship many years ago, I stood in line sheepishly with a long row of teenagers outside the counselling room. When it was my turn I spilled the beans:

> *"I feel like God left me out in the cold. I know I belong to Him, but I'm somewhere on the outside."*

The counsellor helped me to find my way to the footpath that led to the house where Jesus, the glow of the fire and the sweet fellowship with other children of God were all waiting for me. It played out differently to how I thought it would. I thought she would name the different steps and requirements to meet in order to reach the house – even obstacles, barriers and tests that I would have to pass. Instead the counsellor pointed out the lies separating us, like the one that said He didn't love me as much as He loved those on the inside, and that they were better people than I was. The counsellor helped me to own the truth that Jesus truly loved me. She told me to close my eyes while I waited in the dark. Jesus, with a lantern in one hand, came to find me in the cold and lead me to a place inside that already belonged to me.

Since that day I have never again lost my confidence to be close to Jesus and to the Father. I realised once and for all that I wasn't the one who had to figure out how to get close to Him. If there had ever been one human being who was capable of doing that, it wouldn't have been necessary for Jesus to become human.

I recognise in several of the venomous letters the same cynical uncertainty which I had been guilty of while standing out in the cold – saved, believing, but kept far from the warmth of the fire by the lies I believed about Jesus, Christians and myself. That's why the letters don't hurt me – they make me angry instead. I'm not mad at the writers of the letters. They just bleat the bleat of hungry, injured sheep without a shepherd.

I'm angry at the Church for allowing bleeding sheep to continue bleeding, for comforting the hungry sheep with the shallow message that to be spiritually hungry until death is simply a part of life. I'm angry that the Church, who should be busy dressing wounds, is instead busy snuffing out people's last flame of hope by declaring that certain wounds – such as molestation, rape, the death of a child, the murder of a parent, the witnessing of a violent act – are wounds that are virtually impossible to heal, in spite of all that Jesus has accomplished on the cross. He has made no difference to our lives here and know, it would seem. The empty sermons spur us on to wait for heaven, because only heaven is great and life this side of it has not been impacted by what Jesus has done, unfortunately.

I love the images in John 10 of Jesus as a Good Shepherd. He stands looking at sheep whose previous hired shepherds were in it for the money and took off whenever the wolf showed up. His heart bleeds for them because they no longer believe that they can ever be safe and loved and guided well. They have had to fend for themselves and have bloody, gaping wounds under the stained wool to prove that it has not been a stroll in green pastures for them.

The sheep pen is kept shut tightly and guarded closely. Some sheep folds have organized watchmen who keep warning the sheep about this open door here and that unguarded window there. Every hour of every day they wonder where the thief will hit next and when the wolf will take its chance on an unsuspecting sheep who left some or other door open though ignorance or weakness and should take the blame for the whole thing. It is all up to them. Because they have no shepherd. Or could it be that they have One but have not learned to trust Him? Could it be that they forgot that He never sleeps? He stands guard. They think He stands hand clapped over His eyes, peeping through His fingers, saying to Himself: *Oops, there comes the thief. I'd have loved to help them now, but hey, when they leave a door open there is just nothing I can do about it. This is going to be ugly. It's their own fault. I can only step in and help when they do a perfect job. And they just don't.*

Maybe they missed the part about Him being the door. Nothing can come to us until it has come through Him. Almost two millennia ago He shed blood on behalf of every sheep that would ever have to bleed. He bought healing for every sheep that would ever have a run-in with the ferocious wolf. John records the words Jesus said to explain what He does at the very moment when we come to those painful and violent places: "I lay down my life willingly for My sheep." Sheep who miss this little detail bleed with their own blood instead of bleeding with His.

Some sheep just can't stand the thought of a Shepherd who cannot guarantee a wolf-free environment. They prefer staying in the pen. They never hear the sweet sound of the familiar Voice that calls them, that leads them out to go in and out and find pasture. It sounds like freedom, but they would rather be safe than free. They do not trust the Shepherd. They never find the pasture. They eat the trampled weeds that all the other sheep have messed on. Bitterness and undernourishment is their lot. And eternal thirst. I have never seen a stream run through a sheep's pen, have you? To get to the living waters, a sheep has to trust and follow, and leave the safety of the pen. In the wide open space of freedom there is amazing food. There are high places to climb to get to the best of it. The sheep hiding in the pen look at the sheep high on the hills, getting their fill of the best herbs and medicinal shrubs and they bleat: Such arrogance! Now watch them – their fall is certain.

The wide open space is not entirely safe, I know. It is where the thief and wolf roam, but the trusting sheep do not put their focus there at all. They only have eyes for the beautiful Shepherd with the soothing voice and the scars on his hands and feet. They look at those scars and know – if need be, He will bleed for me as He has clearly done before. I have no teeth, no venomous bite, no burning sting or crippling kick. I can't run or burrow into the ground or fly away when the predators come. No fangs, no claws, no impenetrable scales. I am defenceless. Yet, I am not afraid. For He is my defence.

After thinking about all of this, I decide to write a long letter to the man who reprimanded me at church, but I don't send it. With my temperament it's one of the most important lessons I have had to learn: When angry, do not click 'send'.

That evening we enjoy a barbecue with our neighbours, and I proceed to blow off steam regarding the incident at church with a quick flood of words. My wise neighbour helps me to see it from a different perspective: the man who scolded me is simply a disillusioned shepherd who has probably seen too many sheep with broken bones. He has seen how they can trample over one another and is probably afraid that this is what I may do. Every day he sees sheep who have been limping along for a while, which makes your skipping a bit too much for him to swallow.

These are the words I never sent but still want to say, just in case someone needs to think about this with me:

> Dear Sir
>
> I want to ask forgiveness for my impulsive reaction to your criticism. (Or maybe it wasn't criticism but rather advice?) Unfortunately, you had to bear the brunt of my ill-timed explosion. I have been like a pressure cooker having to endure this exact criticism over and over again, and I just became tired of hearing it. I've been repeatedly asked to emphasise, clarify, and expand the point that most people take years to heal, that that's the normal, better and preferred process, and that it doesn't mean people are weak Christians if it takes them a long time to get better. This morning, you asked me to give this disclaimer at the beginning of my testimony rather than at the end. I don't know how to clarify this any better. To tell you the truth, I don't think it's important to emphasise it at all. Everybody knows it. It's because we have repeatedly told people that they will come out broken at the other end, that our testimonies are oftentimes viciously slammed back at us like one does with a weak tennis serve.
>
> Yes, I've seen and heard of people who feel unsure of where they stand with the Lord after hearing my testimony. That's precisely why I've encouraged them to go to the Lord with their discomfort and to battle it out there, in the place where our struggles are never in vain.
>
> Yes, I've thought about the reasons why many Christians and non-Christians react so fiercely to my testimony. I've wondered why some of my statements, like when I said 'what I have experienced doesn't mean I'm a better Christian', have never seemed to reach readers and listeners, even though I've said and written it countless times. The only conclusion that I've been able to make is that

the enemy has closed their ears and eyes to the true meaning of what I'm saying, and that he is busy twisting my words in such a way that it breaks people down instead of building them up.

Can't we consider the possibility that the enemy can't afford for people to be healed quickly and completely? Isn't it possible that he makes them deaf to the hope they have in Jesus? Maybe the enemy actually thinks the baby (the fact that God wants to and can heal people) should be thrown out with the bath water (the unlikely speed with which God heals people). Couldn't sowing this doubt and suspicion be his strategy? If people firmly believe in slow and tedious, partial healing, they would just lie down so much easier to a life in chains, won't they? Satan would only need to lift one finger in order to take people captive through depression, anxiety, anger and bitterness. Very effective.

Can it be that the message Satan tries to keep alive at all costs is this: Christians shouldn't believe that God can really give them peace that surpasses all understanding or joy instead of ashes? It's impossible to reach the healing herbs high up on the cliffs. In the end, He wants you to suffer hopelessly, like everybody else. Even though you're His child, you're not different from everybody else. You have to struggle with the same despair, anxiety and sleeplessness. The type of healing that Louis and Hettie testify about is just a form of self-hypnosis, it's only the first phase of trauma, it's over-spiritualising a very normal experience, it is an irrational response that is typical of survivors of such a shocking experience, it's out of reach for normal Christians, it's a false pretence they feel they have to make as a sort of legitimisation of their ministry, and it's an attempt to promote a God who is doing a bad job at marketing Himself favourably.

We know that what happened to us was surprising. We were also surprised. We believe, however, that our story can present an important message which can only be heard if the noise of the first option (the usual, long road as the only hope of recovery) is tuned down a little bit.

It is only because so many people don't read their Bibles anymore, and don't know the stories of early Christianity, that our story sounds contrived. Any student of the book of Acts or the history of missions would know differently. Any Christian in China today would tell you stories that would make ours sound lacklustre in comparison. It's because we've gotten so used to our cosy Christian life that costs us nothing, that we're satisfied with a Christianity that also doesn't offer anything extraordinary. God can't expect much from today's self-preserving Christians and we don't expect much from Him either. I once read someone describing current Christian living as 'consumer Christianity lite'. As with a sugar-free 'lite' drink, all the ingredients that made up original Christianity – such as fearless faith, selfless sacrifice and perilous adventures through the lion's den – have been taken out to make it more palatable to the postmodern consumer.

Since I also don't know many stories of Christians in other countries, I'll resort to a Bible story or two to illustrate. The puppet theatre story of Paul and Silas in jail should be looked at from all sides. Didn't they go through unfair and horrible trauma? Shouldn't they have been seething with anger? Wouldn't it have been the normal response to start a rebellion against the godless government that allowed all this violence against them and their fellow believers? Instead, Paul repeatedly commands the readers of his many letters to obey and pray for this very government? Why are Paul and Silas praising God at midnight? They should surely be looking for sin in their lives that lead to their predicament or should be feeling rather foolish for trusting in a Jesus that seems to have no power to keep them out of harm's way?

And what about Daniel? He spent a night in a dungeon full of hungry lions. Talk about being let down by the God he prays to day and night! And I dare you to think of something that would cause more psychological damage than a night of such terror. Shouldn't he have come out raging or at least shaken? Where were his nightmares? Where was his depression? Who did his debriefing? Where was his dissatisfaction with God after his repeated suffering under the rule of ungodly kings?

In short: Why were these people still singing? Why were they still worshipping God? We can't find the answers looking at the puppet theatre from the audience's viewpoint. We need to know what happened behind the scenes. We have to ask questions. The right questions. Not the standard ones such as what Paul and Silas and Daniel had done right or what had been unique about their callings or how they had deserved God's special intervention. Such questions put the focus on the recipients of the miracle – on people. That would be a mistake.

In examining a miracle, the focus should be on the One who performed it. Our questions should, therefore, rather be: Who was the God these believers believed in? Who did they know, see and love right through their respective ordeals? The answer to the questions will explain their song at midnight and their praise in times of trauma. To each one of these normal, fallible people, God had been a present, living God – the kind of God who hears, sees, talks and appears in a fiery furnace. A God who commands a host of lock picking angels who happen to carry keys that can lock a lion's mouth, too. And all the believers ever did right was to focus on Him instead of on flames or lions or kings or high priests.

Please don't make the common mistake by looking at Louis or me. Don't ask who we are, what our callings and occupations are, where we live, which church we attend, if we've been baptised or not, if we speak in tongues, or whether or not we proclaim Scriptures over our home and our children every day. Those are the wrong questions.

Rather ask: Who is this God who makes a woman feel like a bride on the night she is raped? Who is it that puts forgiveness in a man's heart towards the robbers who stripped his studio of its most valuable equipment and his wife of her dignity? What does it tell us about God when He takes them through a furnace of trauma and yet brings them out on the other side without even smelling of smoke? Yes, ask the questions we dare not ask. Ask how big this God must be if He can even use a rape for the good of those who love Him. Ask yourself what it says about the Father's heart that He has poured out over us such peace that none of us – not even our children – have had a single nightmare or have shed a single tear about that night until today. Ask, like one of the mocking letter writers asked, why God warned me about the rape only a few minutes ahead of time instead of giving me enough time so that I could escape? Then listen to the unlikely answer: Maybe because He never intended for me to escape, but planned to be powerfully present with me and use my life for something much more as a result of it. He always knew what I know now: the privilege of hearing Him and seeing Him so close was much bigger than the injustice of being raped.

If only we could all rejoice despite our dark nights as Paul did in spite of his floggings and unfair imprisonment and snake bites and near drowning:

> **Oh, how great are God's riches and wisdom and knowledge! How impossible it is for us to understand his decisions and his ways! For who can know the LORD's thoughts? Who knows enough to give him advice? And who has given him so much that he needs to pay it back? For everything comes from him and exists by his power and is intended for his glory. All glory to him forever! Amen.**
>
> (Romans 11:33-36, *New Living Translation*)

It has been spelled out clearly: If we are dealing with the true God, the wise One, the wealthy One, the all-knowing One, we will be dealing with many puzzles. We are guaranteed to see decisions and actions that leave us breathless. Man-made gods are predictable and understandable, but not He. We will never be able to figure out the true God's modus operandi. We will never be able to map out His brain profile in order to predict how He thinks. We are arrogant to use phrases such as "surely His will" and "definitely not His will" as if we could ever predict His purposes. Our perspective is so limited that it is almost laughable when we suggest to Him what we regard as fair and unfair. It is futile to stack up good deeds deserving of a reward in the hope that it would serve as a guarantee of God's special favour in the day of trouble. Doing that would be as silly as stockpiling canned food as a remedy against the Apocalypse. We can't do enough things well enough to ever deserve anything in return from a perfect, powerful God.

The passage from Romans 11 ends with this adjustment in our perspective: Everything done on this earth will ultimately result and culminate in one thing – God's glory. Glory He will share with no-one. Not even with His children. For not even they will have deserved one ray of the light that will shine from the Son. That's why no prosperous person dare explain the grounds of His prosperity nor the grounds for the suffering of those who do not prosper. God does not spin around us as planets around the sun. He is central. We revolve around Him. We may be the centre of His love, but we are not the centre of His existence.

So, let's not look for clues in people to explain what happens to them. Let's not look at people for the reasons God does what He does and allows what He allows. Let's not make fools of ourselves by explaining an inexplicable God. He will do what He wills. He will be unpredictable or He will cease to be God.

By claiming that we were all completely whole immediately and permanently in spite of what happened that night, does not mean I devalue or look down on the long struggle towards restoration that is a reality for many Christians. In fact, it is very real to me in other areas of my life. Some run-ins with the wolf have been very bloody indeed, leaving me cripple for a long time. In fact, I am bleeding right now but not because of the rape. But I bleed with hope now, knowing one thing is certain: The moment I grasp the truth that breaks the power of the last remaining lie that my struggle rests on, my restoration will be immediate, permanent and complete. I've experienced this sort of instant emotional and spiritual healing on more than one occasion. Satan has lost his right to tear into us for as long as he wishes. He uses his one remaining weapon – his deception. When his lies are exposed, God's living truth floods in and destroys every foothold he acquired by his deception. The pain crumbles along with it.

Sir, I urge you to speak to anyone who has been healed of depression, abnormal fears, intense rejection or any other devastating emotional burden (there are many), and they will quote one or two specific revelations of truth, a supernatural moment where they suddenly saw the light, a life-altering event that had made all the difference, or a simple realisation that became a door to healing. They seldom answer that they slowly won back their life-joy one day at a time over a period of years and could not really say what it was that brought them back to a full life. Instant inner healing from the wounds of severe sexual, physical and emotional abuse have been confirmed by many men and women I have spoken to since the rape. Some experienced healing while reading my 'unrealistic' testimony. For some it was the moment in their lives when a pivotal lie finally gave way under the weight of Truth. Here are some of their stories:

> *I'm sorry for what you have gone through. In 2002 we went through the same thing. My husband and I were held up for four hours. This was before our little boy was born.*
>
> *I want to say to you that the way you and your husband testified in today's newspaper, the Beeld, tore open my soul. I cried like a baby because that's exactly how we felt during our ordeal. I cried because I had lost that closeness with God by seeing so much pain and suffering in the world. But this morning when I read the two articles, everything changed.*

Another one writes:

> *Hettie, I want to thank you for that which you suffered for the Body of Christ. Especially that you suffered for me. I got so much from your testimony in the Beeld. I don't know where to start, but I would like to tell you how much it meant for me. Sometimes it's encouraging to know that we don't suffer in vain.*

Another testifies:

I don't even want to think of the possibility of being raped. I always thought, should it ever happen to me, I would rather be murdered by the rapist as well. I thought I would be as good as dead anyway. I never realised how selfish and foolish I was until I read how you testified that God 'kept your soul and spirit in His hand.' I would have given the enemy everything if I were ever raped, but now I know I would not have to – he could only touch my body.

I now realise that the enemy will not be able to hurt me as much as I would hurt myself by holding on to pain. By holding on to things in the past I have done just that: I have allowed pain to consume me; I have allowed bitterness and unforgiveness into my heart. I have even allowed my future to be influenced by things I had decided in the past! My fears paralysed me. I used to be ready to throw in the towel with every small setback I faced because I had already decided that I would not be able to handle it.

Now I realise that my body is temporary. I'm not tossed to and fro by my soul and emotions anymore. I allow my spirit, by the help of God's Spirit, to guide my body and soul. I now understand that it is supposed to happen in that order. I didn't realise how frequently I had allowed my emotions to choke my spirit.

I now know that the enemy can't touch that which is truly important. Nothing can snatch us from the hand of God, but we can remove ourselves by choice. I was ready to give everything to the enemy because I wasn't prepared to walk the road of healing with God.

Thank you for being willing to testify even though it could, and probably has, brought you judgement and persecution from people who don't understand. I can't possibly explain how much I learned from your testimony, but I hope the part I did share means something to you.

If we're on a long road, it does not necessarily mean that our wound is of the kind that has to take years and years to heal. The long road often is not part of our healing at all. Often it is merely a prolonged search for that ultimate truth that will set us free in a moment. In John 8:32 Jesus explains: "... and you will know the truth, and the truth will set you free" (New Living Translation). I believe many people's road to healing will be much shorter and more complete, if we, the Church, believe and preach that Truth heals better and faster than time ever could.

In 1 Thessalonians 5:23-24 Paul blesses the congregation with these words:

Now may the God of peace make you holy in every way, and may your whole spirit and soul and body be kept blameless until our Lord Jesus Christ comes again. God will make this happen, for he who calls you is faithful.

(*New Living Translation*)

To Paul, complete healing in body, soul and spirit was the guaranteed norm and a promise by our faithful God who would be sure to see to it.

Sir, I believe people will find a way to healing much quicker if we stop lying to them. We lie when we tell them that it depends on the amount of faith they can muster up by themselves, or that they have to work through a set of prescribed steps, or that some things just never heal and that they must just learn to live with it. Random time periods are assigned to every aspect of healing: so many months to grow past your anger phase, and then so many months to sleep well again, and then so many months until you're not afraid in the dark anymore. This idea is defended by claiming that experience has taught us this is how it is. Is this advice, which the church so readily accepts, not based on the average recovery period outside the Body of Christ? Is it not founded on unbelieving psychologist's recovery plans which date back decades and even centuries? Don't we have enough faith to prayerfully rewrite this recovery plan?

With all due respect, isn't that taking the unsuccessful search of many and making it the programme others should follow? Isn't it taking the Bible story of the woman who was suffering from an issue of blood until she touched the hem of Jesus' garment and then telling others: "So, what you should do is to go to doctors of every kind until you have tried everything and have not a penny left to your name. Then find Jesus where He is surrounded by a stampeding crowd, push through with all your might and grab His robe. It worked for that women. It will work for you. It took her twenty years, so don't be impatient, now, okay?"

All I am saying is that the twenty years was not part of her healing journey at all. The misdiagnosis was not part of it either. Those things were part of the endless search for the ultimate Truth. Only her very last step was the road to healing. It was not a twenty year journey. It was only a moment. That moment is the entire programme we should propagate: Touch Jesus! Yes, and then, sadly, many will still take twenty years to do it, but at least they will know the truth about where the journey ends.

How can the fact that we are in Jesus not make a difference to our road to healing, Sir? How can we suffer endlessly when all of the riches of God through Jesus have been deposited in us, with the Holy Spirit as our guarantee that we will receive life upon life, truth upon truth, and strength upon strength? How can the resurrection power of Jesus be powerless against emotional trauma?

What would happen if therapists stopped searching for signs of trauma which they can label and write into a schedule, and instead started looking with spiritual eyes for the truths that their patients are close enough to grab a hold of? They should study recoveries, not the 'cases' that stretch over decades, if they are to understand healing. Maybe then they would stop announcing excitedly: "Well done, I can see you are more and more conscious of what you have lost. You're making progress!" Perhaps they will someday announce instead: "I can see you realise that right in the moment of your loss, you have gained something eternally precious in return. You are now finding healing truth!"

In discussing the long road versus the shortcut, a friend of mine, a trauma counsellor and life coach, explained his view like this: "All of us have to cross Beaufort West when we travel from Cape Town to Johannesburg, but sometimes we fly. Those driving the long road need not envy those who are flying."

I want to add: The one who takes the flight doesn't get to see the beautiful wild flowers along the road. Sometimes the slow road is prettier in places. But if we take it, it must be the Lord Himself who chooses it for us, because He will be the One to complete the work He started in us, and He knows exactly how much time is left. We dare not choose to suffer longer than He determines because while we suffer, we have little to give.

Sir, to ban everyone from flying, is to take away grace from many people. For the Church to insist that everyone take the long hard road, and to deny anyone the right to ask for prayer for immediate and total healing, and to believe and proclaim it when they receive it, is in my opinion criminal.

I've come across three types of encouragement in the Bible. The first one is for people who need to go through deep waters and who need assurance that they will not be swept away (Isaiah 43:2). This encouragement has an underlying promise: You have to go through deep waters, but in the waters you will enjoy the privilege of seeing first-hand the power of God. You will pass the endurance test.

The second encouragement is for people who are standing on the edge of a flood, and they're being reminded by God that in the past He turned the waters into dry land (Psalm 66:5-6). They receive a different promise: The waters will open up again because you trust in the God who did it before, and you will cross on dry land.

The third encouragement is for those who have little faith – people like me – who are invited to fix their eyes on Jesus and walk on water (Matthew 14:8). The promise for those of us in this group is that we will learn to keep our eyes on Jesus, because there will be nothing else to stand on. From the outside it might seem impressive that we are not sinking, but we will know that we are really like Peter in this story, who walks on the water one moment and denies Jesus the next. We aren't better than the people who have to walk through the water. In fact, the route through the deep is probably reserved for those who've come far in their faith journey.

Can you see that the shortcut does not depend on the person, but on the life route that God in His wisdom uniquely shows each person on their own life map? Who are we to tell others which route they should take?

Sir, you can see how angry your comments made me. The amount of words that just stream out testify to it. I realise now that I'm not really angry at you. I'm angry because Jesus wants to restore His bride in power and glory, but the institutional church, of which you and I are a part, sometimes denies that He can do this quickly and miraculously. Jesus' bride has an extremely difficult road ahead – a road of trials and tribulation. She will see more blood in her time than the church has seen in any other era. In the past century more people have died for their faith than in the previous ten centuries combined. The trend is not promising. But, Christianity is growing faster than ever before. That is promising, as well as revealing.

It is because we prove Jesus alive by the way we bleed, not by the way we prosper.

I personally don't believe that God will pluck us from this planet to miss the final battle. I believe He is dressing us for the fight. If God can take His bride unharmed through water and fire, then it won't be necessary to rescue her from it. A friend of mine who shares my conviction points out that in the flood there was the ark, in the famine there was the stockpiled wheat of Joseph, in the Egyptian plagues there was Goshen – where God's people were safe, and in the desert there were quails and manna. God's people were never snatched away. Instead they were kept safe in the eye of the storm.

Our testimony is a message to the men and women who make up the Bride of Jesus and perhaps the generation that will see Christ's return: You need not fear hard times or even what the Bible calls tribulation, because that will not be the end of you. You will stay whole in the midst of it all. I experienced this miracle first-hand, and therefore I know and declare that God can do it.

I'm not going to allow anyone to stop me from telling God's people that they can be whole. Instead, I'm going to say it again: You will certainly stay whole in the midst of it all, for that is the will of the Father!

The Church of this era, the Bride of Jesus, will see the glory of her Bridegroom clearer than any other Christian generation has. If each new trauma puts her on the bench or in the sick bay for years, how will she win? No, I believe an end-time church is coming that will not be easily knocked out. An army is coming, who fights in the Spirit and sings praises from inside jail cells, not because they're in denial, but because they're acknowledging who Jesus is. The glorious Bride of Christ is coming, spreading hope through powerful healings, not a Church who gives crippled hope by giving everyone permission to linger indefinitely in the hospital of life.

It might surprise you to know how many people have victoriously gone through traumas in the last couple of years. Few have had a platform from which to testify and many have stopped testifying, because the Church has effectively silenced them. They were laughed at and slandered. Like with us, their psychological condition was questioned. These witnesses kept their mouths shut in order to avoid conflict with other Christians and to evade being tagged as 'spiritually conceited' or 'in denial'. But they are not alone. I pray that my testimony will give them courage to declare, with their heads held high, that they have experienced miracles which they will no longer deny.

I have struggles in my life – even sin – that I haven't been victorious over. In that regard we are all the same. We are like children from the big city, travelling the seemingly endless road to the ocean. We yearn to feel the soft, cool sand of the beach under our feet. If we only see people beside us who have never reached the beach either, we all start walking slower and slower, believing that we are all simply on an endless journey. We fear that nobody ever actually reaches the ocean. Maybe the idea of being whole on this earth is like that elusive shore – a false bay, an unattainable joy.

However, when people are allowed to walk beside us, freely testifying that they have reached the shore beyond the same weaknesses or pain that we now struggle with, we won't ask whether they flew or walked there. We will ask them what the weather was like. How was the view on Table Mountain when they stood on Blouberg Strand? What did the sky look like above Main Beach? Could they smell the salt on the sea breeze? The answers would convince us that the ocean is real after all. We would strengthen our weak knees and run like children – all the way to the white sand.

That's why I, having received instant and complete healing from the events of that night by the grace and will of God alone, have been waking up to the proverbial view of Table Mountain every morning since. And I will continue to tell everyone around me and shout it to those who are still far off:

> *"The mountain is blue today! And so are the sea and the sky. The sun is shining with healing in its rays!"*

Sir, with sincerity and with humble apology that I got so worked up, I invite you and all who still can't see the mountain, to make this poem your own:

Healing in the mountains

Tonight the shoulders of the Mountain
carry off my troubles far
The Mountain breeze sweeps my sighs
To far beyond the trees
The cliffs and crags split my cries
And lay them in ravines below
where waterfalls gently drown out
every sound of sorrow
I choose an end to long lament
I curl up at the Mountain's feet
To sleep and dream in peace
While shadows of the moon slide by
And dove song drips down from above
Tomorrow I will wake the dawn
Singing new joy; cooing *Life*

(Hettie Brittz, March 2010, translated).

16 Have you no scars?

Autumn is turning into winter now and everything, including the trail to the robbers, has gone cold. There is a fleeting news report that the police may have found new suspects based on new evidence. They send me mobile phone pictures of underwear and a watch, wanting to know if I recognise any of them. I sadly don't, and that seems to be it for now. The man in the shadows manages to get past the blockings I have put on my phone and computer. He wants to know if I would at least act like an adult, face him and say good bye properly. I decline. I have gone cold, too.

I am still a little hot and bothered about the letters, though. I see more patterns. Many seem to follow the theme of a very popular theology: *Something bad happened to the Brittz family. God will never let bad things happen. Therefore they are the ones who made this happen; they did something wrong that gave Satan the right to make this happen. It's the same black and white theology that Job's friends held to.* It's a very neat theology – logical, predictable and very just. In my opinion it's the theology of people who haven't dared to walk behind the puppet theatre. (And of those who never read the book of Job properly.)

There are many clues to the truth about suffering everywhere in the Bible. Again, it is never sugar-coated. As a starting point to what I have learned about suffering, I want to quote 1 Peter 1:6-7 (*The Message*):

> **The Day is coming when you'll have it all—life healed and whole. I know how great this makes you feel, even though you have to put up with every kind of aggravation in the meantime. Pure gold put in the fire comes out of it proved pure; genuine faith put through this suffering comes out proved genuine. When Jesus wraps this all up, it's your faith, not your gold, that God will have on display as evidence of his victory.**

I can't help but think how genuine Job's faith was proven by all the fire Satan had piled on him. His gold, among everything else, did not survive – but he did. And ultimately God won the day and proved Satan wrong on his initial charge that Job was only living so righteously because his life was so easy. The god-fearing façade would melt, Satan claimed. God gave the green light to heat up Job's entire world past boiling point (no pun with the boils intended). To his friends all this suffering 'proved' a skeleton in Job's closet, while to the entire spiritual world it proved that true faith in the true God stands through prosperity and adversity – true as gold.

The book of Job is about perspective: God's, Satan's and ours. It is about giving us more than just the human perspective so we can choose our theology wisely. To choose a theology or philosophy to live by is similar to choosing which car to travel in. If I want to know which car is the safest to drive, I look for statistics that were not compiled in the laboratory. I don't care how a car performs in a sterile simulation, connected to a computer. I want to know how it performs on the dangerous South African roads. I want to know how many of this specific model were involved in accidents in which no one was killed. It's my measuring stick. I'm not interested in hearing that a model has never been written off in an accident, because that tells me something about the scarcity of the vehicle or the abilities of the drivers, but nothing about the car. I want to know that even when driven badly or smashed into by a bad driver, the car would give me a fair chance of survival. Show me a wreck from which people have crawled unscathed. I want to invest in that car.

Job's car seemed to have been written off, but on closer inspection you see the brand name or at least the slogan. Far from *Toyota's 'everything keeps going right'*, his vehicle's slogan reads: *'God gives, God takes away, praise God!'* He seems to crawl out alive and his motto never changes. He has a few issues about God as to God's right to take away as much as He eventually did, or at least letting Satan do it, but Job gets right back into the same brand of vehicle when all is said and done. With a little difference that we will get to soon. His friends, as we will see, were driving Toyota's ...

Meaning no disrespect, people should perhaps look at God the way they look at a car. Can He keep me out of trouble completely (which proves very little), or can He – and I think this is much better – take me through serious trouble in one piece? It seems to me that God wants to be a vehicle for us, to take us through the fire smoke-free, with our faith intact. From the outside our lives may look like a horrendous accident, but those who look closer will see that there is no fatalities. In fact, whoever truly looks beyond the mangled metal, will see us stepping out stronger than before.

Like the impurities in gold, our erroneous faith anchors are what needs to be burned away with fire. These may include: "I believe God is pleased with me because He is abundantly blessing my business. I believe God is good because my children and I are healthy. I believe in the power of the cross, because every house on the street has had a break-in except mine with the cross on the front gate. I believe in the blood of Jesus, because every time I have pleaded the blood of Jesus over my car before leaving, I have not been in an accident."

This sounds like a Toyota variation to me. *"Everything keeps going right ... because I keep doing things right."* Will this car survive a wreck? What I mean is, will the blood of Jesus still have meaning to you if your only child dies in the car you just prayed over? Will God still be good if you should be diagnosed with cancer? Will the cross still be your only hope if an accidental fire burns it to a crisp along with your home and all your possessions? A faith anchored to a religious habit or a superstitious symbol is what burns away in a faith crisis. It seems cruel but it is grace. All that's left in the end will be Jesus, if you have Him. Whoever keeps Jesus as his only treasure will not suffer permanent damage, and will gain eternal profit from every temporary loss they suffer.

Pure faith is the faith of Hebrews 11. One should read chapter 10 as an introduction because it talks about unfair suffering and the loss of all things dear as the background to true faith. It describes the kind of carnage that our faith is strong enough to survive. Like Noah, who built an ark even though he didn't know what rain was, or like Abraham, who moved to a new country even though he had no heir to leave it to, like Moses, who chose to suffer with slaves rather than eat from Pharaoh's table – our faith convinces us that God is true and good and faithful. The early Christians did not drive Toyota's. They were sawed in half and understood that their salvation and their love for God did not exempt them from such suffering. True faith can help believers win wars, but it can also permit believers to die heroically in battle. True faith, Hebrews 11 teaches us, is not insurance – it is *assurance*.

The test of true faith is locked up in suffering as well as in prosperity. Both can take our focus off God. Prosperity can move our focus from His face to His hands. We become like spoiled children waiting at the airport for their dad's return from overseas – their eyes fixed on an invisible mark between the two sliding doors at the approximate height of the expected gift bags.

Prosperity tests our love of things, and hardship tests our love of God. If we only love God when it's going well, we will find that things become our gods; however, if we love God in spite of hardship, we will find that God is always good. We don't measure Him against the happenings in our lives or by our material prosperity. To quote a pastor I know: "God is always good. When He is not good, He's fantastic." Does this quote seem like a cheap cliché? This pastor saw his daughter raped by his best friend, and subsequently saw the inside of a prison where he served a long sentence for murdering that friend. His "always" does not come from a place of blissful ignorance. "God is good, always good" is the slogan on the wreck that he crawled out of alive, because it is solid theology, clearly not because he did everything right.

I walk around constantly preaching to an invisible audience, thinking how grateful everyone should be that God is still holding me back from talking in public. I have to cool down a bit first, but I find it hard to do because I am so thrilled that the car I picked so many years ago has turned out to be the safe one. I know better than anyone else that God gave it to me for free. I want everyone to return their Toyota's to the shady dealer that sold them the counterfeit. Everything cannot always go right, no matter which car you drive.

I try to mind my own business and pray about God's journey with me once He lets me minister to others again. It is only the 22nd of May, so there are many months still left in this year to try and string my words together properly. I write these words of Spurgeon in my journal, as he seems to have a sound response to bad events figured out clearly and simply:

> *Is this part of God's plan for me? Can this be the way in which God would bring me to heaven? Yes, it is even so! The eclipse of your faith, the darkness of your mind, the fainting of your hope – all these things are but part of God's method of making you ready for the great inheritance into which you will soon enter. These trials are for the testing and strengthening of your faith. They are waves that wash you further upon the Rock.*

The morning after the rape I read these words of Charles Spurgeon, which mean more to me now that I see people's faith dying when their Toyota's crash:

> **The Christian more often disgraces his profession of faith in prosperity than in adversity. It's a dangerous thing to be prosperous. The crucible of adversity is a less severe trial to the Christian than the refinery of prosperity ... More than human skill is needed to carry an overflowing cup of mortal joy with a steady hand ... Satisfied with earth, we are content to do without heaven.**

What sort of faith can only accept the good in life? It's the sort of faith the devil had thought Job had, and it turned out his wife and friends did have. It's a faith that believes everything keeps going right when we do everything right and things go wrong because someone has made a mistake.

A friend of mine spent most of her life as a missionary in countries where poverty, suffering and rape are old news. Without writing another word, she simply sent me this poem when she heard our news:

Have you no scar?

Have you no scar? No hidden scar on foot, or side, or hand?
I hear you sung as mighty in the land.
I hear them hail your bright ascendant star.
Have you no scar?
Have you no wound?

Yet, I was wounded by the archers, spent,
leaned me against the tree to die,
and rent – by ravenous beasts that encompassed me
I swooned.
Have you no wound?
No wound? No scar?

Yes, as the master shall the servant be,
and pierced are the feet that follow Me,
but yours are whole.
Can he have followed far – who has no wound? No scar?
Can she have followed far – who has no wound? No scar?

(Amy Carmichael)

Could it be that it is part of the plan for every follower of Jesus to bear scars? If I read 1 Peter 4 correctly, then yes, it could be:

> **Since Jesus went through everything you're going through and more, learn to think like Him. Think of your suffering as a weaning from that old sinful habit of always expecting to get your own way. Then you'll be able to live out your days free to pursue what God wants instead of being tyrannized by what you want.**
>
> (*The Message*)

It's a fresh perspective when we realise that to want what we want essentially amounts to slavery. When we realise that our desires and comforts are tyrants ruling over us, then suffering becomes a key that can help us shed our shackles. It's through suffering that we can gain true freedom. The type of suffering I'm talking about here is different from the robbery and rape. I'm referring to the hard, extended suffering that we experience when it takes a long time to achieve victory. It's when our flesh is slowly being tortured to death and when we decide how long we want to drag it out by whether or not we continue to hold onto our self-interest. That's the road I have learned to walk, in fact sometimes crawl, to get rid of my own rebellious self. This kind of growth always takes time.

Growth and healing are not always the same thing. In verse 12 Peter continues to explain this:

> **Friends, when life gets really difficult, don't jump to the conclusion that God isn't on the job. Instead, be glad that you are in the very thick of what Christ experienced. This is a spiritual refining process, with glory just around the corner.**

In Peter 5:10-11 the good news arrives: Suffering won't last forever because Jesus has the final say.

That's why I confront people when it seems like Jesus has called out the final healing words over them, yet instead of receiving their healing, they shackle their own feet together again. Because they are so upset about being cuffed in the first place – something their theology did not leave room for -- that the miracle of the lock-picking angels passes them by.

When you start talking about the book of Job, many people, especially the 'adults' that I talked about in my introduction, fly up from their seats to stop you. There are those who feel we are not allowed to look behind the puppet theatre. They say: "Job's tale is only a disturbing myth, and it doesn't tell us much. Just keep looking at the puppets and the décor. Look carefully at Job. In some ways, Job brought this on himself. You have to watch carefully and you will find proof to confirm his friends' suspicions. He has hidden secrets that will explain everything!"

Many Christians, usually those who adhere to the neat theology wherein God is predictable, use the argument that everything happened to Job because he feared that it would happen. They base this on Job's cry that everything he feared had come over him, conveniently ignoring that God Himself said Job had done nothing to deserve it. Some of these Toyota drivers have listened to our testimony, nodding their heads like they had just figured the whole thing out. One even came to me to help me answer the 'why- question:

> *"It is because you were afraid of rape that you were raped. Your own fear came over you. Moving into the security complex was an act of not trusting God. It opened the door for the enemy to come in."*

If this line of thinking were true, then all of my teeth should have fallen out by now, because I have been afraid that I would lose all my teeth since I lost my very first tooth. And every single woman in South Africa should have been raped by now, except of course those who aren't afraid of being raped, if such a woman exists. Every mom who was ever afraid that she would lose her child should have lost her child by now and the only teenagers alive would be those whose moms never cautioned: 'drive safely' and 'call when you get there!'

If our fears are the cause of our suffering, then one can argue that Jesus' anxiety in Gethsemane caused His violent death. It's absurd theology. The Word of God is clear about this: Only the fears of the *faithless* materialise, not ours, since they fear that there is no God and then end up in eternity without Him. Our hope, on the other hand, will never disappoint us.

Proverbs 10:24 says:

> **The fears of the wicked will be fulfilled; the hopes of the godly will be granted.**
>
> (*New Living Translation*)

Other people read the book of Job differently and are even more convinced of the irrelevance of the whole story. They are the learned who very wisely quote what they were taught in Bible school: Job is a collection of beautiful poems, mainly about animals. It's not historically correct. It is wisdom literature at best, but more likely poetry, and if you think carefully you will realise it shares the type of wisdom typical of that era's world view – naive. Simply put, the introductory line should read "for entertainment purposes only." We need to calm down, go back to our seats in the theatre, and stop alarming others by claiming that this book contains revelation from God, and that it tells of His plans and Satan's.

I believe it is no use trying to read it as a mere story, although I have to admit that the poetry is indeed exceptional. In Job the puppet theatre is turned back to front from the very first chapter. Or maybe I should say it is set up as an open stage with the readers' seats in a circle for a full 360 degree view. The curtains between the earthly stage and the heavenly backstage are lifted. The danger lies not in perhaps spotting God, or even worse – the devil – behind the curtains. The danger lies in not seeing the hairy arms at all and thinking the story is just about puppet Job and his boils, his puppet children and their parties, his puppet wife who can't stand the sight of him, or his dear puppet friends that he could have done without. No, the whole idea is to look past the puppets and décor and to stare into the forbidden backstage area. It gives a rare opportunity to walk around the theatre and gain a helpful perspective on the unjust pain of this life.

In The Message, Eugene Peterson writes the introduction to Job in such a way that it's impossible for readers to overlook the Puppet Master and the Dragon. The way in which God's actions are portrayed will definitely make a few heads turn or even spin. But those who choose to watch until the end will be happy they did.

> *It's not suffering as such that troubles us. It's undeserved suffering. This is the suffering that first bewilders us and then outrages us. Job makes poetry out of what in many of us is only a tangle of confused whimpers. Job does not curse God as his wife suggests he should do, getting rid of the problem by getting rid of God.*

But neither does Job explain *suffering. Suffering is a mystery, and Job comes to respect the mystery. Perhaps the greatest mystery in suffering is how it can bring a person into the presence of God in a state of worship, full of wonder, love and praise. Suffering does not inevitably do that, but it does it far more often than we would expect.*

Peterson adds that the reasons for suffering are not being avoided by Job because Job thinks the answers are forbidden. Rather, he believes Job rejected the human tone with which we sing the answers:

The book of Job does not reject answers as such. It's the secularisation of the answers that is rejected – answers severed from their Source, the living God, the Word that both batters us and heals us. We cannot have truth about *God divorced from the mind and heart* of *God. The ironic fact of the matter is that more often than not, people do not suffer less when they are committed to following God, but more. When these people go through suffering, their lives are often transformed, deepened, marked with beauty and holiness, in remarkable ways that could never have been anticipated before the suffering.*

I read this a few days after being a guest on a TV insert with a particular pastor I had not met before. He personified this transformed beauty to me. He was a picture of humility, soft-heartedness, patience, warmth, friendliness, wisdom and generosity. I shared this with a friend who happens to know him well. I learned from her that his son had committed suicide a few years earlier. This clarified what I saw in him – the beautiful scar which suffering leaves on us. A scar that is by no means disfiguring.

Louis and I pray that the scar of suffering in our lives will be beautiful. For that reason we can never wish away the robbery, rape, or the temptations we've had to fight and mountains we've had to climb. The gain has simply been immeasurable.

If we could ask Job today about his suffering, how would he answer us? Would he shake his head, clasp his hands together, sigh, roll his eyes, and then with a shrug of his shoulders declare that he has no idea why it all happened? No! With a mysterious twinkle in his eye, he would tell us how his suffering had saved him from great foolishness, and then he might repeat what he had told God back then:

I now realise that I'm only a living doll, and You're not a mere character in my story. You write the script and no one can hijack the pen with which it is written. Dear me, that's precisely what I tried to do, wasn't it? Was I really crazy enough to think I could prescribe to You the course my life should have taken? How I put my folly on display by speaking out of turn on things I didn't have a clue about! What You did and still do is in another dimension altogether and my doll-head is too flat to take it all in. You did and still do miracles which I attempt to unravel in vain.

You put a finger to my lips that day to silence me so I wouldn't make a complete fool of myself by putting You in the hot seat with all my questions. You swapped our seats around and peppered me with the real questions at hand. Through my clumsy attempts at smart answers I finally arrived at the truth: I'm a puppet man;

You are God.

Growing up, I heard stories in which You were nothing more than one of the characters, and I believed them. But then, suddenly plucked into backstage by my suffering, my eyes popped with new perspective. I saw who I am and who You are. All the animal stories made no sense then. Looking back I now know You wanted me to see Your hand in the ostrich puppet, the hippopotamus puppet and the crocodile puppet. Those were very good clues, but I had been too busy preparing my defence to connect the dots ...

Then I handed the pen back to You. I begged You to write my story Your way. You have one hand firmly inside my life and the other on paper. You write much better life stories than I ever could. I was too embarrassed to make any more proposals for the script. I still am. Thank you for excusing my presumptuousness.

(My own paraphrase of Job 42 verses 2-6.)

17 *Pitching tents*

Our news has now had months to reach a few people who missed it when it happened, many of them former South Africans who had always known this country was unsafe. They keep inviting us to move our home to higher grounds, so to speak. It makes me think about hope and what that means. If I had lost hope for a meaningful life here, I certainly would consider it, but I haven't. The opposite happened.

> **I saw God before me for all time. Nothing can shake me; He's right by my side. I'm glad from the inside out, ecstatic; I've pitched my tent in the land of hope. I know You'll never dump me in Hades; I'll never even smell the stench of death. You've got my feet on the life-path, with your face shining sun-joy all around.**
>
> (Acts 2:27-28, *The Message*)

A friend of ours from Tennessee shared this piece of Scripture with us one evening. I strongly identify with it, since I have this joy now. A joy that does not come from my circumstances but one that springs up inside and pours out, changing my view on my circumstances. I have a deeper hope now that I know the life God has for me is indestructible. I'm certain that my feet will permanently be on a path of life, even when I give those last few steps to the other side. In this life and the next I know with certainty that God's face will shine over me with joy and favour. Death has lost its grip on the way I think and live. The stench of the grave will never cling to me, because I now live in Christ who was the first to succeed in giving death a slip.

When we pitch a tent, it means that we won't be staying forever. Tents are temporary. They are also fragile. They can't be insured against fire or theft. I've never seen one with burglar proofing or an alarm system. They are never really a hundred percent waterproof, either. Living in a tent means making peace with the frailty of life as well. Paul, a tentmaker by trade and an apostle by calling, understood these things about tents and about life. He very poetically wrote about our earthly bodies as tents that will someday be dismantled, folded up and set aside so that we can go to live with God for eternity. He encourages us to always keep this perspective.

> **For instance, we know that when these bodies of ours are taken down like tents and folded away, they will be replaced by resurrection bodies in heaven—God-made, not handmade—and we'll never have to relocate our**

"tents" again. Sometimes we can hardly wait to move—and so we cry out in frustration. Compared to what's coming, living conditions around here seem like a stopover in an unfurnished shack, and we're tired of it! We've been given a glimpse of the real thing, our true home, our resurrection bodies! The Spirit of God whets our appetite by giving us a taste of what's ahead. He puts a little of heaven in our hearts so that we'll never settle for less.

That's why we live with such good cheer. You won't see us drooping our heads or dragging our feet! Cramped conditions here don't get us down. They only remind us of the spacious living conditions ahead. It's what we trust in but don't yet see that keeps us going. Do you suppose a few ruts in the road or rocks in the path are going to stop us? When the time comes, we'll be plenty ready to exchange exile for homecoming.

(2 Corinthians 5:1-8, *The Message*)

This is one of the most important mind shifts we have to make if we wish to be able to correctly handle life's onslaughts against our bodies, our possessions, and our finances. When we look only at the temporary, then our loss of health, status, and possessions can be very traumatic. When we forget, even for a moment, that we're only in our temporary tent now, we can easily start holding onto something of very little value as if our lives depended on it.

We can react to a crisis in one of three ways – with our flesh alone, with our soul on the front lines, or with our spirit as a shield. For example, what would our reaction be if someone insulted us? The fleshly reaction would be to hit back, without even thinking. A reaction from the soul would be to think about it, get emotional, maybe even follow someone's advice, and then collect our thoughts, will and words to plan the best possible reaction. The spiritual response would be to react in the opposite spirit. It might mean that we answer softly, push our own feelings aside, and listen to what comes from the other person's heart. It may even include a range of actions that Jesus would call 'turning the other cheek'.

People who respond from a healthy, mature spirit would probably be able to stay calm and not even let the insult affect them. Such people would be able to see the insulting ones from God's perspective, and would love them. A healthy spirit can trumps one's soul and body when it comes to our responses to life's hard knocks.

We need lots of practice to learn how to put our spirits on the frontlines of life's battles, because it is as unnatural and illogical to us as the war strategy of Jehoshaphat that we read of in 2 Chronicles 20. His first response to the news of a fast advancing enemy troop that far outnumbered them should surely be to recruit more forces, to forge more weapons, to instruct his soldiers to stock up, dress up, fill up on nutritious food and head out. Instead, he calls a fast and a prayer meeting. He admits in front of his entire nation that he does not have the first clue how to win the war. And then he waits for God's instruction.

The Holy Spirit stirs up a young prophet to speak words of encouragement. Jehoshaphat believes the prophesy that God would defeat the impossibly large enemy army on their behalf. His next step, after seemingly weakening his forces and wasting valuable time to assemble everyone for prayer, he sends for the praise and worship team to go ahead of the soldiers into battle. Imagine your army recruiting your church choir as front liners. Please do not cheer the thought, no matter how off-key your choir is. I know some church choirs could potentially sing the enemy to death, but this is not our topic, now.

By praising God and declaring the simple but profound truth *'his love endures forever,'* they effectively had their spirit out in front like a shield. They defeated the enemy without lifting a single sword. Or rather, God did it for them by confusing the troops and making them turn on one another until not a single soldier was left alive. It took Jehoshaphat's army three days to collect the loot. That is what a spiritual victory looks like: illogical, effective, and full of rich rewards. Oddly, it may at times require keeping the soldiers, which we can probably compare with our bodies and souls – out of the picture. We have to believe verse 17:

> **You won't have to lift a hand in this battle; just stand firm, Judah and Jerusalem, and watch GOD's saving work for you take shape. Don't be afraid, don't waver. March out boldly tomorrow—GOD is with you.**
>
> (*The Message*)

When we decide where we pitch our tents, we take a position in which we acknowledge that we are only travellers on this earth and our eternal homes are in heaven. Where we position ourselves on this earth will either aid or hinder our spirit from leading the battle on the frontlines.

Many Christians struggle to pitch their tents beside mine in the land of hope – even Christians that I believe are spiritually more mature than I am. Each of us walks a different road through life. Our faith journeys are not straight lines on which we can indicate our progress in percentages. It would be silly to say that I'm now 30%, 50% or 60% spiritually mature. Our faith journeys look more like a toddler's scribbling – full of loops and turns that cut through the same point numerous times. The Israelites followed a circle route of wandering around like this on their journey through the desert, before arriving at their land of hope.

How we respond 'in the desert' reveals a lot about our pain, but it also reveals a lot about where we stand with the Lord on our journey of growth. Each of us needs to stop at certain wells in the wilderness, and I believe the Lord will take us there again and again until we drink enough of that particular well's living water. We need those truths to sink in to the point where we really live them out, or God will make sure we go around the mountain and back to the well as many times as it takes. Hopefully we will remember every life-altering truth. The Israelites built altars or monuments at each well of truth as a memorial to the liberating revelations they didn't want to forget. We should probably at least journal what we learn.

On our journey from well to well, we will meet truth every time but also death. At each one of these wells yet another piece of our flesh must die.

Everyone who hears our testimony reacts from the places they are at on their spiritual journeys. Some people have been at the same wells that we have and recognise the monuments. They understand what we are trying to remember. Some are at different wells, drinking other truths. That's why I have learned from many of the writers behind even the most aggressive letters. They are at a different well, or have perhaps forgotten a truth they once knew. Some have been hurt so many times that they don't dare lower their shields, sing praises and let their spirits live out front.

The story of our spiritual fathers – Abraham, Isaac, and Jacob – is a very interesting one, with continual references to the wells and altars they made in their desert land. The writer of their story went to a lot of trouble to mention every well and altar and to emphasize the meanings of each well's name. Through following their struggle from well to well, we can gage where we are and where we might want to head next in our own thirst for living truth.

The story starts in Genesis 21. Abraham is already living in the land of promise; Isaac has been born, and God is making them prosper. Hagar and Ishmael have just been chased off into the desert like dogs after a jealousy-driven argument with Sarah. Now, for the first time we come to know the well of Beersheba – 'the well of promise'. Hagar is sitting on the ground beside it, sobbing. Her son is dying of thirst under a bush nearby. She can't bear to see it. And she can't see the well to save her life – quite literally. It is completely invisible until the Lord opens her eyes by speaking the life-giving promise to her:

> *"I have an inheritance for you too!"* (Genesis 21:19).

Some years later Isaac and Rebekah stayed at Beer-Lahai-Roi, which means 'well of the Living One who sees me', which was the same well. Hagar might very well have given it this name after her wonderful encounter with God[1].

It is at this well, the place where we feel like Hagar – utterly hopeless, rejected like a slave's child – where we often discover that the Lord hears and sees us after all. It is here that our blindfolds, woven out of the many lies we believe about ourselves and God, suddenly fall off our eyes. We see the well. We hear a sound that drowns out the sobbing. We hear a promise that starts with our name. There we drink of the life-saving water from the well of promise – Beersheba.

I believe this is where the journey should start for all of us. The moment we are noticed among the billions of people on this earth, and given the assurance that the God who counts people *'one, one, one ...'* has counted us, is the moment our spirit jumps to life. Until then we cannot even see the well and life's journey makes no sense. Until then we hate or are at least a little annoyed by the Sarahs and Isaacs who seem to live with a promise, even though we don't quite know why. Until then, we may be some of the angry letter writers, needing to hear someone say: *"I don't want to see you feel rejected. I want to see generations of our children playing together in the land of hope. God has more than enough riches for all of us to take part in this inheritance. Get up, find the well, drink the truth and start living your promise."*

---

[1] According to the International Standard Bible Encyclopaedia

Charles Spurgeon explains it like this:

> **If I have any suspicion that Christ is not mine, then there is vinegar mingled with the gall of death, but if I know that Jesus lives for me, then the darkness is not dark. Even the night is light about me!**

Abraham starts here at Beersheba, too. After making a covenant with the Philistines, he calls Abimelech to be his witness that the well of Beersheba is his. Abraham claims that he had dug it himself, and he warns Abimelech's shepherds not to take it again, as they had done once before. Abraham erects his first altar here by planting a tamarisk tree. This well of promise embodies the legacy that Abraham knows God had promised him. He would not stand by and see it stolen.

As the story continues Jacob and his twin brother Esau are born. Their father, Isaac, had a difficult journey of his own. Like his father Abraham, he found himself at odds with Abimelech over a 'sister' who was in fact a wife, and over wells with disputed ownership. The Philistines played dirty and filled the wells with waste. One of these wells was the well of promise at Beersheba. Isaac abandoned that well and decided to dig others. In his frustration he gave them the names 'Quarrel' and 'Accusation' because of the conflict he experienced during the whole process. We get the impression that he felt short-changed and threatened. There was no sign of joy even in this highly favoured son of the promise! He had his eyes on others and their wells, instead of on God and his promises.

These wells are symbolic of a place we may find ourselves on our journey. Some of us may even get stuck here in a permanent quarrel, envying so much the cool, fresh water we see others drinking and feeling threatened by it, instead of minding our own thirst. The wells of our lives get clogged up in the way the Philistines clogged up the well of promise. Disputes over temporary matters, personality clashes and conflicting views lead to a constant state of discontent. All because we lose perspective in the way Isaac did here. All because we do not hold onto our own well of promise, trusting God to be good to us in time.

The third well that Isaac dug he named Rehoboth which means 'open space'. This time around nobody argued, because Isaac discovered that there was more than enough space for everyone in the land of hope. Subsequently Isaac's servants and shepherds unblocked the well at Beersheba and called him with the news that they had found water. Of course the water had always been there, but it had to be opened up once again. In a way we don't simply inherit our forefather's water. I suspect that each new generation needs to dig out the Lord's promises from the mud and dirt themselves. But the promises stay the same, in the same place, unchanged because of the faithful character of the One who made the promises.

Isaac finally arrived at the place where he could continue building on the Lord's covenant without fear and without striving. He was no longer fighting for a place in the sun. He was now living the spirit life in a wide open space of grace and God's favour.

Unfortunately, the next generation lost the well again as Jacob had to flee from there because, through lies and betrayal, he robbed his brother Esau of his birth right and the precious firstborn blessing. It's no coincidence that Jacob's name meant 'Supplanter' –

one who uproots another from his rightful place with deceit, and then takes his place. This is precisely what he did.

Jacob fled to Haran which means 'crossroads'. On his way to this important crossroads he had the famous dream of the ladder and the angels. He planted his stone pillow in the ground as an altar and called it Bethel – 'The house of the Lord'. Something interesting took place here. God gave him the same promises He had given his ancestors, and at first it seemed as if this convinced Jacob to build on the Lord as his Rock. But, if we listen carefully, we discover that he was planning on checking things out first, before deciding whether or not he would take the candle that was being held out to him. He wanted a Toyota as his god. He made a vow: *"If* God will indeed be with me and protect me on this journey, and *if* he will provide me with food and clothing, and *if* I return safely to my father's home, *then* the LORD will certainly be my God." (Genesis 28:20-21, *New Living Translation, italics mine*).

He seemed to want to take the car for a test drive, didn't he? And he arrogantly made the vow attractive by promising the Lord that he would give Him a tenth of everything the Lord gave him. Didn't he hear the nature of the promise? God already vowed to be his God, unconditionally, yet Jacob chose to set conditions. God had to earn the title first, and the list of pre-requisites that Jacob had was very specific. He might as well have said: "If I'm safe, fed, clothed and always prosperous, we can talk about this again. Let's see how it goes first." Jacob chose the temporary. He chose to live from his flesh and to measure God by counting material and temporary blessings.

Many people live at Bethel, every Sunday they sit in the house of the Lord, metaphorically speaking, still sussing things out. Even though they're showing up and even tithing, some are still testing God to see if He is doing enough to earn the title of "my God". People who are here look at what happened to me and Louis and say in so many words: "My God would never have allowed that. I don't know what God they serve, but mine is too loving to allow a woman to be raped." Some go even further: "I would never worship a God that allows something like that." Disillusioned, others write: "If God can't protect us from violence like this, what hope do we have left?"

All of these reactions are emotional reactions. While our tents are still pitched at Bethel, we will struggle to differentiate between our will and God's will. We expect God to act in line with our will, thoughts and emotions. In other words, if He acts according to our will, our thoughts and what we are comfortable with emotionally, then we will agree that He is good. If his actions don't please these three dimensions of our soul being, we're unsure and unsettled. We fear God may not be God at all. Or not good after all.

We can get stuck here, never growing beyond an existence where our circumstances define our view of God. Our lives will be like a leaky tent leaving us wet inside whenever it is wet outside. We can only live with real hope when we embrace the fact that God's will is one of those mysteries theologians try to understand and explain with clever words but never will get quite right. In Bible School I learned of God's 'perfect' and 'permissive' will; his 'active' and 'passive' will. His permissive will, I was taught, includes all the things He allows to happen even though He doesn't really want them to happen. His passive will includes the things He wants but does not force to happen. His active will are things

He does because He wants to. Some people can get themselves to the point where they agree that my rape fell within God's permissive will but that my never getting hurt is his passive will. But the idea that it was part of a plan or that one could ever say it was God's will, is too much for most to bear. It would rip the entire puppet theatre to shreds if it were true.

Reading Isaiah 53:10, does it sound like an example of God's active or passive will? Would you think it is God's permissive will or his perfect will?

> **But it was the LORD's good plan to crush him and cause him grief.**
>
> (*New Living Translation*)

It seems to me that more than a permissive will is at work here. Is it not true that God *wanted* Jesus to die for us? Is it not true that it was his *fixed intention* for it to be a humiliating, crushing death? God *chose* and *foretold* it that way because He looked at it not with the eyes of a human soul, but with the insight of his eternal Spirit. God is a timeless Being, seeing everything for all it was, is or can be – all at once, and calls it good or bad based on that complete perspective. He is never short-sighted. He does not judge things based on feeling or thought. He bases His will, I believe, on what I want to call spiritual *all-sight*. The consequence of the death of his Son is eternal life! That *all-sight* makes him call that horrible day a good plan! Some wise church father understood this when he decided to call crucifixion Friday "Good Friday".

Is it perhaps possible that other seemingly horrible things could be God's will, because the end result would be something wonderful and even glorious?

Jesus himself said the following about the will of God:

> **This, in a nutshell, is that will: that everything handed over to me by the Father be completed—not a single detail missed—and at the wrap-up of time I have everything and everyone put together, upright and whole. This is what my Father wants: that anyone who sees the Son and trusts who he is and what he does and then aligns with him will enter real life, eternal life. My part is to put them on their feet alive and whole at the completion of time.**
>
> (John 6:39-41, *The Message*).

The tone we pick up here is "Whatever it takes." Can you hear it? Jesus is going to do the will of the Father, no matter what obstacles are in His way. He will put us on our feet. This suggests we may be knocked down at times. He will make us whole. This means we may experience brokenness. He will put us before the Father fully alive. This He will do in spite of death.

Isaiah 53:10 also says that Jesus will successfully complete his Father's will:

> **Still, it's what God had in mind all along, to crush him with pain. The plan was that he give himself as an offering for sin so that he'd see life come from it – life, life and more life. And God's plan will deeply prosper through him.**
>
> (*The Message*)

God has the bigger picture in mind: We need to be saved, resurrected on the last day, and placed in front of the Father, whole and holy. The finer details of this process aren't that important. Does it really matter if we arrive at the end goal via poverty, riches, popularity, obscurity, sickness or health? Isn't everything that happens to us done in order to reach this one goal – our complete salvation? From our perspective, the details seem awfully important. Like Jacob we have a list of minimum requirements. We want to journey to the end that is promised, but we want to have all the say in the journey.

Imagine for a moment that your tent is already dismantled and you are already on the other side of death, eternally with God. If then, excited and saved, you look back from that viewpoint to today's pain, how relevant would the question – *was my suffering God's permitted, perfect, active or passive will?* – be? Would you still base your conclusion whether God is God and a good God at that, on whether you had suffered a car crash, a robbery, the loss of a child, cancer or a rape? Would your soul still be protesting or would your spirit finally have the *all-sight* that God has had all along?

I believe in a God who is much bigger than my own insight – that's why He is GOD. I refuse to worship one who can't see further than I can, who doesn't have deeper understanding than I have, or who can't do more than I could ever think of or imagine doing. My life view is this: This life is temporary – God's Life is eternal. Our so-called realities can only really be understood from God's eternal bird's eye view. C. S. Lewis said it well:

> **I believe in Christianity as I believe that the sun has risen: not only because I see it, but because by it I see everything else.**

I strive to look at my life in the light of a heavenly reality. Even though we don't understand much about it, it still remains the determining reality. A spiritual perspective on life is like the rising sun Lewis spoke of – it sheds light on things we would not have understood in the light of just our own insight.

The way we handle the things that happen to us can take us closer to or further away from God's will for us – our salvation. Paul wrote this truth about the suffering church community in Corinth had undergone:

> **And now, isn't it wonderful all the ways in which this distress has goaded you closer to God? You're more alive, more concerned, more sensitive, more reverent, more human, more passionate, more responsible. Looked at from any angle you've come out of this with purity of heart.**
>
> (2 Corinthians 7:11-13, *The Message*)

Could one say that God willed them to have sensitive, pure hearts and chose for them this difficult journey to get there?

Many people, who are still at Bethel, might not want to hear the truth that we can't test-drive this vehicle called true faith without getting into it, and that we won't know if God will be our God if we don't surrender everything into His hands. Many Bethel Christians don't like this idea of blind and boundless abdication. They want to know the privileges and rights they will be able to claim for themselves. They would like to know which of God's rights are restricted, too. It's dangerous to enter into a contract with a partner with unrestricted rights! This is where we are confronted with a new way of thinking. The undertaking between us and God is not an equal contract between two business partners. It's a covenant of grace. We don't bring anything, because we have nothing God needs. We receive everything we need, even though we may not even know that we do. Everything that is locked up in Jesus becomes ours. We're shocked by the inequality of it all when we realise what this means. It leaves us questioning exactly what it is that we're going to get from all of this if we were to sign our lives away.

God's rights to our lives will be unlimited. It is daunting for sure. The truth that can sway our decision, though, is the fact that our access to God's eternal riches and favour will also be unlimited.

Jacob underwent a few lessons to discover this for himself. He had his own plans and was very excited about the life he would build for himself. Opportunities and a beautiful girl presented themselves right at the offset. He was going to execute his first plan: work very hard for the woman of his dreams. It didn't work out well since he was tricked into working another seven years for her. When he married her, we didn't see him praying for his barren wife the way Abraham and Isaac had prayed for theirs. Instead, we see him angry and frustrated with her. He showed the clear symptoms of a manipulator who discovered some things were beyond his manipulation.

We also see Jacob talking about God, but not to God. A key signature of a Bethel believer. A test driver.

In Genesis 30:26-27 we see his take on what had become spectacular prosperity. He believed he had achieved it all by the sweat of his brow and the brilliance of his brain. Even Laban could see that it was the Lord's favour on Jacob, but Jacob was too busy with his own life script to realise that it was God doing everything. The puppet thought he was pulling the strings.

He went on pulling even more by putting his next plan into action: He peeled strips of bark from branches to create white stripes so that the mating flocks of sheep would produce striped and spotted young when they mate while seeing the striped branches in the watering troughs. Unless my understanding of genetics is flawed, there is no way that simply looking at white striped branches would produce striped and spotted flocks. Jacob danced wildly, convinced he had made his own rain. God allowed him to dance wilder and wilder for a while, but behind the curtains of his puppet theatre there was something else going on. God was increasing Jacob's wealth, just as He had promised He would, while waiting for Jacob to grow tired of all his dancing.

Now wealthy and blessed, God called him back to his own country. Instead of realising that God was behind it all, Jacob sang his wives a very self-centred and conceited song about dreams and visions and moments with the angel of the Lord. He claimed that he had walked the straight and narrow, and that Laban had been the one trying to cheat him. He claimed that Laban wanted to harm him but that God had never allowed it because Jacob had been in the right and Laban in the wrong all along. Jacob's wives were so impressed by his version of the story that they agreed their father was the crook. They vowed to follow wherever the Lord told their husband to go. But he did not follow God home. He ran, fleeing across the river into the mountains, not like one who knew he was favoured but like one who fought for himself and planned to escape by the same cunning as he had always made his own rain. He boasted about God on his side but ran like one who had no God.

Even when Laban caught up with him, Jacob showed no signs of gratitude. All of his arguments were based on what he thought he deserved. He spoke of all the hard times he had had, to prove that he had earned all of his wealth. Not for one moment was he willing to confess the truth that Laban had been trying to help him realise: Jacob, you had nothing when you arrived here. Everything you own came from my abundance through the Lord's favour upon you.

Jacob's self-righteous stance underscores the irony of the altar that is erected next. In an attempt to settle their difference, they made a monument to justice. They called it Galeed, which means 'witness pile'. They also call it Mizpah, which means 'watchtower'. They called upon God to be a witness between them. God had to pick sides, actually, by watching them for any sign of injustice towards one another. By implication I think they expected God to punish or at least judge the one who was in the wrong. Two frauds insisting on fairness. It was almost laughable.

This insistence on absolute justice and fairness is something many Christians do, believing it is godly. I will call them Mizpah Christians. They respond to a testimony like ours by saying: *"Don't worry, the Lord will judge this and expose the criminals. They will definitely be caught and given their just deserts."* These people believe that as long as Louis and I had done nothing to deserve this, God would be on our side and act against the robbers. Therefore, they believe, our forgiveness of the robbers and rapist is unnecessary and misplaced. We don't have to forgive them. God won't either. The robbers are guilty and deserve to be punished. God's judgement seat will see to it if the legal system doesn't get to them first.

This is similar to when people think they know exactly what mistakes other people have made to cause the suffering they are experiencing. When we think like this, we are saying that we know the answers for why God acts, and that we can advise Him on what He may or may not do. Certainly He would be fair in our understanding of fairness?

Jacob wanted to ensure that he and Laban both got what they deserved. If Jacob would have only asked himself if he really wanted to get what he deserved, he might have remembered what he had done in the past. Then he would have spoken differently. Perhaps he would have realised that justice might not be kind to him. But instead, Jacob claimed to be in the right, never sparing one thought for all he had done in the past.

Jacob went further to a place called Mahanaim, which means double camp. Many commentaries attribute this name to the fact that Jacob saw his own camp and the camp of angels and was encouraged by the fact that he was not camping alone. His actions don't seem to me like the actions of an assured and encouraged man at all, though. He is about to head into his brother Esau's territory next. His party was outnumbered by Esau's 400. He was very scared, and found himself at a place that was a 'double camp' for him in another way. Like his family, who had been split into two groups, he was also double-minded about how to handle this crisis.

He had his own camp and the camp of angels almost as a visual choice set before him. Choose what is seen or what is (normally) unseen, choose soul or spirit, your own plans or God's favour. Rely on your numbers or the numbers of God's heavenly host. Perhaps Jacob should have looked back to the place he had just left. Padan-Aram does not mean 'crossroads' for nothing. All along he had been given the choice whether to simply embrace the promise, or to work himself to a standstill to earn it.

Reading this chapter in Genesis we see him still not making the choice. He did both. On the one hand he prayed passionately to God and finally acknowledged that he had crossed the Jordan with nothing more than a staff in his hand. After many years he was returning with two whole family groups. In this panicked prayer, he attributed this prosperity to God. On the other hand, he planned his most complex and manipulative plan to date. All of the classic elements of scheming were present: false humility, bribery and flattery – all in an attempt to soften Esau's heart. It's interesting to note that he doesn't try confession and remorse. A realisation of your own personal sin is always far from your thoughts when you are making your own way without God ...

He stayed back alone on his side of the Jordan while everybody else and everything he owned crossed to the other side. Finally, this was the perfect time for the Angel of the Lord to wrestle with him. He was alone, stripped of all he had done his rain dance for, and at the end of all his plans. He had done all he could and could very well lose all he ever had. The Angel grabbed him and wrestled with him. So down and out, God seems to want to finish him off rather than grace him with encouragement.

I want to think it was as if God wanted to wrestle his last dance out of him. When Jacob still wouldn't choose to surrender, his hip is put out of joint. I love how it is written that the Angel did this by merely *touching* his hip socket. By this time Jacob had already realised his assailant wasn't merely a man and more than an angel. It was never an equal fight. The Angel did not play dirty because he felt Jacob was getting the better of him; rather, God himself saw that Jacob would not bend the knee. God could not bless a man so firmly on his own two feet. He had to break him to save him. It took very little. Finally dancing was out of the question. All Jacob could do was hold on and plead for God's blessing. He finally knew the key! His efforts were not it. He could know nothing for himself. He finally chose to pitch his tent in the right camp.

At this point – limping but blessed – his name is changed. We see God only changing a name after the moment of true faith – with Abram, Sarai, Saul and others we see that they first believed before being renamed Abraham, Sarah and Paul. This further proves that up until this moment of absolute surrender, Jacob had in fact not been a believer, he had been a test-driver.

Oftentimes we are brought to this point of suffering through a God-given test. We are brought here when our prayers, fasting, spiritual rituals, and whatever other plans we might have trusted in, don't work anymore. Many of us wrestle with God here. We feel that we first need to show what we are capable of. We bring our Christian achievements and all of the things we've been doing right to the fight, but they don't help us. It's in this place where we can spill litres of oil anointing on anything and everyone, beg, fast, pray with thousands around the world at the exact same moment, prophesy positivity, and proclaim every promise we know, only to find that we can't make God do what we want Him to do.

Each one of us will have an encounter with God's *"godness."* Here, we will struggle until our own power fails, and we receive a touch on our hip to remind us of how foolish we are to trust our own two legs to sustain us. Here we will finally collapse, no longer claiming our rights, or blaming our abusers, or dancing for rain, but humbly crying: *"He will be my God because He promised He would."*

Renewed on the inside and despite his sleepless night and a hip that must have been throbbing, Jacob ran to overtake everyone he had sent on ahead. His spirit was alive and his soul and body could but do everything to keep up. He knelt – finally! – before Esau. At long last he confessed with sincerity that it was only the favour of the Lord that had made him prosperous. No longer any mention of hard work, being cheated, having to fend for himself or any of his schemes. Only God, only grace. Esau answered this with more grace. We see a moment that no amount of justice done could have made any more beautiful.

Jacob built an altar called El-Elohe-Israel – 'God, the God of Israel'. Israel being his own name, we witness the moment where Jacob ends his test-drive in the Toyota. He is no longer trying God on for size. He is essentially confessing "God, not any God, not anyone's God – God, the God of me!" It may be bad grammar, but it is solid theology.

This entire episode is a lesson in the true nature of forgiveness. Jacob is so relieved about the forgiveness he received from God and Esau that we never hear him complain again about what Laban had done to him. He's fully aware of his own undeserved acquittal. He doesn't claim to be righteous anymore.

Forgiveness is difficult – perhaps quite impossible – when we still believe the lie that we are right and others wrong. We can forgive at El-Elohe-Israel where we finally get a grip on grace, but not at Mizpah where we plant our feet for justice.

In the last verses of Matthew 18 we find the story of the master who forgave his servant a huge debt. The servant ran into a colleague who owed him an insignificant debt compared to the one he had owed his master. Quickly forgetting all about grace, he grabbed his debtor by the throat, shaking him down for whatever he could cough up. The other servants overheard and told the master about it. Angered, the master handed this ungrateful servant over to the torturers, who made sure he was dealt with justly. He had insisted on justice, after all. The master forced him to repay his own debt because it was fair. He wanted fairness and he was granted his wish. This story ends with shocking words from the mouth of Jesus:

> *"My Father will do the same to you, if you don't truly forgive your brothers."*

What will His Father do? He will hold us to the total of all our debt before Him if we are as fickle as to think anyone owes us more than we owe God. If we are shown grace, we are expected to show it to others.

The anger of the master in this parable is quite telling. He is insulted. Not forgiving those whose sins are covered by the blood of Jesus can be compared to looking at Jesus nailed to the cross, tortured and shamed, covered in wounds for all our sakes and saying:

"Yes, I can see You paid quite well for my sins, thank you, but not quite enough for the sins committed against me. I'd still prefer that my offender pay a little more, please? Your grace is great, but can we please top it up with some good Old Testament justice? Please make my enemy pay dearly!"

Those who choose grace for themselves but justice for others will find their choice is not available. Either justice for you and justice for me, or grace to us both. There are no two ways about it: people who don't forgive will pay for their own debt – it will be torturous, and the one giving the orders for torture will be God himself. Even in that torture there is grace, though. I firmly believe when we are tortured long enough by the fangs of fairness we will finally realise our foolish choice and cry for mercy. Our ever gracious God will grant it as He granted the blessing to Jacob when he finally saw fairness for the unsatisfactory fraud that it is.

That's why I don't appease people who are bitter; I don't give them a hug and a pat while they continue spewing gall and hating their perpetrators, waiting for fairness and justice in court. Apparently, many believe we need to soothe people who are disgruntled about the wrongs that have been committed against them by saying,

"It's good; you need to be angry now. It's the phase you are in. You are going to feel like this for a while."

If I read Matthew 18:34 correctly, we are saying this then:

"No, it's too early to come out of jail. Hang around for more torture."

Shouldn't we encourage people who find themselves there, to escape? That's the reason Louis and I keep on insisting that we forgave our attackers and the reporters and the people who have insulted us and were instantly free – not because what they had done had been fair or just, for that it certainly wasn't. We forgave them because we know we would have had our huge debt in God's books reinstated if we chose justice. We know justice could never have given us the freedom and lightness that grace did.

Many around us are waiting for justice on our behalf, hoping to hear an arrest has been made. They are sure a long sentence for the offenders will give them peace of mind. Their tents are pitched in the land of justice. They make me think of mothers whose children were killed and who are interviewed at court right after the sentencing of the murderers.

"Now that justice has been done, I will find peace."

I want to cry when I hear this, because these mothers won't even find a good night's sleep unless they travel to better places in the desert.

There are two more important keys hidden in the last section of this passage in Matthew 18. Jesus spoke about the forgiveness of "brothers", in other words fellow believers. Some people quote this as a handy loophole. We should forgive the good people in our church, but there is no obligation to forgive the bad people out there on the streets. Unfortunately, Matthew 6:14 – 15, among other passages in Scripture, says that we can't expect forgiveness if we don't forgive. It makes no distinction between "brothers" and "others". The forgiveness we have extended to our attackers doesn't make them innocent before God; it makes *us* innocent before God.

The second key from this passage is a bit of bad news for us – God expects us to forgive wholeheartedly. Many people think it's good enough to make the choice to forgive and utter the words "I forgive you" while still seething or cringing inwardly. It seems from this passage, though, that God expects far more than that because He is willing to give us much more than such a fickle love. He expects the sort of forgiveness that changes our mind as well as our feelings toward our offenders. I have heard of people who whisper forgiveness out of obedience, whose hearts are instantly filled with compassion that they did not have before uttering the words. Uttering the words without having your heart follow them, is not enough.

Our pulse and blood pressure shouldn't go either up or down when we see those who offended us. We should not become hot nor cold. Our hearts should be light when we think of them. Every desire to see them suffer should be gone. This is not hard for a person to do – it is impossible. Without God, that is. We need His heart, and He is willing to give it to us. He gives it to us in the way He gave it to Jacob. He gives us an experience of His boundless grace in spite of our indelible guilt. Sometimes this can be a very uncomfortable experience because it involves seeing our shame in full colour. Do you struggle to forgive? Ask God to show you your sin in full colour. Suddenly, you may find yourself willing to let others go free.

It is easier to forgive when we can see the profit we gain from our suffering and realise that we are already living in the land of hope, despite our pain, while our offenders are perhaps still living in judgement and poverty. It was with this perspective that a Jewish woman in the Ravensbruck concentration camp died, with this note in her pocket:

> **Oh Lord, remember not only the men and women of goodwill,**
> **but also those of ill will.**
> **Do not remember all the suffering they have inflicted on us;**
> **remember the fruits we bear, thanks to this suffering –**
> **our comradeship, our loyalty, courage, generosity,**
> **the greatness of heart which has grown out of all of this.**
> **And when they come to judgement,**
> **let all the fruits that we have borne be their forgiveness.**

Let's return to the story of Jacob for one last glimpse. A short sentence catches my eye. *Later, Jacob moved back to Bethel.* Even though this was the same place he had been at before, this time he wasn't here to negotiate with God, or to test Him. He renamed the place El-Bethel. No longer was it an altar for the house of God. Now, it was an altar for the God of the house of God. It's as if Jacob no longer viewed God as small; nor did he think that God was limited to a place where he had once planted a rock.

At this place in our spiritual journeys, we are challenged again and again to think about God in a new way. Every event that makes a deep impression on us can broaden our perspectives of God. The forefront of missions where darkness and light clash in the fiercest way is often the best place to see more of God. It is like going to the countryside to find the stars are so much brighter there. They appear dim when we're in a place with too many city lights. God seems dim and grey and the candle He holds out seems almost insulting until, by grace, everything gets very dark and we see the light for what it is.

During our student years and our first years of marriage, Louis and I often joined missions work and went on several outreaches. In countries like Egypt, Turkey, and Bosnia, we saw first-hand what God was capable of doing against the backdrop of such evil darkness. We had to humbly declare that we only knew a small part of who God really was, because during those outreaches He showed us aspects of Himself that had been new and sometimes shockingly different from the picture we had of Him in the past.

In Egypt, for example, I saw a Coptic priest splashing so-called holy water on people and swinging a cross around while the altar boys lit candles to the religious icons. He screamed. People cried. Demons shrieked. I did not quite understand what he was up to but had seen enough to be certain that everything was wrong with this priest and his church. Judgemental but intrigued, I stepped closer to the mayhem. I literally rubbed my eyes a few times in disbelief, thinking my eyelids were playing tricks on me because as the priest was carrying on, a young quadriplegic's contracted body started unfolding almost like sped-up footage of a budding rose. I saw muscles swelling out around his twiggy limbs. Sweat was almost streaming off his body as a by-product of all this sped-up formation of new cells, I suppose. He was quivering and stared at his body in shock, weeping for joy. He kept becoming straighter and shapelier until he stood without support on his own two legs with a well-formed body. Even his face changed as the muscle tone that rendered his mouth and tongue useless, normalised and he could speak.

I asked our translator what he was saying. Surely his first words would be worth hearing.

> *"He is asking for Jesus. This is a problem. His parents brought him here because he was born this way and was getting weaker with age. They heard about the miracles happening here, but they are Muslims."*

I asked what would happen now, and she said they would join the underground Evangelical church as it was a crime to convert to Christianity. They'd be as good as dead to all their friends and family. They'd hide for the rest of their lives.

If we could have asked them today whether it was worth it, they would be able to tell us a story of great gain. Would they be angry at God for giving them a disabled son? I doubt it. This Coptic Church in Cairo seemed so wrong but turned out to be visited by God with a power that made so many lives right with God. I learned that I could not trust my own judgement.

During a worship service in Turkey, Louis experienced how Muslims, who had never before heard of Jesus, fell over under the power of the Holy Spirit. We never believed that people were supposed to fall over like that. We were convinced it was powerful suggestions if not evil spirits that cause that. But Louis heard with his own ears someone getting up from the floor say:

> *"While I was lying on the floor, I saw two pieces of wood that were bound together – one upright and one sideways. Someone put nails through a man's hands and feet to fix him to the wood. What does it mean and who is it?"*

On another trip a Muslim woman listened to the English worship songs that she could not understand one word of. She asked a translator to ask Louis why the music seemed like water that could take away her thirst forever. She wanted to know where she could find more of that thirst-quenching water music.

In these precious glimpses of God-at-work we learned that He is much bigger than the spaces we created for Him in our churches and larger than the spaces we think He should fit into in the lives of others. He is not a boxable God, is what we learned, I suppose. We can build little Bethels, and think He will live within the confines of what we think He may do or be, but He will be bigger. He is the God above all. Even when people don't believe or understand, He remains God, and nothing will be impossible for Him. God will always break out of our boxes. If He were to fit into our frames, or into the embrace of our short arms, we would be holding a God too small for us. We need to put arms of faith around Him knowing our embrace can never lock Him in. He is simply uncontainable. Not even our thoughts can hold together when we try to get our minds around just who He really is.

If our tents are still pitched far from water, a promise, grace and "the God of *me*", we are not lost, we are just on the journey, still travelling. And my prayer is that we will have the courage to seek out the right wells and altars until we find what we are hungry for. As our path crosses with other wilderness wanderers, let us look at them with compassion. They may be looking for a better well, too.

18 *Underwear and tests*

My struggle with the letters is over. It's the 22nd of April. My publisher paid my royalties early, so the curtains that should have been paid by the money in the safe are now being delivered and installed. The measurements were taken weeks ago, and the drills are screeching in our bedroom. I hear them feeding the curtain railings through the metal rings. It's quiet for a moment. Then I hear them shifting around our bed and a two-seater couch in our bedroom. They finally announce that the curtains are ready for inspection. I run expectantly up the stairs and into the bedroom.

I don't even see the curtains. Something else has caught my eye. Several items that the curtain installers found who-knows-where are now on display in a neat row on our bed. An old paper bag with a few greasy popcorn kernels is the least of my embarrassments. Next to the popcorn, neatly folded, is my torn underwear from the night of the rape. It looks worse than I thought it would. The word 'carnage' comes to mind, even though it does not have a drop of blood on it. It tells a story more shocking than what had actually happened that early morning. I know the tearing should speak of the rapists hastiness, but instead it speaks of brutality. The synthetic lace unravelled in wild tufts, making what's left of the garment look as if an animal had gotten hold of it.

I sigh. Once again the parallel stories. I say "torn off hastily without hurting me." People's imaginations will always make them believe "ripped off viciously in a violent rape." The latter certainly fits with what all three of us are now staring at. I ask the curtain installer to tell me where he found the underwear, since it could now be used as potential evidence in my rape case. He is knocked for six. The horror in his face and the step backwards reveal that he's afraid of possibly being implicated in the crime because he had touched the torn underwear. I'll never know where he found it because he is gone in a flash. Less embarrassment for both of us, so I don't mind too much.

I call Louis to ask if he thinks that after more than two months I should still hand the underwear over to the police. Any forensic evidence would be gone by now and proving that it was torn that night by that man would be impossible anyway. I put it in the garbage can along with the left-over popcorn; Louis probably does not really want to see it either. I smile inwardly as I remember the care we took in describing the missing item in great detail and even submitting a similar panty to be photographed. We all thought the rapist had taken it as a souvenir. The police should employ Mr Curtain Installer. He's better at collecting evidence than the investigators.

I know how upset I should be about this grisly discovery. It's an embarrassment and a portrait of how I could have been shredded that night, but it is not traumatic. I am filled with gratitude that it, too, has not brought on any post traumatic breakdown. It confirms what I already know – I am never going to crack over this. God has truly done a perfect and complete healing miracle inside me and Louis. I realise I had skipped the morning's devotion, so I take Spurgeon's book off my bedside table to catch up on the passage for the 22nd of April:

> *Thou shalt not be afraid of the terror by night (Psalm 91:5).*
>
> WHAT is this terror? It may be the cry of fire, or the noise of thieves, or fancied appearances, or the shriek of sudden sickness or death. We live in the world of death and sorrow, we may therefore look for ills as well in the night-watches as beneath the glare of the broiling sun. Nor should this alarm us, for be the terror what it may, the promise is that the believer shall not be afraid. Why should he? Let us put it more closely, why should we? God our Father is here, and will be here all through the lonely hours; He is an almighty Watcher, a sleepless Guardian, a faithful Friend. Nothing can happen without His direction, for even hell itself is under His control. Darkness is not dark to Him. He has promised to be a wall of fire around His people – and who can break through such a barrier? Worldlings may well be afraid, for they have an angry God above them, a guilty conscience within them, and a yawning hell beneath them; but we who rest in Jesus are saved from all these through rich mercy. If we give way to foolish fear we shall dishonour our profession (*the claim that we are Christians*), and lead others to doubt the reality of godliness. We ought to be afraid of being afraid, lest we should vex the Holy Spirit by foolish distrust. Down, then, ye dismal forebodings and groundless apprehensions, God has not forgotten to be gracious, nor shut up His tender mercies, it may be night in the soul, but there need be no terror, for the God of love changes not. Children of light may walk in darkness, but they are not therefore cast away, no, they are now enabled to prove their adoption by trusting in their heavenly Father as hypocrites cannot do.
>
> **Though the night be dark and dreary,**
> **Darkness cannot hide from Thee;**
> **Thou art He, who, never weary,**
> **Watchest where Thy people be**
>
> (James Edmeston)

Louis is home. We are sitting like two naughty children in the lounge with our feet on the coffee table. I ask him whether or not he has any secret desire to leave the country. The initial euphoria of all the support and love, the white bedroom, the jewels, the free burglar bars and so forth, is starting to fade, although I still feel the same peace and thankfulness. But I'm wondering about my husband and whether he may be contemplating a move. He confesses thinking of perhaps living in America sometime in the future. We already know that all of us have left a bigger part of our hearts there every time we went on tour. It is harder to come back to South Africa every time we leave the USA. We never went sightseeing. In fact, we have never been to Disney World or the Grand Canyon or New

York City. We visited churches on invitation and upon clear promptings from the Lord to go with a particular mission or message. We have no invitation now, no prompting, no message. Even though we would love to go again, it's financially impossible. And even if we had the money, we'd feel guilty to spend it on an overseas trip simply for our own pleasure. We have been overseas many times, but always for ministry purposes.

Louis gets a twinkle in his eye, flips open his laptop, and like a lover dreaming up a honeymoon he maps out an imaginary three week trip for us. For the first time ever, we would love to take the expensive direct flight into Atlanta, we would visit our dear friends in Loganville, Georgia, rent a van, travel across four or five states in a circle route past our friends in Iowa and Tennessee and then back again. Our fantasy makes us intensely happy for half an hour or so. Then we sober up, slam the laptop shut on the dream and go to bed silently.

Louis is out of town for a concert. He calls me and I can hear he is talking faster and breathing deeper than usual.

> *"Honey, do you remember the family in Kingsport that we stayed with a few years ago? I know we haven't seen them or spoken to them for years, but they called today! They say God told them to bring us to America. They feel we need to get away and rest. They'd love for me to come and lead worship at that same church and for us to share our testimony if we want to. They offered an amount that will almost cover our flight expenses. I'm going to let all our friends know that we may be coming. Perhaps they can arrange for me to sing at their churches? If a few donations come in to cover cost we may be able to actually do this".*

Within three weeks a five–week long visit is booked, and everything seems to be working out perfectly. We will be able to see everybody we wanted to at exactly the times it suits them and their churches' schedules. We get all of our passports and visas in order, and we struggle to appear as though we have mixed feelings about missing the Soccer World Cup here in South Africa. Aagh, we're not going to hear the noise of a thousand vuvuzelas!

Only one thing dampens my enthusiasm. Against what I have already decided, I realise that this will mean having absolutely no communication with the forbidden man. I know I shouldn't anyway, but now I would not be able to. It is not the same thing. Mixed-up thoughts swarm around in my mind: *It is God intervening because I am too weak to stop it all by myself. It is punishment. I will fail and be weak and send an email or something and then I will be caught out. Maybe I should be caught out so that this horrible tension can end. I'd rather have it all out in the open than have it all eat me from within. Maybe after the five weeks I'll be free.*

Keeping busy helps, and sitting in church for the first of a series of sermons by a visiting American pastor, I feel as if I am in a safe house. His message is interesting. It is about what he calls backlash. He explains that there is often a spiritual backlash after significant spiritual victories. He claims that during this time God seemingly takes His protective hand away for some time. We can fast and pray for all we're worth, but it will remain a time of testing, during which the enemy will be at play. I listen attentively and imagine the dragon coming onto the stage of the puppet theatre. But, this is also a time during which God has a very specific agenda, he says. After the time of testing, the breakthroughs will come, as well as the long-awaited spiritual inheritance.

The words resonate in my ears. So that's what's been happening to me? Maybe the victory over the rape was my spiritual breakthrough and the emotional battle I'm struggling with now is the backlash? I really hope so because that means that I will have a legacy if I can only remain standing. And that would explain why nothing I said, tried or prayed has helped. No wonder the Lord asked me if I were serious about my spiritual inheritance. He saw that I was willing to fail my most important test.

The preacher's next point really hits home:

> *"Research shows that 90% of spiritual leaders that go through this time of backlash, will sadly fail the most important test of their lives and never receive their inheritance."*

Once again, I find myself in a hot seat in this big church. I'm scared to death. I'm not going to wait for my car to die on me again. I'm going to speak up. After the service I'm in the long line of people to talk to the preacher. It's not like me. Normally I'm too proud to go to the front for any sort of help, but I've been flat on my face for a while now, totally convinced of my own weaknesses, and I don't care what people think of me anymore. When I arrive at the front I immediately confess that I think I am right there in the place of the ultimate test. He smiles:

> *"Is it money, an addiction, or a man?"*

Wow, I think to myself, so it is that simple? Apparently it's always the same pattern. We make an appointment to talk about it tomorrow evening after the service.

I am sitting behind my computer. The little green light that just went on in the corner of my screen means that I need to disconnect now or face the temptation that has me in its grip. I freeze. A message pops up immediately. I fail to ignore it, but this time I decide not to fall back into the usual friendly banter. I type a brave reply: *You know I am struggling with this, although you think it is not a big deal. I am going to talk to the preacher tonight to figure out what to do. I'm going to follow his advice. I want you to know that if he says that this frequent communication has to stop, then I'm stopping it. He is older and wiser than us.*

A response appears on the screen within seconds: *Fine. Talk to him. Just don't mention my name.*

The sermon was good, but I did not take much in. I am in the long line. An hour has passed. I am sure the pastor is exhausted, but I am desperate and he promised to see me. I am finally in front. I sit down, embarrassed. He smiles without judgement and asks a few questions. He sits quietly, with his head slightly tilted as if listening to something I can't hear. God must be speaking to him. He says:

> *"Satan is not central in this picture. This is not a temptation. It's not lust. You have a wonderful marriage, don't you? God is central in this picture. It's your big test. God tells me that you asked for this. What did you ask for?"*

"I asked for the families of South Africa."

"And you thought you would get such an inheritance for free? You are full of your own desires, and you are following your heart. I know about the rape. When the pastor introduced me to your husband and the rest of the worship team, he told me about it. Your spirit is strong, but you are not leading from your spirit. You are leading from your heart. You want to be a ministry leader, but you are far behind schedule in this area. You have to stop your rebellion and wilfulness. Satan isn't fighting you. Jesus is fighting you. He is fighting you for your heart. That is why it's so painful. He wants you to give Him your emotions and desires. They should belong to Him alone."

We talk for some time, and I begin to understand. The enemy likes to attack us in our weak spots. He is a coward, coming from behind. Even in the Garden of Eden he was called the heel-biter. He wants to see us defeated and destroyed. But that's not what's happening with me – my marriage is strong and my relationship with God stronger than ever. If this is a temptation to cheat on my husband and betray Jesus, then it's happening at the worst possible time, a time when I am strong and intensely aware of how much I love both Louis and Jesus. Their love for me is also tangible every day. This, according to the pastor, shows that this may not be a temptation, but rather a test, which would explain why my will is not enough to help me escape this time. We can walk away from temptations by making a firm choice and using our willpower, but we can't get away from tests in the same way. We can't run – we have to pass them. They will recur until we do.

It seems that God tests us in areas where we are strong because that is where our pride and self-confidence – two very dangerous things – are nestled. In a test God asks of us to sacrifice all of our Isaacs, too, because it is in them that our future and dreams are tied up. The tests also come in the area of our strengths, because they are often gifts that equip us for our spiritual inheritance. Abraham's strong points were his obedience and trust in God. His inheritance was Isaac. No wonder God wanted to test whether Abraham would sacrifice his own son. It wasn't because God was uncertain how deep his faith was; it was so that Abraham could see how real his own faith was. This test would show me the truth about myself in the area I most desire to leave a legacy – family.

I ask the preacher my burning question:

"But why so long and when will the test be over?"

"God will test you in this until you have seen everything that is in your heart. What have you seen so far?"

I name all the vices, including my rebellion. The ugliest one is probably that even though I'm married to someone as wonderful as Louis, I have the audacity to enjoy and even invite another man's attention. The pastor warns me that the frequent communication may not feel like it's leading to adultery, but that he has seen innocent talk cross the line and progress into full-on sexual affairs so many times that he can guarantee me that it is just a matter of time. I could not have heard him clearer.

Jesus' temptation in the desert is a classic example of a test. Sometimes Satan gets a role in the story. But it's the Holy Spirit Himself who led Jesus into the desert to be tempted in the first place. The devil's temptations were only a side show, because Jesus' heart was being tested by God Himself before He could receive His ministry and inheritance. Was there any stubborn self-will in His heart? Would He change stones into bread simply because He could? Would He play with His godly powers like a child would with a set of magic tricks? Would He use His power to make life a little more comfortable for Himself? Would he succumb to the attraction of power and riches? Would He force His Father to catch Him when He jumped off the temple's roof? Or was He submissive in His heart to His Father's Word and will? Would He love and serve God only? His legacy was about to take shape, and even He had to have His heart stripped of everything that could snare Him during his time in ministry.

A spiritual legacy rests on spiritual authority. Spiritual authority in any sphere comes through spiritual victory in that sphere. We shouldn't be allowed to preach to people who are merely making the same mistakes we are making, should we? If we can overcome those mistakes, though, we'd be the ideal ones to help others through the snare. In every area where families get hurt, I will have to walk the walk if I'm going to be able to serve them with true authority, not just book knowledge or eloquent talk. I will have authority to talk to women about their families only if I successfully fight for mine with all that I have.

The preacher adds one more encouragement before I leave:

> *"You will end this, because now you know Who is fighting you. You dare not win. Abdicate. Therein lies the victory."*

Sometimes we think that every struggle is with the devil, only to discover, like Jacob, that we are often wrestling with God's Angel. Then it's to our advantage to limp out of the fight and always carry the reminder with us that we aren't supposed to win against God. He gives us what we need. Sometimes we need a good fight.

As I'm walking away, I think of how many times I've already tried to end this. What if it's not possible? I fear I will be part of the 90% who fail the test. I see my candle before me – melted and snuffed out. As if he could read my thoughts, the preacher calls after me:

> *"No, you can do it. You really can. In fact, you will do it* tonight*!"*

Such incredibly motivating words of wisdom and knowledge, I think to myself while walking to my car. Just like the words of the man in the Drakensberg inn. It stirs the desire in me to one day be able to speak that clearly and accurately into people's lives, because of the tremendous freedom and relief it brings straight from God Himself.

By the time I arrive back home it's late. I tell Louis that I have just found the answer that he has seen me struggling for months to find. The inexplicability of my struggle has become explicable. All I need to do now is gather the courage to do what I have to. Reading the words of my spiritual travelling companion, Charles Spurgeon, may help, so I decide to read from it before logging onto Skype to pull the final plug. Today, on the 19th of May, the message is simply a amplification of my talk with the wise man:

Let us not fall into the error of letting our passions and carnal appetites ride in triumph while our nobler powers walk in the dust. We were not newly created to allow our passions to rule over us, but that we, as kings, may reign in Christ Jesus over the triple kingdom of spirit, soul and body, to the glory of God the Father.

I follow through with my decision, and the next day I hand the American preacher the printed Skype conversation as proof of my obedience. He looks at me intently:

"You are not done. You will be done when God has shown you everything that is in your heart. And let me warn you: If you ever go back, you will cross the line and throw away everything you fought for. You will lose it all in 24 hours. I have seen people do that many times."

Am I not done? Is there more behind the rebellion and wilfulness that I have already seen and confessed? I'm sure I have no pride left. Having confessed to half the world, I've made sure I'm not hiding behind any self-righteousness, either. I can't think of anything else I might be missing, except maybe one thing. I haven't revealed the man's name to Louis. I had promised not to. My mentors and one or two of the counsellors I saw agreed that it would only stir up trouble. He is out of my life, and just in time. I'll rather let sleeping dogs lie. We'll go to America. All will fizzle out.

We've reached the three month mark, and once again it's time for a blood test. The pathologist sends in a girl who looks like she should still be in high school. She confirms my suspicions when I ask her if she draws blood regularly:

"Not really, Ma'am. I shouldn't actually be on duty but with all the strikes and things going on I'm working overtime for extra spending money."

"Well, if you're not absolutely sure you'll be able to find a vein on the first try, we should rather leave it, because we need to draw four vials full today. My GP wants to run other tests, too, so I arranged for all of it to happen at the same time. You will only have one chance, because after that anything is possible – I may run away, attack you, or faint. I can never quite predict whether it will be fight or flight."

She seems to be contemplating flight, but we're both trapped by obligation. She promises to do her best. I turn my head away and violently pump the rubber ball in an attempt to call forth a plump vein; the rubber pipe stretches tightly around my bicep. We may be in luck. She stabs, withdraws quickly and stabs again. Something feels really strange. I'm pretty sure the needle is straight through my vein and lodged in something deeper. I wait a few seconds and glance bravely to gage the progress. There is not a drop of blood in the vial.

"Pull that thing out immediately! You're not even close to a vein! Is the needle bent? How did you manage to do that?!"

"I'm sorry, it probably hit a sinew or bone."

"Call a doctor! You have two minutes at the most before I run out those doors. I can feel my adrenalin pumping."

Within seconds the doctor arrives. Luckily she finds the vein with her first attempt and the four vials promptly fill up. I'm very relieved that I don't have to return for another three months. The vein the first needle had gone through makes a tiny bubble like an angry puffer fish and within a few hours it grows into a purple bruise the size of my palm. I can't bend my arm without wincing. She really went all the way into my joint with that needle. Someone pays her to do it. I want to throw up.

The 24 hour wait is over. My Dad and I drive to the hospital to get the HIV result. This will probably be conclusive. We wait for hours. They are very apologetic, blaming it on the strikes once again. Someone may have misplaced the file, and they can't find it anywhere. We wait some more. They return with bad news. They have the results for all the tests the GP had requested but there is no HIV result. They think with all the excitement someone forgot to request the most important test of all. I'd have to have more blood drawn now. In utter dismay I show them the purple proof of yesterday's brutality and beg for mercy.

They are unmoved. The adrenalin pumps on the side of fight:

"I want to see the head of the hospital, because this is unbelievable. The incompetence is ridiculous! I simply refuse. I'm not having blood taken today!"

After more than half an hour the good news arrives. There has been a simple mix-up. The HIV result was sent to my doctor and the other test results erroneously ended up here. And there is more good news: the result is negative, again.

This time around I have no mixed feelings – only pure joy!

After a week of peace, today feels like a scavenger party with me as the main dish. My phone and my computer take bites out of me. I am like an addict. I start texting the forbidden man, then remember that I can't do this anymore and put down the phone, resisting the physical pain it causes to fight the urge to pick it up again. A few minutes later, I do the same. I realise I am in withdrawal. This is like drug rehab. Only, I am both doctor and patient. I try to think like a doctor. I have to delete all the unsent mails and the address I used. I wipe Skype from my hard drive. I set up a blocking protocol on my other email address. I delete the phone number even though I know it well. I move my computer to the family room. I will only go online when I am not alone. I give Louis all my passwords so that we both know there are no dark corners left. This seems pathetic, but I'm determined to be one of the 10% who make it.

I think it is easier to quit drinking when you start smoking instead. I don't know what to replace my addiction with. I miss talking to someone in secret and having them talk back. So I start reading my Bible and praying as the closest alternative. Some days are so hard that I have to do it ten times in one day to keep myself from falling off the wagon. I know I am not, but I feel so alone. Even though I've won back my freedom, it still feels like I've lost something. Over and over, I say the same words that I had struggled months ago to say:

"Jesus, I prefer You. Jesus, I prefer You!"

I also miss the mind games – the intellectual heroin I had been fed, so I buy a book of Mensa puzzles and fry my brain trying to figure them out. I buy one for each bathroom. It is those quiet, private times that I need to fill most proactively.

At my lowest point the cyber stalker reaches a new level of perversion. He sends me a detestable text message describing what he would like to do to me. It's much worse than what the rapist had done. I feel dirty. That evening I read how David had to cross the Kidron Valley before he could achieve his ultimate victory. The Kidron Valley was the city's sewerage outlet. I probably need to cross this vile thing as well. I only pray that I will be able to get rid of the pollution it dumped in my mind. I wonder about the tests of life and the sequence in which they hit us. Mine arrived in the following sequence:

- Will you love sin?
- Will you hate Me because of what happened to you?
- Will you love Me above everything and everyone else?
- Will you hate sin by fighting every foothold it has with everything in you?

Today's text messages are even worse than yesterday's. I've had enough. I want to know who this is, and then I want to send someone to his house with a baseball bat. I know it is not the solution, but my spirit is worn out from all the fighting and I feel like acting out my animal instinct. I phone the detective who handles our case. He is in the area. Within an hour he arrives at our house and I show him the worst of it all. He gives me bad news. I'd have to print out every message on my cell phone and hand it over to the police before any cell phone company would block calls from his number to my phone. The problem is that these print-outs would end up at the same police station that leaked our incident to the newspaper. The same informant probably won't be able to withstand the juicy content. There is enough slime here to keep the popular weeklies busy for weeks. It's not going to work. Besides, I won't be able to charge him with anything unless he directly threatens me and I can prove it.

I receive another text message, and I decide to set a trap by provoking him a little bit. I answer that I would meet him. Then I add that I would bring Louis along. It works. He uses a very unique phrase that rings a bell:

"If he is a pastor, please don't bring him along. Pastors are as dense as dung."

I suddenly remember who said those exact words to me over my cell phone in February, right after the rape. Someone referred a man to me, and I tried to send him to a pastor for counselling but he was not keen to go, using the "dense as dung" defence. I know who the cyber stalker is now, but I still have no idea where he lives and of course, this "proof" would never hold water.

I call the person who gave him my number and tip-toe around with a few questions. It takes no more than five minutes to get his address. I end the call, burst into tears and scream before I can even think properly:

"None of this is funny anymore!"

He lives walking distance from us.

For the first time since the rape, I don't feel safe. Then I realise it's the same old song of the enemy. He has tried so many things to catch me in a snare of fear. It's verse two of the same song. If I won't fear men, darkness, being alone, HIV, or my own weakness, then he would try and make me fear a perverted stalker.

I make an appointment with a psychologist friend of mine. She may be able to look at his messages and know if I have reason to feel unsafe. She is uncertain but gives a few pointers. We chat over coffee, and as we take the last sips of our coffee my phone beeps. There is a message:

Is there any space in your universe to greet an old friend before you go overseas?

How can it be that for weeks there is no attempt to contact me, but on the day I finally discover my stalker is practically my neighbour, the attractive man shoves a candle into my hand? I need comfort and he shows up as an "old friend." I answer with one word that's never been this hard to type:

No.

19 Sand castles, cheese, and keys

It is finally time to board the airplane bound for America. My phone will stay behind. I experience indescribable relief as we take off. Five weeks away from the battle will really do me good. On top of it all, it's Louis's birthday today. All is right with the world.
Atlanta is beautiful in the spring. We share some unforgettable experiences with friends in lovely places and I almost feel guilty for enjoying it this much. I had gotten so used to the battle back home that being spoiled like this has caught me by surprise. A friend from Atlanta hands us his car keys along with a map to a holiday destination. We are feel so blessed.

It is a perfect day on Hilton Head's beach on the coast of North Carolina, I am reading a book by Dr Bruce Wilkinson: *You were born for this.* It teaches how to co-operate with God in everyday miracles in people's lives. I'm not finished with the book yet, but I'm impatient and eager to try out the concept. I'd love to experience God using me in one of His miracles. I fire off a short prayer and report for duty. Now I wait to see if what the book says is true. It claims that those who report for duty almost always get a job, since God has too few volunteers on His list.

I notice my son building sand castles with two dark-haired boys who look like they may be from India. Coming from Africa as part of a white minority, it feels so strange to see only white people for weeks on end. I almost feel at home as I spot these two boys. Next to them is a man who is lily white. Interesting. I move a bit closer to take a picture of the sand castles. We greet one another. I can hardly believe it: he recognises my South African accent! The book I am reading says God will bring people to our attention in an obvious way so that we will know who He wants to touch through us. I get the feeling that God wants to give this man a message. Americans normally think we are Dutch or British. How did he know?

He explains that his wife's family is from Durban and that they have South African neighbours. Now I am certain he's the one, but what should I tell him? I'm still thinking of something to say, when he lets out words I'd forgive you for not believing:

> *"South-Africa is such a violent place. My wife has been back to see family, but I don't care to go. In February this year you had such a terrible wave of crime and violence."*

No kidding, I think to myself.

> *"There was this one report that my neighbours from up the street showed me. It was about this lady who was raped during an armed robbery. Her husband was*

abducted. I am so worried for her. I'm a doctor, and I just know that HIV is such a terrible risk for her. She and her husband must be devastated."

There are many people in South Africa who don't know what happened to us, but here I'm standing on a beach in North Carolina and a man is telling me my story. Of all the dozens of news articles every day, this one had shaken him four months ago and still bothers him. All I can get out is:

"We are fine, I am not HIV positive."

It's his turn to give me a strange look. I can see his mind is doing back flips. He's processing the pronouns and probably thinking what I thought a moment ago. What are the chances? He mumbles that he is not a believer, but that he is happy we are OK.

"But what about mentally and emotionally? People don't recover from such a thing."

"We really are fine. Africa may be a violent place, but many of us live close to God. Probably because we really need to. Our faith and the prayers of many people made a huge difference to us."

He asks to take a photo of me and my son with his boys and the sandcastle. I can already see him on Google comparing my photo with the one in the newspaper article. Hopefully that is exactly what he will do and hopefully he will find our testimony and encounter a God who would love to show a sceptic doctor who He truly is.

Excitedly, I share the miracle with Louis, and I lie back down on my towel. I think I now understand what Dr Bruce Wilkinson means when he promises in his book that the Lord will use you in a supernatural way to give what you already have, what you already know, and what you already are to someone who needs exactly that. He says it will look so improbable that you will know only God could have orchestrated it. I can't wait for the next moment I will see God work in this way.

After two weeks at Hilton head, we are in Tennessee visiting our friends and spending time at the congregation we have come to love. They invited us to testify at the Saturday evening service. After the service a woman walks up to me. She mumbles an excuse for bothering me and says how incredibly sorry she is for what happened to us. I wonder if she really heard our message. I try to explain again that she need not feel sorry as we aren't sorry. We are thankful for having had the opportunity to experience God's goodness so tangibly, and we are thankful that we are alive. She interrupts me and blurts out incoherently:

"I really blame myself. God is going to let me starve because I provide for myself. I am going to hell because I have lost my salvation. God can no longer forgive me."

I pray for her, but she shakes me by the shoulders to make me stop and reminds me with eyes full of visible dread that she had committed the unpardonable sin and that my prayers won't make a difference. She tells me how many times she had tried to commit suicide. I quote from the Bible in an attempt to assure her that she can be forgiven for sure, but she seems to have a spiritual blindfold and earplugs to keep the truth out. She can't even make eye-contact with me. I advise her to speak to her pastor because I clearly can't help her. I tell her quite candidly that I believe she may need deliverance. I leave the conversation flustered and feeling useless for not being able to encourage her. I forgot to ask the Lord what He wanted to tell her.

She bugs me as I go to bed and as I awake, she is the first person on my mind. I'm ashamed to admit that I hope she does not attend this morning's service. I secretly hope for easier conversations today. But halfway through the service I notice her in the front row to my left. I smile at her faintly, and she motions to me that she will see me after the service. I am instantly exasperated by the mere thought that we'll have to talk again.

This time around she keeps me busy for the full hour between the two services. We talk round and round in circles. She has no hope for herself and would rather die. I wish there was something I could do to help her, but she can't take in any truth. Louis calls me as the second service is about to begin. I feel frustrated as I exit the prayer room to find a row of women waiting outside for a chance to pray with me. I should have prioritised them.

During the second service I realise I need to pray and ask the Lord to give me a word that will unlock her heart. She is still sitting there to hear the same message for the third time. She will probably come back for a third time, too. I plead for a word for her, hoping it would work the way it did on the beach a few weeks ago. The thought comes from nowhere:

> *"She steals."*

I assume it is God telling me this and I ask:

> *"Lord, if this is the case, what do I have to tell her?"*

I hear one word:

> *"Cheese."*

It can't be. I'm probably hearing last night's dinner.

> *"Lord, if this is You speaking, would You at least give me a complete sentence to say to her?"*

> *"Tell her I will give her cheese again."*

I feel as if I am moving in the wrong direction now. This isn't working. Perhaps my imagination is too productive. I'm making up nonsense in my desperation to hear something – anything.

Sure enough she is first in line to corner me. I immediately bring my defence:

> *"I have absolutely nothing more to say that could possibly make a difference. You can't and won't hear the truth. I can't spend any more time talking to you. There are other women waiting for prayer. Please talk to your pastor this week."*

She starts crying and clings to me like a frightened child. I decide to test if I had heard the Lord correctly:

"How much money have you stolen?"

Without blinking she starts telling me. I stop her before she can give me information that would incriminate her and force me to report her. I want her to confess, but she is suddenly shaking with panic.

> *"How did you know? Who told you about the stealing? Are you going to let me go to prison now?"*
>
> *"God told me, not to expose you, but to show you that He knows all about you and is able to help. He is forcing you to confess so He can heal you."*
>
> *"I never hear Him like that. Did He say anything else?"*

I realise I might as well say something about the cheese because nothing is making any difference, and by this time she already knows that I'm a dismal failure as a counsellor. Perhaps my crazy words will get her to leave. Carefully I put it on the table:

> *"What does the word 'cheese' mean to you?"*
>
> *"It's my absolute favourite food. I eat it on everything – even on my cereal and on fruit, not just on bread, meat and vegetables. I always say if I have coffee and cheese, I'm okay. I don't need anything else to live on."*

I take it as my sign to give her the full sentence:

> *"God says He will give you cheese again."*
>
> *"Really? Did He say that?"*

I see her ears and eyes and heart open up. It looks as though demons are leaving her. Her eyes are no longer darting around wildly. She seems focussed. She is making sense for the first time:

> *"I once decided not to steal for a month and to test God. I wanted to see if He would take care of me if I stopped stealing. My money ran out and then my food. I went to a church for help. They had already handed out the food parcels for the month. All they had left was a bulk delivery of cheese that had arrived too late to be distributed into the parcels. They were happy to let me stock up on as much cheese as I could carry. Walking home with the load, I wondered if, perhaps, God actually saw me and knew me. Maybe He would care for me. After all, He had given me my favourite food! But I got scared again. I couldn't take the chance so I went back to stealing. Now you are telling me that He promises to give me cheese again!"*

She is looking me straight in the eye. She is no longer shaking. She even has a smile on her face. I see in her body the evidence of the power of God's love for her. The lies that kept her spirit shrivelled up in a dark corner of her being have just been dispelled by the truth. The scars of her suicide attempts and her misconceptions of Him didn't disqualify her from a supernatural encounter with Him. And my awkwardness as a helper didn't disqualify me from being a vehicle for the little miracle God wanted to do in the heart of this precious but weak little woman. I would have written her off. But God sent her

someone from another continent to give her the most unlikely message. God wants to give her another chance. How can she continue doubting?

She prays with me and confesses her sin. She is now willing to accept help. She decides to trust the Lord and to take a leap of faith that He would provide everything she might need. She even walks with me to the church office where we leave her details and notes about her qualifications and the type of positions she could be employed in. After believing for years that she could never find work and that she was worth nothing, she is now confident and eager to try to earn an honest income.

The American trip ends on a high note for me. I am thrilled with what I am learning about God's love for every individual and His desire to speak to those who are desperate to hear from Him. I am also hopeful for myself. Having enjoyed every moment of five glorious weeks with my family, I know now that the lie that I need anyone else has been broken. I am no longer scared of a relapse. I am ready to go home. I am no longer scared of my own phone.

South Africa is almost back to normal after a successful Soccer World Cup, during which no foreigners were raped or murdered – a miracle in itself. I switch on my cell phone. The long silence has apparently bored my cyber stalker. It probably also helped that my assistant sent him a text message warning him that we know who he is.

Freedom and peace. I couldn't have won it back with any fight. The preacher was right. Giving up and simply resting in God brought on the victory.

It is August and the winter is not yet letting up. We missed the worst of it while being in America, but we are still snowed in with work that has piled up in our absence. Among the mail there is a letter from the cheese woman. My heart breaks as I read her letter. She is too afraid to continue walking on the water. She regrets wasting my time. She hopes God and I will forgive her. She wants to go back to her old life. She simply can't trust God to provide for her.

God's heart must be breaking, too. He isn't the one who is mysterious and elusive. He reveals himself very clearly. He isn't the one who doesn't give us enough love. In a miraculous way He gives in abundance. Mountains of cheese for our souls, so to speak. He even knows our favourite food! I am sure to hear God's voice for ourselves and for others shouldn't be difficult at all, because God is a God who speaks. The error is on our side: We struggle to hear, and we are reluctant to receive. And even when we hear Him we fail to hold on to those word and to build our lives on them. We listen with forgetful ears instead of faithful hearts.

Perhaps it is so difficult to hear because there are so many voices in our lives. We have limited capacity when it comes to our ears. It may have been so difficult for me to hear God in the past because I had given attention to the voices of many people who should never have had a say. I should have ignored those detestable text messages from the very first one. And I should never have allowed the voice of another man to gain such prominence in my life. If I had been wise the last few months wouldn't have been dominated by my own battles. Instead, I would have been able to love and support others.

The voices that have prominence seem to prime our ears. We hear and believe more of the same lies or truths and find it hard to hear anything that conflicts with that. This may be why our testimony causes some to plug their ears. It strikes a dissonant chord with what they want to hear and are used to hearing and even hurts them. We cause the screeching sound of a fingernail across the blackboard of their hearts.

Some words are plucked from our hearts before they can take root. Perhaps that is what happened to the lady in Tennessee. The seed was lying on the surface because her heart wasn't ploughed well and the seed was sown but never watered. Sowing a single seed is not enough.

Even the truths I learned from the robbery and rape should not be the only truths I share with others ten years from now. By then the Lord will have taught me newer, better things if I choose to listen even to what may be a fingernail's scratch across my heart. The manna in the desert lasted one day and had worms in it the next morning. This story is my story, but it's not my whole story and it certainly should not become my identity. I want to learn new things, to bring fresh manna.

I'm invited to share my testimony with a group of women who meet monthly. I pray about it since I'm not supposed to be on stage. The organiser explains that they don't advertise, and that no one will know beforehand that I'm coming. They are, like I had been commanded to do, following what they believe to be a call to come together to sit at Jesus' feet. They usually don't invite speakers. They simply minister to one another. They call these meetings 'Mary evenings.'

Louis agrees that I should go. In my guesthouse room is a beautifully decorated cake, flowers, and a lipstick holder with a note inside:

"Look in the mirror and listen to what God is whispering in your ear."

I prepare myself for the evening and look in the mirror, without really expecting to hear anything. The name of a woman pops into my head. Nobody I know, but a common name. I feel a nudge to take her a gift, so I decide to take one of the roses in my room along with me. On the way to the meeting, however, I realise I had forgotten to bring it along. I hear in the same way I heard the name:

"Her gift is already there."

The women are busy with the last of the preparations. The hall is lit with a few candles. There are no lights where I'm going to be standing. The women will truly be able to focus on the Lord since my face will be invisible. I notice that these women are leaving lots of space for God to be who He is and do what He wants to do. There is no fixed program. They want me to talk as God leads me, and they are sure that God will do the rest. I ask if they are expecting someone by the name I heard in front of the mirror, but no-one knows anyone by that name.

The chairs are filling up and a woman approaches me with a wrapped present that looks like a book:

> *"Hettie, the Lord told me to bring this with me. I'm not sure if you might want to give it to someone as a gift?"*

Ah, it must be for the woman whose name I heard, I realise. All we need to do now is find her. I keep on asking around while the women arrive. There is still no-one by that name.

There are exactly the same number of women as the number of chairs they had put out even though they didn't take bookings or names beforehand. I give my testimony, and for the first time I reluctantly talk about the emotional relationship and the fierce struggle to escape from its grip. It's such volatile information that could easily be used against me and it doesn't completely fit with what I wanted to share. I may have gone off track here. The theme I had in mind was how only Jesus can wash us clean.

Before we end I ask again if there is someone in the audience by the name I had heard. No-one responds. Then I hear the rest of the message:

> *"The gift is for her, and the person who betrayed her should give it to her."*

No one seems to have any idea what I'm talking about. After some time of awkward silence a woman comes to the front and takes the gift, claiming that she has a friend by that name who is really going through a difficult time. She will give it to her. I feel as if I fired at a target but hit the wall next to it. I really wanted the message to hit the bull's eye. It may have confused us all more than it helped anyone. I realise that perhaps I will have to practice and hone this gift. I don't for a minute consider the possibility that the person that this message is meant for, is simply too embarrassed to step forward ...

Two women that I saw crying while I was speaking come to me for a hug afterwards. They say the message brought healing, answers, and comfort. Both their daughters were recently raped – one less than a week ago. I am now convinced that I did not have to talk about the emotional affair and regret having said anything about it. Clearly my message was for these two heartbroken mothers who needed to know that rape needs not be the end of a joyful life.

Behind them in line, a women is clearly struggling to contain her excitement. She felt the Lord telling her to make white heart-shaped bars of homemade soap and to put it on each seat. It was an unusual choice for a gift. But when she heard the theme of my message – Jesus washes us clean – she was so excited that she had heard the Lord correctly. I wonder if there is a bigger joy than that – the experience that we are one of His sheep and that we know His voice.

It is September and the six month mark is already behind us. I'm pretending I don't know I should have another HIV test done. No-one else remembers. Life has gone on, and it is a relief not be the centre of everyone's concern anymore. Two young students call to invite me, as a victim of crime, to take part in the Sycamore Tree project of Prison Fellowship Ministries. It is a restorative justice programme in which they guide prisoners and victims to reconciliation through weekly sessions that run for a couple of months. I accept the invitation, thinking to myself that the rape has really broadened and deepened my life in many ways. This opportunity is a door that may never have opened if it weren't for the events of that night.

Each week the one to two hours amongst the prisoners bring a confrontation with truths which I understood in theory, but had never seen in operation with my own eyes. Without exception every woman I meet behind these bars is a victim of lies she believed. They are no worse or better than I am. Most of them have simply made one or two more mistakes than I have. Many of them are there because they gave their heart to the wrong man and couldn't get out before the boat sank with both on board. Their stories are confidential, so I can't get them out of my system by talking to a friend or to Louis. Their brokenness traumatises me to such an extent that some days I have to go for a drive, or sit for a while in a quiet place before I can go home.

But, even in this dark place there are women living in complete victory. One of them declares with a beaming smile: *"Jesus is just as real inside of this place as He is on the outside. I would never have known Him were it not for these bars. I'm very thankful to be here."* Her words resonate beautifully with Spurgeon's words about Christian's suffering:

> **Blessed is the fact that Christians can rejoice even in the deepest distress. Although trouble may surround them, they still sing; and, like many birds, they sing best in their cages ... Truly, the presence of Jesus is all the heaven we desire. He is at once 'the glory of our brightest days; the comfort of our nights.'**

One particular woman touches my heart, even though I don't even know her story. All sharing is voluntary and she is not opening up. Still, her hurt oozes out of every pore. I find her magnetic and scary at the same time. One afternoon the Lord clearly tells me:

> *"I came for her. She's why you are here."*

During the session I have the uncanny urge to stand behind her, put my arms around her and say the words:

> *"I know that nobody ever touched you without taking from you. I want to touch you just to make you feel loved and without taking anything from you."*

I could not get myself to act on this impulse.

It's the 27th of September. One of the students calls to let me know the prison phoned, and would I please come to the prison because this intriguing woman wants to talk to me. On the way to the prison I send up a barrage of prayers, because I fear I won't know what to tell her or how to help her. I hear myself talking to her as I pray:

> *"God can restore everything that has been stolen from you in twenty years!"*

I feel the Lord prompting me to say only that. That would be enough to unlock her heart.

She comes after a long wait. We have a tiny back office at our disposal. She is clearly not deemed dangerous as no-one is watching us. She gets up from her chair, makes a dismissive gesture with her hand as if to say "it won't make a difference anyway" and apologizes for having us come all the way. She had changed her mind and did not want to talk anymore. I insist on saying the only sentence I have:

> *"God can restore everything that has been stolen from you in twenty years!"*

She looks shocked and tells me the twenty-year old secret that started the slippery slope that spewed her out here. Her story is the worst I've heard. I struggle to keep the lump in my throat down.

After some prayer and what must have been one of the clumsiest attempts ever to drive out demons, she is relaxed and ready to talk about growing in her relationship with the Lord. We talk about hope and her future, and for a while she seems hopeful too.

She asks me whether a life as broken as hers can ever be repaired. I hand her my Bible with the very bold words:

> *"The Lord Himself wants to answer you. Open it and start reading. Keep on reading in the days and weeks ahead and expect the Lord to speak to you directly and personally. If the words stir your heart, believe them."*

While explaining to her that she needs to feast on God's words, she opens my Bible on a random page without reading and presses it against her chest.

> *"I would like to do what I did before I was sent to prison. I like renovating things. I worked in a construction company where others did the rough construction and I did the restoration work. But I still think my life is wrecked."*

> *"Read something. I want to see you practice living from the words of the Lord. You can borrow my Bible until I bring you another one."*

She reads where she had opened the Bible:

> **Your lives will begin to glow in the darkness,**
> **your shadowed lives will be bathed in sunlight.**
> **I will always show you where to go.**
> **I'll give you a full life in the emptiest of places –**
> **firm muscles, strong bones.**
> **You'll be like a well-watered garden,**
> **a gurgling spring that never runs dry.**
> **You'll use the old rubble of past lives to build anew,**
> **rebuild the foundations from out of your past.**
> **You'll be known as those who can fix anything,**
> **restore old ruins, rebuild and renovate,**
> **make the community liveable again.**
>
> (Isaiah 58:11-12, *The Message*)

She lowers the Bible and smiles.

> *"He just spoke to me, didn't He?"*

I look at the joy on her face and am sure she will take this key and turn it in the lock of the prison she is in.

It is October. It should be warming up, but I'm cold. I'm sitting in a church where Louis is leading the worship, contemplating the experiences in the prison. My friend Marietjie, who debriefed my kids after the robbery, sees me as I leave the church.

> *"Why are you looking worse now than you did in February after the rape?"*

I explain to her that the enemy is taunting me with words of fear to a new tune. He is now threatening me with the idea that newspapers will discover what I did and who the man in the shadows is. Then I will fall on my face and everyone would mock God's work in my life. The credibility of both our ministries – Louis's and mine – would be lost.

> *"It doesn't make sense, Hettie. You are innocent. Your side of the story is clean. Everything is in the light and forgiven. The relationship was stopped in time. Why do you keep feeling as if someone is watching your every move? I think you should come for a therapy session with me, because you look just like the children I do play therapy with every day. Forgive me for saying this, but you look like a child that was groomed for sexual abuse."*

A few days later I take a seat on one of those kiddie chairs one would expect to find in a play therapy room. It is fitting. She is right, I feel extremely vulnerable but don't know why. She knows. Without needing me to tell her how it all started, she starts telling me how this man did what he did to get such a hold on me.

> *"He would throw you a bone emotionally and pat your head as you come to chew on it. Then he would fling it further away so you would work a little harder for his approval, give a little more of your time and your heart, stroke his ego more. He'd push boundaries and then apologise for it, making you feel safe, yet leaving you with boundaries that have shifted anyway. And he'd do what any abuser does: he'd threaten you to never tell anyone his name."*

The realisation that I had been easy prey makes me fly off the little chair to throw up in the little basin.

> *"You have to tell Louis the man's name. It is the key."*

I know she's right. I fiddle with the key, not sure if it's going to open Pandora's Box or my prison. I realise the American preacher was right. I was not done, because I had to see one more thing in my own heart. Yes, it was fear and his threat that kept me from revealing the man's name, but there was more to it. Pride also stopped me. I got burnt by a fire Louis had warned me about. He is a trusting man and has only ever expressed his distrust in one man – this man. At the time I thought I could handle a charmer and dismissed his warning, trusting my own judgement that as long as I entered the relationship with pure intentions everything would be fine. Revealing the name now would be admitting that Louis was right and that I was weaker than I thought.

I drive home, ready to turn the key in the lock. I look for the perfect moment for two agonising days. It is time. I sit down with Louis and take the direct route:

> *"Honey, I still owe you part of the truth. I am ready to tell you the name even though you never asked for it."*

The name tears through my lips.

> *"I knew all along it was him. I was waiting for you to confess it. If I confronted you and you lied, I would not have been able to stand it. If you admitted it, I'd still never know if you did it because you have true remorse or because you were caught out. I knew the day you come to me of your own accord, I would know you are done with this nonsense."*

He has only one question. Both of us are relieved that I can answer honestly that the relationship did not turn into a sexual one. It does not reduce the amount of regret I feel, because I believe that an emotional bond can be an even deeper betrayal. I also know that I could have crossed the line. There was a lot of grace involved and I have no moral high ground to pride myself on. I am disappointed in myself for not figuring out sooner that this *'keep quiet'* lie was the key deception that kept the stronghold in place. It ate away at intimacy and kept me out of paradise as long as I allowed it to.

November has come and my heart is warm. I receive a Facebook message referring to that day I shared my testimony and gave the strange message that a person who had wronged another, has to take her a gift. That day when I regretted talking about the emotional affair.

> *"I was too embarrassed to tell you the truth that evening. When you said the woman's name, I cringed. I am the one who wronged her. I have an affair with her husband. How do I get out?"*

I realise that talking about the affair was necessary for this snared women. She had to hear my confession in order to have the courage to make a confession of her own. It seems I will often be exposed in my own brokenness so that others will have the courage to reveal theirs.

20 *No place too dark*

Our financial adviser announces that I have a policy that will pay out if I should test positive for HIV. The claim period is about to lapse, so he will send a nurse from the insurance company to draw blood. We are halfway between the test I should have had and the one I must still have at the one year mark. I decide that this test will serve well to replace both.

The test comes back negative and I can already taste the party food we'll share on the official date. My year of no stage appearances is almost over, and my calendar for next year is filling up fast. Most events I'm invited to speak at are *oestrogen fests*. Who would have thought? I'm going to have the privilege of flying them a white flag just as my friend from long ago said I would. My heart for women has changed to such an extent that I'm honestly looking forward to these events, and I sometimes even find myself crying when I think of the brokenness and lies that so many women struggle with every day. In the past their brokenness struck me as pathetic and evoked irritation rather than compassion.

I start organising my thoughts in order to write this book. The December school vacation time will make it easier to find the time. I try to remember all the important details and am glad that I kept a journal all year long. I decide that I will write honestly and candidly about all the dark places, places where I have seen the light and the hope we have in Jesus. The dark place, where crime had paid me a visit, was but one of my dark places. I could not write about that only. I had to see the darkness in forbidden relationships and the darkness in prisons, because that is where the families I so desperately want to serve find themselves. It was necessary to see that we can have victory in each of these dark places once we embrace the truths that dispel the lies we used to believe. I have to write about all of these places.

It's early on a Sunday morning in December. I receive a phone call from my best friend's brother. They were involved in an accident earlier this morning. She and two of her children are critical. The youngest and her husband seem fine. They are on their way to a better hospital via ambulance and helicopter. He asks for my prayers and suggests that I may want to fly down to be there in case things take a turn for the worst. Their injuries were extensive and all three of them would need brain surgery upon arrival at the hospital. The little girl already had to be resuscitated once.

I feel like a zombie all day, trying to figure out what to do. I cry myself to sleep, because even though I would like to see her recover miraculously, the Lord is telling me to say my farewells and crawl into His arms tonight so that He can comfort me. Tomorrow I will be on the first flight. I will try to speak the healing truth to her husband and to support the rest of the family, if I can find the words.

I'm so exhausted that I don't even hear my alarm go off at 5.00 am. By the time I am really awake, it is after six and I should have been on my way to the airport already. I can't miss this flight! Without showering or combing my hair, I grab some clothes, shove them in a bag, and run out to the car. As if I'm not already looking dishevelled enough, I get soaked to the bone while loading everything into the car. The rain is coming down so hard that I can't see a thing. I'm going fast enough on the freeway to make the flight even though I should probably not be driving at all. I contemplate how morbidly poetic it would be if I made an accident now.

I'm forced to park in the short term parking lot where a shocking parking fee would be getting larger by the hour for who knows how many days before I can return. I only booked a one way ticket. I reach the boarding gate with only moments to spare. I feel like I did that night when I ran out into the cool morning air with only my pyjamas on. Just as I did that night, I make humble excuses for my appearance, dab on a little make-up as soon as I reach my seat and try to comb my unwashed hair as best I can without elbowing the person in the seat next to me. In truth, I don't really care what I look like now. I am going to say goodbye to my best friend of twenty five years. The thought flies round and round in my head like a mosquito that won't sit still long enough that I can swat it:

"Say your farewells. Say your farewells. Say your farewells."

I rent a car and rush from the airport straight to the hospital. Nothing could have prepared me for seeing her and her children lying there unrecognisably swollen, bruised and with tubes protruding everywhere. Her husband has many questions and is wrestling with God. I don't have any words for him. I beg the Lord for something to say, but I don't hear anything. After spending most of the day there I flee to the beach near the hospital. I want to cry but I can't. I just want to get the imprints of the emergency room out of my mind. I'm not praying, either. I'm just blank. I hear the words:

"He doesn't know that I care. I will show him what it means to have a Father."

I go back early to kidnap my friend's husband for breakfast. He seems relieved for the break from hospital food and needs to get out anyway. I can hear he has heard some truth in the past 24 hours. He tells of the support and prayers of so many friends, and even the local church who doesn't know him from a bar of soap has taken him under their wings.

We return to be there when the neurologist is expected to show us the results of this morning's scan. My friend's mother and I both had enough exposure to anatomy and neurology during our studies to see the obvious. Half of her brain matter is dead. We are all crushed beneath the weight of the unbearable news. I am the first to find my voice. As I pray aloud for my friend's husband, I see the Father standing next to him saying: "This is my beloved son and I am pleased with him." I hear this broken man exhale in a long sigh.

His father in law prays next. Upon opening my eyes I can see the difference in my friend's husband. From being visibly and understandably upset, he has changed into a portrait of peace, though laced with the sadness one would expect.

> *"I felt the Father's hands on my shoulders while we prayed. I've never felt Him touch me before. I have peace."*

Two days later my friend's earthly tent is dismantled. She is home. The pastor says it well at her funeral service:

> *"For thirty eight years Jesus lived with her, and now she's living with Him."*

I see her husband making a daily choice to see the Lord's grace in every little bit of progress that his injured children are making. His question is no longer *"why?"* Each day he asks *"Show me where You are, Father; I don't want to miss You."* I see him making the crucial decision that every person hoping to recover from trauma should make – to look for signs of the Lord's goodness and presence and to testify about those. Every morning I excitedly read his phone and Facebook messages. He reports joyfully about what the Lord is doing. Some think he is in denial, but he is simply in awe of the bigger reality. He sees his Father at work for the first time and it brings him comfort.

From everything I've experienced throughout this year, I can see that the principles of freedom are the same in every dark place. Distinguish between the lie and the voice of truth. Seek God in the eye of the storm where it is dead quiet. Don't ask too many questions. Never ask why. Even if you got the answer, it would not bring you healing. God's ways are higher than ours. Listen to the questions He is asking you in the middle of your pain. He always asks the same questions: "Who am I to you?" and "Will you love Me above all, despite your pain?"

Today is the 10th of February. Late last night I sat next to the window where the robbers had entered our house exactly a year ago. I wasn't sitting there morbidly, the way that some people sit next to a grave. I sat there because the wireless internet signal was the strongest there. A few metres behind me, in the studio, Louis was editing a production just like he was doing that night. This production will simply be called Psalms; he had just set music to Psalm 18. Its declaration was streaming from the same room where the enemy grabbed him and told him that he would die.

I call to God for help and mercy
And in His palace He hears my cry
The earth is shaking, trembling, quaking
and God comes flying
wrapped in thunder and fire

The Lord God is my Rock my Fortress
My Saviour and my God
The Shelter of my soul, my Shield
My strong Deliverer and my Tower of refuge

I can take on enemy armies
I can vault the highest wall
My feet can run on hills and mountains

You trained me well for victory in this war
The Lord God is my Rock my Fortress
My Saviour and my God
The Shelter of my soul, my Shield
My strong Deliverer and my Tower of refuge

Tonight we celebrate, because every arrow of evil was snapped in two in this past year. In every dark place we've seen our Knight come to our rescue, and to the rescue of many others we know. We celebrate the freeing truths we've discovered behind the puppet theatre. As a family we sit around the dining room table and each one prays. Louis and I pray with grown-up insight into the magnitude of the miracle, but each of our children also join in with childlike sincerity. Our oldest praises the Lord that we are all still together. My son, our second, prays faithfully, like he does every morning and evening, for two of our family members who haven't pitched their tents in the land of hope yet, because they don't yet believe the land exists. Our youngest prays:

"Jesus, allow us to do everything we want to in tonight's family party."

I suspect her prayer is aimed more at our ears than God's.

We feast on all our favourite snacks. I'm not sure you can call it communion, in the strictest sense, but we drink grape juice and eat cake and all of us share a better understanding of what Jesus' blood and broken body has bought for us.

After our feast, our son suggests a dance competition as the main activity for the celebration, and our youngest just wants to race around the house. We have a desire to relax, of course, being a little older than they are. A compromise is negotiated. Louis and I sit on the veranda like an old couple. The sun is setting, and we watch thankfully as our children dance and race around the house. The running is followed by exuberant and carefree splashing in their inflatable swimming pool.

We share future dreams and a few kisses that are drawn out just long enough to evoke a disgusted response from our twelve year old. We have many dreams about all that may still lie ahead, knowing an adventure with Jesus could hold anything. With our bodies we are living in the same dark and dangerous world, in a puppet theatre that may be shaken again at any moment, but Louis's spirit and mine are both eternally and fearlessly free – living in the land of hope.

CPSIA information can be obtained
at www.ICGtesting.com
Printed in the USA
LVOW09s0211151116
512997LV00009B/190/P

9 780620 697361